SUCCESSFUL GARDENING
THE PRACTICAL GARDENER

Published by The Reader's Digest Association Limited.

First Edition Copyright © 1991
The Reader's Digest Association Limited,
Berkeley Square House, Berkeley Square, London W1X 6AB

Copyright © 1991
The Reader's Digest Association Far East Limited
Philippines Copyright 1991
The Reader's Digest Association Far East Limited
Reprinted 1992

Consultant editor: Lizzie Boyd

Typeset by SX Composing Limited in Century Schoolbook

PRINTED IN SPAIN

ISBN 0 276 42042 X

Opposite: A narrow path snakes its way between beds
resplendent with rhododendrons and azaleas,
suggesting that the soil in this garden is acid. Glowing
tulips and lemon-coloured primroses complete the
picture of a healthy garden.

Overleaf: Healthy plants, abundant flowers and a
well-tended lawn are a reflection of the gardener's
practical experience and know-how.

PUBLISHED BY THE READER'S DIGEST ASSOCIATION LIMITED
LONDON NEW YORK MONTREAL SYDNEY CAPE TOWN

Originally published in partwork form
by Eaglemoss Publications Limited

SUCCESSFUL GARDENING

THE PRACTICAL
GARDENER

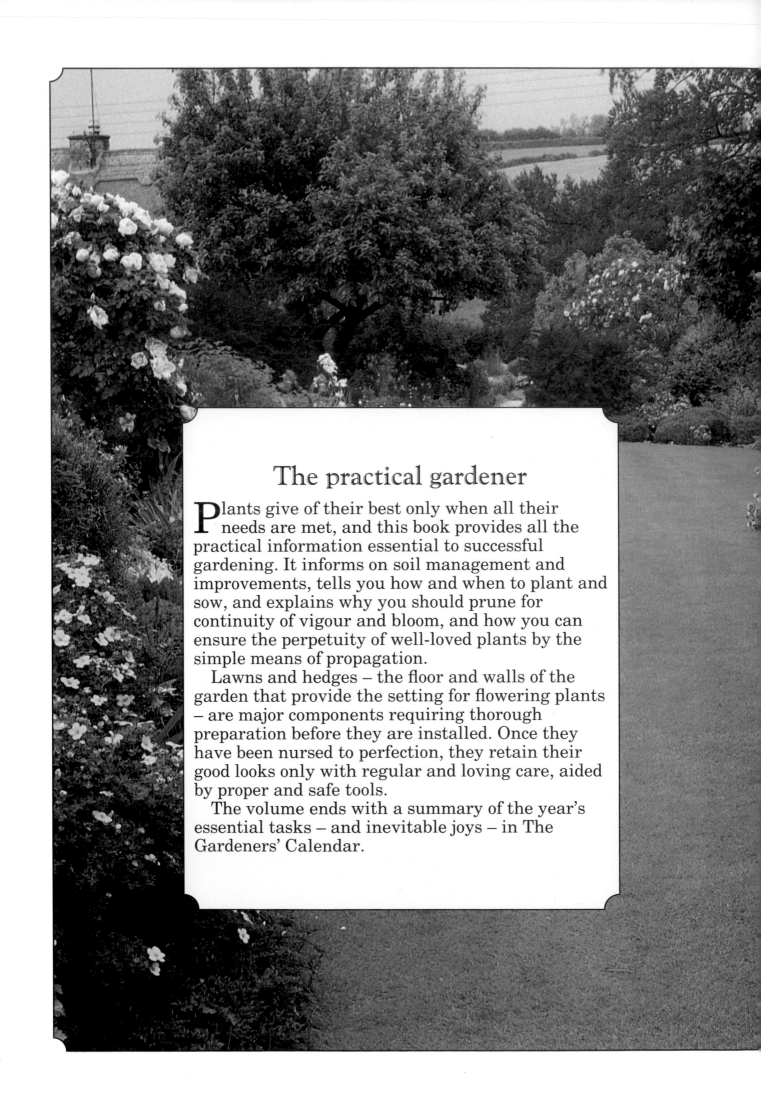

The practical gardener

Plants give of their best only when all their needs are met, and this book provides all the practical information essential to successful gardening. It informs on soil management and improvements, tells you how and when to plant and sow, and explains why you should prune for continuity of vigour and bloom, and how you can ensure the perpetuity of well-loved plants by the simple means of propagation.

Lawns and hedges – the floor and walls of the garden that provide the setting for flowering plants – are major components requiring thorough preparation before they are installed. Once they have been nursed to perfection, they retain their good looks only with regular and loving care, aided by proper and safe tools.

The volume ends with a summary of the year's essential tasks – and inevitable joys – in The Gardeners' Calendar.

CONTENTS

Understanding your soil

Soil – a complex mixture of disintegrated mineral rock, organic remains, air and bacteria – is literally the foundation on which any successful garden is built. Whether you grow flowers, grass, shrubs and ornamental trees, or vegetable and fruit crops, strong vigorous plants need good soil to thrive and perform well. Soils vary, however, and while fertile, moisture-retentive but well-drained loam is considered ideal, most soils can benefit from basic improvement.

Understanding your soil type is the key to this, and to choosing the most compatible plants. Simple soil-testing kits can assess acidity and alkalinity; other equally simple tests can determine soil texture and water content. From there, it's an easy step to correcting chemical imbalances and improving structure and drainage if necessary.

All soils benefit from regular enrichment to maintain their fertility and moisture content. Bulky organic matter such as well rotted manure, garden compost, leaf mould and spent mushroom compost add both vital humus and food. These are environmentally far preferable to the heavy use of chemical fertilizers, which add nothing to soil structure and can build up to harmful levels in the soil. Slow-acting organic fertilizers such as bone meal are beneficial in moderation. Peat has no value as a fertilizer and is in very short supply. It should be used sparingly.

Organic matter used as a surface cover, or mulch, provides extra benefits: mulched soil requires less weeding, and less watering in droughts. Mulch is also a natural insulator, keeping roots cool in summer and warm in winter.

Lime-haters Rhododendrons — and azaleas — will flourish only on moist, acid soils.

RECOGNIZING YOUR SOIL

**Once you know your soil type, you can do much
to improve it and maintain it in good health to give plants
optimum growing conditions.**

Not all plants will grow well in the type of soil in your garden – soil type varies widely and there is little point trying to alter it. However, once you have found out what type your soil is, there are many ways it can be improved. The better the soil, the easier it is to grow a variety of beautiful and productive plants.

Knowing your soil
To improve a soil you must first identify whether it is basically chalky, clayey, sandy or a mixture. You can find out a lot about the soil in your area by talking to neighbours and by working the soil yourself. Most libraries also stock copies of The Soil Survey of Great Britain which gives more detailed information.

In addition, consider soil-testing for chemical content and acidity/alkalinity. You can buy kits that are easy to use and give reasonably accurate readings. It's a good idea to get one jointly with a friend (with different soil) so you both benefit.

Your soil will fall roughly into one of four categories:

Chalk soils, formed from the breaking down of limestone, are strongly alkaline. Fuchsias, pinks and alliums thrive on them, but acid-loving plants such as azaleas, rhododendrons and most heathers hate them. These soils usually have little topsoil – you'll hit bedrock quickly if you start digging – and are poor at retaining both water and plant nutrients. This means you need to keep on applying organic matter and fertilizers frequently.

Clay soil is made up of minute mineral particles that tend to clog together. It is probably heavy and sticky to dig since clay soils are generally poorly drained and aerated. When clay dries out, it sets rock-hard and cracks. To make the most of its natural fertility, you need to improve drainage and aeration by working in leafmould, shredded bark or horticultural grit, so that the texture becomes more open.

Sandy soils are light and easy to work. Although they warm up quickly in spring, giving plants a good start, they are so free draining that nutrients are washed out. Like chalky soils, they need plenty of organic matter and liberal dressings of fertilizer.

Loam You are lucky if your soil is a well-drained loam, containing a

Loam

Clay

Sand

Chalk

Soil textures The particles of clay soils are so close that they can retain water even in mid summer – but they are cold and heavy to work in winter. Sandy soils, on the other hand, have larger particles through which water and nutrients drain away. They warm up and cool down quickly and are easy to work. Chalky soils easily lose water and nutrients, are strongly alkaline and usually shallow and stony as well. The ideal soil is loam, which is well-balanced, humus-rich and retains water and nutrients.

good balance of clay and sand particles and a high humus content. Loams are the most easily cultivated of all soil types and hold water and nutrients well.

Acid and alkaline soils

The ideal soil, a fertile, moisture-retentive loam, is slightly acid. Acidity or alkalinity is measured on a pH scale. Something neutral, such as pure water, measures 7. Anything above that is alkaline, below, acid. A pH reading which is between 6.5 and 7 suits the widest range of plants. Moderately acid soils measure about pH6, moderately alkaline soils about pH7.5.

Sour (extremely acid) soils are often found in town gardens, and can be corrected with garden lime. Use 200g (½lb) per sq m (sq yd), depending on how bad the problem is. Hydrated lime, available from garden centres, is the most convenient form.

Slight acidity is, however, preferable to a strong alkaline content – it's much easier to modify. A bucketful of peat per sq m (sq yd) will increase the acidity of alkaline soils but, as peat has become an endangered commodity, reserve this treatment for the worst afflicted areas of soil. Plants on alkaline soil often show poor growth because they are unable to absorb trace nutrients such as iron and manganese. If you have alkaline soil, and still want to grow acid-loving plants such as azaleas and rhododendrons, the best solution is to create raised beds of acid soil, or to grow such plants in containers filled with an appropriate soil mixture.

Humus for good soil

Good soil is living soil. Based on an accumulation of weathered rock, soil also contains a combination of chemicals and humus. This ingredient – organic matter such as dead leaves broken down by bacteria – holds vital nutrients in a form that plants can absorb.

Two conditions are essential in forming humus: an adequate supply of air and a balanced provision of water. Waterlogged soils, or those with very close textures, prevent the air from circulating freely, and so stop the beneficial process of decay.

▲ **Earthworm activity** This is essential for healthy soil. Earthworms' tunnels aerate heavy soils, and their feeding habits pull leaf litter underground to form humus — vital for plant growth.

Some water is needed, though, both for the action of soil bacteria and to dissolve nutrients. Fast draining soil, which holds little or no moisture, parches easily and also suffers from leaching – plant nutrients and minerals are washed out of the topsoil.

As well as containing humus, a good soil must have a balanced

SOIL IMPROVER: WHAT TO DO WHEN

	SPRING	SUMMER	AUTUMN
Dig/fork/ hoe	Fork ground to loosen and aerate soil.	Hoe beds to keep down weeds and to aerate soil.	Dig beds before ground becomes too wet.
Manure	Mulch existing beds not dug and manured in autumn. If planning to use farmyard manure in autumn, order and stack now.	None needed.	Incorporate manure at the bottom of trenches when digging new beds, beds for ornamentals and vegetable beds (once every two years). If planning to use farmyard manure in spring, order and stack now.
Fertilize	Sprinkle powdered general slow-acting fertilizers on to soil and fork lightly in. Apply quick-acting fertilizers to specific plants to encourage their leaf growth and bud formation.	Apply quick-acting fertilizers, watering in or spraying as foliar feed, particularly to roses and tomatoes and on 'hungry' sandy and chalky soils.	Apply slow-release organic fertilizers when planting shrubs and trees.
Condition	Incorporate organic material, such as compost, leaf-mould or shredded bark, to improve soil's texture and/or spread on a layer (mulch) to conserve moisture, particularly on sandy and chalky soils.	None needed.	If soil is too dense or too free draining, incorporate bulky organic material when digging to improve texture. Every second year add about 200g (½lb) of hydrated lime per sq m (sq yd) to acid soils to decrease acidity, and to clay soils to make them more crumbly.
Water	In prolonged dry spells in late spring, water thoroughly, particularly sand or clay.	Water ground thoroughly in dry weather, in morning or evening not at midday.	Continue watering into mid autumn in dry spells.
Drain	Incorporate grit and/or bulky organic material in poorly drained clay soils.	None needed.	In poorly drained soils, particularly clay, lay drainage pipes or add grit and/or bulky organic material.

HOW TO DIG

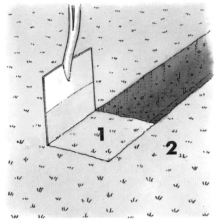

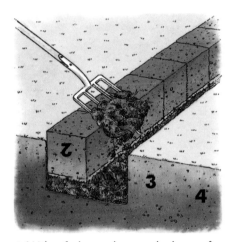

1 Dig a trench (**1**) 30cm (12in) wide and one spit (spade's depth) deep: drive in the spade upright on all four sides of a square of earth; slide your hand down the shaft and bend your knees; lift the soil by straightening your legs to take the strain off your back. Move the dug soil from the first trench to the end of plot.

2 With a fork, evenly spread a layer of well-rotted manure in the trench. Dig the next strip (**2**) and turn it upside down into the trench. Remove any perennial weeds such as dandelions and nettles.

3 Continue in this way, trench by trench (**3, 4** etc), to the end of the plot, filling the final trench with the soil from the first one. Dig methodically and don't overdo it – it's tiring work.

chemical composition, including not only the prime nutrients required by plants – nitrogen, phosphorus and potassium – but traces of others such as copper and zinc.

Aerating the soil

Working the ground with a spade or fork is the most effective way of aerating waterlogged or dense compacted soils.

It's best to dig after annual flowers and vegetables have been cleared and before the ground becomes too wet. Wet soils are heavy to work and there is a danger of compacting the ground, particularly on clay, while tramping backwards and forwards.

The action of the weather in winter helps to break down the soil turned over in autumn. Raking in spring produces the fine, crumbly surface layer known as tilth – perfect for seed sowing or planting.

In established beds, such as a shrubbery or border, aerate the soil by forking it over in spring – before growth starts. Throughout the summer use a hoe to break up the soil, let the air in and clear the ground of weeds.

Adjusting the water balance

If an area of the garden is seriously waterlogged, water will lie in puddles after rain; it eventually evaporates rather than drains away. The simplest solution is to dig in plenty of manure to improve drainage, or you could create a

Soil testing kits Adding drops of the chemicals in the kit to a sample of soil produces a liquid which, when it is matched against the colour chart provided, indicates the acidity or alkalinity (pH) of the soil, as well as the presence or absence of nutrients such as phosphates, potassium and nitrates.

scree bed. Otherwise you may need to lay drainage pipes to carry excess water away. Fortunately, problems this serious are unusual.

Conditioning soil texture

Bulky organic materials, such as compost or well rotted farmyard manure, help to open up the structure. They also give substance to soils that are too free draining, so increasing the soil's capacity to retain water.

If you have a clay soil, add grit to break up the density (make sure it's horticultural grit from a garden centre, and not builder's grit). A half to a full bucketful per sq m (sq yd) is the correct proportion, according to how poor the drainage and how acid the soil is. Alternatively, use 200g (½lb) of hydrated lime per sq m (sq yd) – this binds the particles together in larger lumps.

Mulching – covering the soil with an organic material such as compost, leaf-mould or composted bark – conserves moisture and discourages weeds. Apply in spring or early summer when the sun has taken the chill off the ground and while it's still moist. As it works its way into the soil, the mulch also improves the texture.

Peat – vegetable matter prevented from decomposing by lack of oxygen – is no longer recommended for general use in the garden because of its increasing scarcity. It has little nutrient value, and coir (coconut) fibre and spent mushroom compost can be substituted as soil conditioners, as they both improve qualities of aeration and water retention.

Enriching the soil

Adding organic material such as manure (from animals) and compost (from plants) aerates the soil and improves its texture and ability to retain moisture. But their value goes a great deal further – they produce humus.

You can make your own compost by recycling kitchen vegetable peelings and tea leaves, and garden waste, particularly dead leaves, on a compost heap. But avoid adding woody material, which doesn't break down, and also diseased plants or perennial weeds such as ground elder.

Alternatively, you can buy manure. Farmyard manure is an extremely rich dressing but never use it fresh – it needs to be stacked for several months before use. Other options, which may not sound appealing but are effective additions to the soil, include hop manure, poultry manure, seaweed, sewage sludge and shoddy, which is a waste material from wool factories.

Feeding plants

Applying chemical fertilizers – the inorganic answer to manure and compost – is the easiest way to boost the nutrient content of soils. But don't rely solely on fertilizers – they don't produce humus. Treat them as supplements to organic materials rather than as substitutes.

Fertilizers come in various forms and perform different functions. Add slow acting general fertilizers to the soil in early spring. Throughout the summer, apply quicker acting general fertilizers. These are either liquid feeds watered into the ground around plants, or leaf feeds applied with a watering can or spray. There are also special formulas for some categories of plants, such as tomatoes and roses.

▲ **Alkaline soil hydrangeas** The flowers of *Hydrangea macrophylla* are affected by soil pH. On alkaline or neutral soil they are pink or red.

◄ **Acid soil hydrangeas** The same species on acid soil will have blue flowers. Blueing compounds containing aluminium sulphate can be added to neutral soils for a blue tint.

▼ **Lime haters** Acid-loving plants such as heathers and conifers can create a magnificent and colourful display on a very acid soil.

DRAINAGE SYSTEMS

**Waterlogged gardens are a misery. They are
impossible to cultivate and plants won't thrive in such infertile soils.
What is needed is a good garden drainage system.**

Every garden needs moisture to enable plants to flourish, and in most gardens the balance is about right; rain falls, seeps into the soil and drains away naturally. But if something disturbs this natural balance, the result is a garden that is a soggy swamp most of the time.

Few plants can thrive with waterlogged roots, and wet soil is very hard to work when it comes to digging and planting. Worst of all is a lawn that is always soft and wet underfoot; every footfall leaves a mark and mud is constantly carried round the house from the garden.

Waterlogging occurs for a variety of reasons. One of the commonest problems – and the easiest to put right – is soil that has become compacted because it has not been recently worked. Heavy

clay soils are particularly bad in this respect.

Compacted soil keeps water standing on the surface so that it cannot reach plant roots. The solution is a vigorous programme of double digging, incorporating plenty of organic matter such as manure, straw or compost to help break up the soil and improve its water-holding capacity.

A similar problem is common in the gardens of newly built houses. When clearing a site builders often remove the topsoil and spread excavated material over the garden area. They then inadvertently compact it with the movement of heavy machinery, and later cover everything up with a thin layer of topsoil or poor quality subsoil. The result is an impermeable layer just below the

surface, preventing adequate drainage. Again, the solution is to double-dig and to incorporate organic matter.

However natural problems are the worst, such as a layer of non-permeable rock close to the surface, or an area where the water table – the natural level of ground water – is particularly high.

In the latter case, prolonged rainfall causes the water table to rise until it reaches the surface, resulting in standing water. With both these problems, the only practical solution is to install a land-drainage system.

If you move house in the summer, you may not discover that you have a drainage problem until winter. The best way of spotting a potential disaster area is to look at what is growing in the garden;

HERRINGBONE DRAINAGE

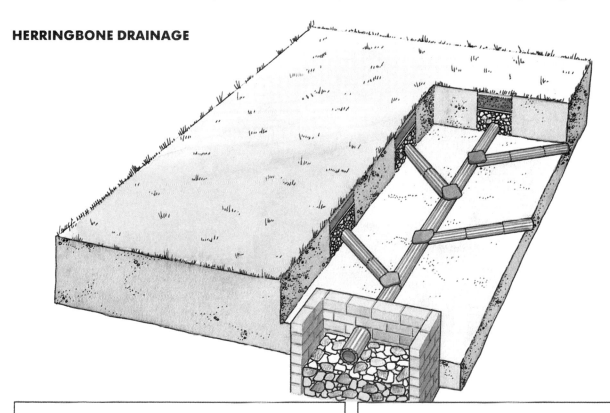

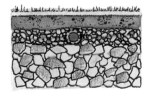

Simple but effective soakaways consist of two levels: a layer of rubble on which the last pipe in the drain run rests, and an upper layer of gravel between the soil and turf.

In the herringbone system, pipes are laid on a bed of gravel. A glass fibre membrane is sometimes placed between the gravel and subsoil to stop soil seeping into the pipes.

LAYING A DRAINAGE SYSTEM

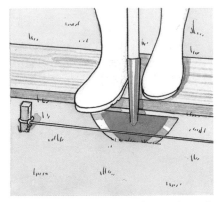

1 Mark out the position of the side and main drain pipes using pegs and a string line. With an edging tool, cut into the turf along the line, making right-angled cuts at 60cm (2ft) intervals.

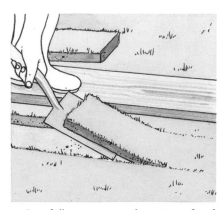

2 Carefully remove each section of turf with a spade, and lay them neatly along one side of the trench ready for replacing when all the drainage pipes have been installed.

3 Dig out the soil to the required depth, removing the topsoil and subsoil separately and storing them in separate piles ready to be replaced in the correct sequence.

4 Using a ruler, check the trench at regular intervals, making sure that it is deep enough to give the necessary fall. The gradient must be constant to keep the water flowing in the pipes.

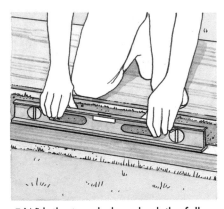

5 With the trench dug, check the fall again along its length. Place a piece of batten on the bottom of the trench and rest a spirit level on it. The bubble should be just off centre.

6 Prepare the bottom of the trench to receive the pipes by coating the soil base with a 5cm (2in) layer of fine gravel, or a cushioning mixture of sand and gravel.

---

stunted sickly looking shrubs, rushy grass and bare patches of lawn are all tell-tale signs of drainage trouble.

Gauging soil porosity
To gauge how well the garden drains, dig a hole about 60cm (2ft) square and 60cm (2ft) deep. Leave it for 24 hours to see if any water collects in it; if it does, the garden is suffering from impeded drainage caused by a high water table or non-porous subsoil, and definitely needs drainage. If the hole remains dry, fill it with water and see how quickly it drains away. If it empties in about 12 hours drainage is very good – in fact too good – probably because the soil is very sandy. Rapid drainage can be slowed down by enriching the soil with lots of organic matter.

If the hole takes 24 hours to empty, drainage is adequate; if the water is still standing in the hole after 48 hours, the soil is probably too dense and needs breaking up thoroughly by double-digging. Some simple drainage may also be necessary.

Simple drainage techniques
Soggy areas can sometimes be improved by installing drainage trenches. These help to divert water running across the garden from higher ground, conveying it to a soakaway or a natural outlet such as a ditch or stream.

On no account must any land drainage system be connected to the main sewage system.

The simplest type of drainage system is a trench about 75cm (2½ft) deep with a lining of coarse rubble (brushwood is less satisfactory because it eventually rots and allows the trench to collapse under the weight of the covering soil). Unless you have access to a reasonable quantity of rubble, contact a local demolition firm and arrange to have a load delivered.

Give the trench a fall along its length of about 1 in 100, running to the ditch or soakaway. This is just a hole about 90cm (3ft) deep and filled to within about 30cm (1ft) of the surface with loose-packed brick rubble or clinkers.

Spread the hardcore to a depth of about 30cm (1ft) along the base of the trench. To prevent soil washing in and clogging up the hardcore, cover it with polythene sheeting or glass fibre matting before back-filling the trench with the excavated soil.

Herringbone drainage
In extreme cases of waterlogging, install a series of land drains running across the whole property. They should discharge into a natural outlet, a ditch for example, or a soakaway. Drainage trenches are laid out in a herringbone pattern, running from the highest point of the garden to the lowest and then into a soakaway.

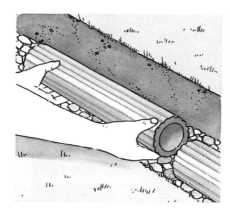

7 If you are using earthenware pipes, lay them end-to-end on the bed of gravel leaving a small gap between each unit. Try to keep the gaps even, and the line of pipes straight.

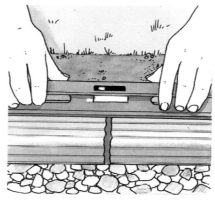

8 Check once again that the fall and alignment of each drain run is correct. Check consecutive pipes against a spirit level to avoid discrepancies occurring from pipe to pipe.

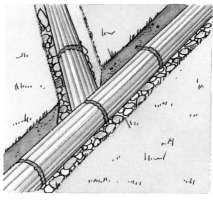

9 Lead the branch pipes to the main pipe line. Make a hole in the side of the pipe in the main drain run and angle the end of the branch pipe so that it butts up as close as possible.

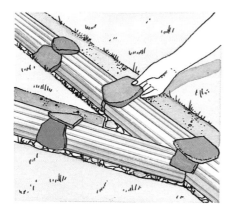

10 If you are laying earthenware pipes, protect them from excessive soil filtration by covering the joints with pieces of old tile. The sides and bottom of the joints remain open.

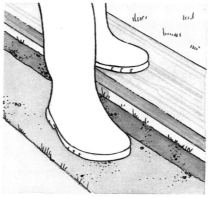

11 Replace the subsoil and then the topsoil, compacting each layer in turn using the flat side of a garden spade or the underside of your boot. Level off to an accurate depth for the turf.

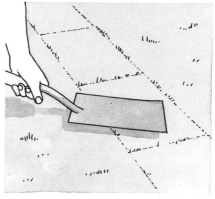

12 Replace the sections of turf, and tamp them very carefully into position with the back of the spade. Fit the pieces of turf as precisely as possible, flush against the lawn edge.

On level sites the trenches should have a fall of about 1 in 100 to ensure that the water flows comfortably through the system.

The depth of the trenches depends on the soil porosity. Dig down to about 75cm (2½ft) in clay, 90cm (3ft) in loam and 90-120cm (3-4ft) in sandy soil to compensate for the differing rates of drainage of each soil type. The side drains should be spaced about 3m (10ft) apart in clay, 6m (20ft) apart in loam and 15m (50ft) apart in sand, and should join the main drain at an angle of about 45°.

Start by marking out the positions of the side and main drains with pegs and string lines. The main trench needs to be about 30cm (1ft) wide, the side branches about 15cm (6in) across. Then, lift the turf along each drain line, setting it aside so that you can replace it later, and excavate the trenches. Give them sloping sides so that they don't collapse, and

store lawn turf, topsoil and subsoil separately on tarpaulin sheets as you dig.

After digging each trench, use a spirit level on a long batten – or a water level made from a length of garden hose and two pieces of clear plastic pipe – to check the fall. Then lay a 5cm (2in) thick bed of sand and gravel along the bottom of the trenches ready for the drainpipes to be laid.

You can use plastic, concrete or earthenware pipes. Plastic pipes are perforated, and are laid with the perforations facing downwards so that water can enter the pipe without washing in fine soil and causing a blockage. Successive lengths are linked with straight couplers, and tees are available to make connections into the main drain run. Plastic pipes are best – they are easy to lay and the joints help keep the system clear of blockages.

Concrete and earthenware

pipes are laid with 12mm (½in) gaps between successive lengths. The joins are covered with pieces of slate or roof tile to stop soil falling in. However, they are more difficult to lay and silt up easily.

Whichever sort of pipe you choose, lay 7.5cm (3in) diameter runs for the side branches of the system, and 10cm (4in) diameter pipe for the main drain leading to the soakaway. This should be dug

Tool list

wooden pegs
string
edging tool
spade
ruler
shovel
tarpaulin sheets
spirit level
long batten or garden hose and
    two pieces of clear plastic pipe
tamper

so its base is about 1m (3ft) below the bottom of the main drain run (or 2m/6½ft) deep on sandy soils. Slope the sides and shore with sheets of plywood or similar materials to help prevent the trenches from caving in.

Then fill up the soakaway with rubble to the level of the main drain and start laying the pipework. The last length of the main drain run should project into the centre of the soakaway.

As you reach each branch drain, fit a tee piece (with plastic piping) and carry on laying the pipes until you reach the top end of the system. Check that all the pipes are laid correctly and that the joints are secure. Then cover them with 15cm (6in) of gravel, then a layer of glass fibre matting to help prevent soil seeping into the pipes. Finish off by backfilling the trenches with subsoil and topsoil tamped firmly into place, and replace the turf. Lastly, complete filling the soakaway with gravel to within about 30cm (1ft) of the surface and lay soil and turf over the top. A sheet of polythene placed between the soil and the rubble will prevent soil from being washed in by rainwater or forced into the hardcore base by people walking across the lawn or the movement of garden implements over the surface.

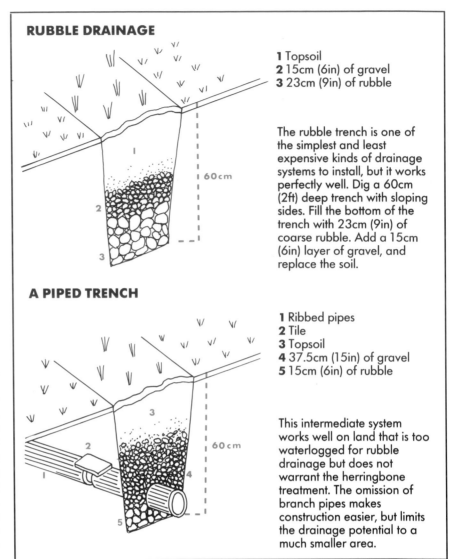

RUBBLE DRAINAGE

1 Topsoil
2 15cm (6in) of gravel
3 23cm (9in) of rubble

60cm

The rubble trench is one of the simplest and least expensive kinds of drainage systems to install, but it works perfectly well. Dig a 60cm (2ft) deep trench with sloping sides. Fill the bottom of the trench with 23cm (9in) of coarse rubble. Add a 15cm (6in) layer of gravel, and replace the soil.

A PIPED TRENCH

1 Ribbed pipes
2 Tile
3 Topsoil
4 37.5cm (15in) of gravel
5 15cm (6in) of rubble

60cm

This intermediate system works well on land that is too waterlogged for rubble drainage but does not warrant the herringbone treatment. The omission of branch pipes makes construction easier, but limits the drainage potential to a much smaller area.

A BRICK AND CONCRETE SOAKAWAY

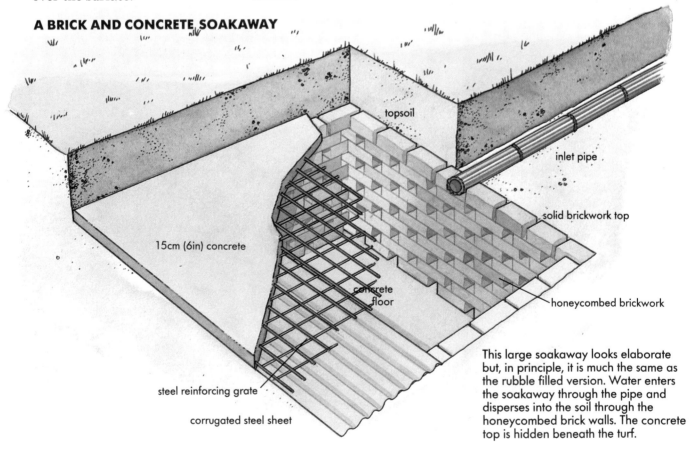

topsoil

inlet pipe

solid brickwork top

honeycombed brickwork

15cm (6in) concrete

concrete floor

steel reinforcing grate

corrugated steel sheet

This large soakaway looks elaborate but, in principle, it is much the same as the rubble filled version. Water enters the soakaway through the pipe and disperses into the soil through the honeycombed brick walls. The concrete top is hidden beneath the turf.

USING FERTILIZERS

**Plants, like people, thrive on a balanced
diet – the soil they grow in must be enriched with
all the foods needed for healthy growth.**

Plants manufacture their own body-building substances from raw materials in the soil – weathered rock and humus. Several of the essential chemical elements for plants are readily obtainable from the air and the soil and do not need supplementing under normal conditions – these are carbon, hydrogen and oxygen.

Other essential nutrients, dissolved in water, are taken up as a 'drink' by hairs growing near the tips of the roots. The three principal elements on which plant life depends nitrogen (abbreviated to N), phosphorus (P) and potassium (K) – are absorbed in this way. A well-tended soil will be rich in all these, together with the so-called 'trace elements'. These are required in very small quantities only – or a trace – but are just as essential as the big three, N, P and K. Nitrogen is 'fixed' in the soil – and so rendered available to plants – by the action of various soil-borne bacteria.

In time, a plant will use up most of the available nutrients, so it is essential to supply more if the plant is to thrive. Nitrogen is leached rapidly from the soil by drainage water following rainfall.

All the complex needs of a plant could be met by enriching the soil with farmyard manure – animal droppings mixed with straw. The highly productive kitchen gardens of Victorian times received huge quantities of stable manure, and the natural processes of the soil, assisted by enough lime to keep it 'sweet', made it unnecessary for the gardener to worry about details of plant nutrition.

This simple method of maintaining fertility is no longer practicable for most gardeners, who must now rely on whatever organic material is available and on supplementing it with organic or inorganic chemical fertilizers. Manures do a combined job of feeding the soil and improving its structure, but are slow-acting in building up fertility.

Chemical fertilizers feed plants more directly, supplying nutrients that can be absorbed immediately, but they do nothing to improve soil structure and may even deplete its reserves of organic material.

Aim to strike a balance, adding as much organic material as is possible, and using fertilizers to remedy known deficiencies.

Fertilizer types

Each of the essential nutrients – nitrogen, phosphorus (in phosphate) and potassium (in potash) – can be bought separately as so-called 'straight' fertilizers, or in balanced mixtures known as 'compound' or 'general' fertilizers. The latter type generally include the most important trace elements.

Nitrogen sources Some fertilizers derived from dead animals, including dried blood and hoof and horn mix, are rich in nitrogen. But they are expensive and are normally used only in special circumstances, such as in sowing and potting composts.

Less expensive sources of nitrogen are the inorganic fertilizers – the cheapest being sulphate of ammonia. More expensive are nitro-chalk, nitrate of ammonia and nitrate of soda. These work faster than sulphate of ammonia because they are already in the nitrate form which roots absorb and use.

When plants need a quick-acting stimulant, it is usually best supplied by nitrogen alone. For example, spring cabbages respond quickly to a top-dressing of a nitrate fertilizer at 15g (½oz) per sq m/yd once growth starts.

Other overwintered vegetables also need added nitrogen in spring to replace that lost from the soil by winter rains or not yet made available by the action of bacteria because of low soil temperature.

◄ **Organic fertilizers** Bonemeal is a slow-release general fertilizer which can be added to soil around perennials and shrubs at planting time to supply essential nitrates and phosphates.

PLANT NUTRITION		
SOIL NUTRIENT	**MAIN PLANT USERS**	**REQUIREMENTS**
Nitrogen (N)	All plants, especially leaf vegetables and grasses	For leaf and stem growth. Soon washed out of the soil by rain, especially on sandy soils. Replenish every year.
Phosphorus (P) as phosphate (P_2O_5)	Root crops and all young plants; also flowering, fruiting and seeding plants	For root growth and the production of flowers and seeds. Remains in the soil for two or three years after application; less so in sandy soils
Potassium (K) as potash (K_2O)	Flowering and fruiting plants	For flower and fruit formation, maintaining general growth and providing resistance to disease. Remains in the soil for two or three years after application; less so in sandy soils
Calcium (Ca) in lime	All plants	For general plant growth; encourages the growth of soil bacteria which are responsible for producing certain plant foods. Deficient in acid (lime-free) and potash-rich soils
Magnesium (Mg)	All plants, especially tomatoes and roses	For the production of the green pigment chlorophyll. Deficient in well-drained or potash-rich soils
Trace elements: Iron (Fe), Boron (B), Cobalt (Co), Copper (Cu), Sulphur (S), Manganese (Mn), Zinc (Zn), Molybdenum (Mo)	All plants	For general plant growth. Rarely deficient in well-tended soils. Certain plants have higher demands for certain trace elements – supplied by specially formulated fertilizers, such as rhododendron feed which has added iron and manganese. Sulphur is more likely to be deficient in rural areas than in urban ones. Soil type may affect the availability of certain elements – the calcium in chalky soils may render iron and manganese unusable by plants, for instance

FERTILIZER APPLICATION METHODS

1 Broadcast base dressings of pre-planting or pre-seeding fertilizers at an even rate over the bed, then rake in. Follow manufacturer's instructions for application rates – use canes to mark out 1 sq m/yd areas as a guide.

2 When planting shrubs in soil that has not been well-cultivated, prepare a planting mix consisting of good garden soil with a couple of handfuls per bucketful of a slow-release general fertilizer such as Growmore.

3 Sprinkle top-dressing fertilizers around the roots of plants to promote strong growth, a good show of flowers or a high yield of fruits. Water in if the soil is dry or if it does not rain for several days after application.

4 Special fertilizer blocks are available to meet the needs of every plant group. These are put into a dissolver canister attached to a hosepipe – a precise way of applying liquid fertilizer to leaves and roots.

5 Liquid fertilizers can be applied simply to moist soil using an ordinary watering can with the sprinkler rose removed. This is the best way of giving garden plants and crops a feed during dry weather, after initial watering.

6 Liquid foliar feeds should be applied to the leaves using a pressure sprayer. This is a good way of giving a rapid boost to plants, and is ideal for applying trace element plant tonics. Don't spray in hot weather.

Most fruit crops appreciate a dressing of sulphate of ammonia in spring. A more active source of nitrogen is urea, sprayed on to the foliage of starved fruit trees and bushes in the spring. Urea spray can be bought from a nurseryman, but be sure to follow the manufacturer's instructions carefully.

Phosphorus sources Phosphorus, in the form of soluble phosphates, is particularly important to plants in the seedling stage and in the formation of roots. When the soil has too little phosphate the leaves turn dull purple, they are smaller and the growth of the plant slows down. Too much phosphate will cause a premature ripening of the plant.

Phosphatic fertilizers include slow-release bonemeal, which is popular because it is organic and readily available, and superphosphate of lime.

When seeds are sown out of doors, a dressing of superphosphate at two tablespoons per sq m/yd should be applied before sowing, and lightly raked in.

Potassium sources Potassium, in the form of potash, increases the intensity of flower colour and is sometimes given as a top-dressing to improve the formation of flowers and the ripening of fruits. It also increases a plant's resistance to pests and diseases and hardens the tissues. Potash is especially required for fruit crops, tomatoes and potatoes.

Light soils in particular are likely to need added potash, and the most suitable form for the gardener is sulphate of potash.

Compound fertilizers Growmore is a very popular and well-tried compound fertilizer, containing 7% nitrogen, 7% phosphorus and 7% potassium. The ingredients are sulphate of ammonia, superphosphate of lime and sulphate of potash.

Another compound formula is John Innes base fertilizer containing hoof and horn mixture, superphosphate and sulphate of potash. The N, P and K content is more carefully balanced and, since the nitrogen is of organic (natural) source, this fertilizer is usually more expensive.

Fertilizers are also available in formulations for special purposes – there are quick-absorption liquid feeds for potash-loving plants such as tomatoes and carnations, for instance.

NUTRIENT DEFICIENCY SYMPTOMS

1 Nitrogen deficiency is indicated by poor, stunted growth with pale leaves and weak stems. Leaves often turn orange, red or purplish and may fall prematurely. Fruit trees and vegetables are most commonly affected.

2 Potassium deficiency is indicated by brown scorching around the edges of the leaves. Flowers may be dull and sparse, and fruit yield may be low and of poor quality. Tissues are soft and more prone to pests and diseases.

3 Magnesium deficiency is indicated by yellow patches between the leaf veins which later turn brown. The affected leaves may wither. Roses and tomatoes are often affected. Magnesium sulphate (Epsom salts) spray is the best cure.

4 Manganese deficiency is indicated by yellowing between the veins of older leaves. Leaf edges may become slightly in-curled and brown. Many types of plant may be affected occasionally. Apply a sequestrine plant tonic.

Liquid fertilizers Concentrated compound fertilizers, sold in both solid and liquid form, must be diluted before use. They are easy to apply as a top-dressing and are quickly absorbed by plants.

Some liquid fertilizers are derived from seaweed and humus extracts; others are made solely from chemical elements. They are mixed in various proportions to suit the needs of various plants and soils.

Foliar feeds Plants take several days to make use of nutrients absorbed through their roots. However, if their leaves are sprayed with dilute solutions of fertilizers the process is accelerated. Special fertilizers for foliar feeding are available, some being based on soluble, inorganic fertilizers while others are all-organic preparations with a seaweed base. All types are quickly absorbed.

Foliar feeds should be regarded as a supplement to manures or fertilizers rather than as the sole means of feeding the crop. They are particularly useful, however, if the plants have a poor root system or during dry spells when the plants have difficulty in drawing nutrients from the soil.

Applying fertilizers
Never apply more fertilizer than recommended. Measure roughly the area to be fed, then weigh the required amount of fertilizer on a kitchen scale – line the scale with paper and wash it out thoroughly afterwards, or preferably keep an old scale solely for this purpose. Halve the amount of fertilizer when farmyard manure or garden compost has been dug in.

A fortnight before sowing seeds, spread a compound fertilizer evenly over the soil and hoe or rake it into the surface. Do not dig it in or it will soon wash down out of reach of the roots.

Do not scatter fertilizers along a seed drill as they may injure the germinating seedlings. Apply top-dressings along the sides of the rows or around plant roots and lightly hoe them in. Do not allow inorganic fertilizers – except the foliar feeds – to touch the plant's foliage or it will be scorched.

In dry weather follow the application of fertilizers with a good watering because they cannot be aborbed by the plants until they are dissolved. The condition of the soil and the weather also dictates the types of fertilizers to use. A light, sandy soil, for example, needs more potash than heavier soils, especially in gardens where soft fruits are grown. In districts with a heavy rainfall, nitrogenous

fertilizers wash out quickly and should be replaced by regular top-dressings of sulphate of ammonia or nitrate of soda.

Storing fertilizers
Store fertilizers in a dry place as they quickly absorb moisture. If you transfer a chemical to a new container, label it clearly. Store out of reach of children – some fertilizers are poisonous.

FERTILIZER TYPES AND THEIR CONTENT

FERTILIZER	NUTRIENT CONTENT (approx.)	APPLICATION METHOD	SPECIAL FEATURES
INORGANIC Magnesium sulphate (Epsom salts)	10% magnesium; sulphur	Top dressing	Effective against chlorosis
Nitrate of ammonia	35% nitrogen	Liquid feed	Do not mix with lime
Nitrate of soda (sodium nitrate)	16% nitrogen; trace elements	Top dressing	Fast-acting but quickly washed out of the soil. Keep off foliage
Nitro-chalk	16% nitrogen; calcium	Top dressing	Contains 48% lime. Long-lasting, fast-acting; useful on acid soils. Can be used to aid rotting of compost
Potassium nitrate	12-14% nitrogen; 44-46% potash	Top dressing/ liquid feed	A general spring fertilizer. Impure Chilean potash nitrate contains only 15% K_2O
Sulphate of ammonia	21% nitrogen; sulphur	Top dressing	Best source of N, but makes soil more acid. Do not mix with lime. Fast-acting
Sulphate of iron	Iron; sulphur	Top dressing	Effective against iron-induced chlorosis. Acidifies the soil
Sulphate of potash	48% potash	Base or top dressing	Best general source of potash. Fast-acting for flowers and fruit. Acidifies the soil
Superphosphate	13-20% phosphate	Base dressing	Best source of phosphates. Keep off delicate leaves. Do not mix with sodium nitrate
Urea	46% nitrogen	Liquid/foliar feed	Very rich source of N. Apply in spring
ORGANIC Bonemeal	2-5% nitrogen; 20-30% phosphate; calcium	Base or top dressing	Slow-release fertilizer; apply in spring or autumn. Contains lime. Ensure it is sterilized
Dried blood	10-13% nitrogen	Top dressing/ liquid feed	Fairly fast-acting. Apply in late spring or summer. Ideal for leaf vegetables
Fish meal	6-10% nitrogen; 5-12% phosphate; 1-2% potash	Base dressing	Fairly slow-release; apply during spring cultivation, one spade's depth
Hoof and horn	7-15% nitrogen; 1-10% phosphate; calcium	Base dressing	Fairly slow-release, though speed depends on fineness of grinding. Apply in spring
Wood ash	2-9% potash	Top dressing	Must be kept dry to retain potash. Young wood produces the richest ash. Not for chalky soil
COMPOUND Growmore	7% nitrogen; 7% phosphate; 7% potash	Base or top dressing	Good general-purpose fertilizer. Apply in spring. Now available also in liquid form
John Innes base	5% nitrogen; 7% phosphate; 10% potash	Base or top dressing	Contains hoof and horn; slow-release of N. Used mainly in potting mixtures
Rose fertilizer	5% nitrogen; 6% phosphate; 12% potash; iron; magnesium	Top dressing	Fairly fast-acting. Apply in summer. Specially formulated for roses, but suitable for others
Sequestrine tonic	Magnesium, manganese, iron	Top dressing	Cures yellowing. May include other trace elements
Tomato fertilizer	6% nitrogen; 5% phosphate; 9% potash	Liquid feed	Used as weekly feed throughout the growing period to promote a high yield. Ideal for growing bags

COMPOST AND MANURES

**All plants, especially food crops, benefit from
regular applications of compost or manure, as well as
of fertilizers, to promote strong growth.**

The requirements for compost or manure go hand-in-hand with those for organic or inorganic fertilizers. If heavily cropped land is supplied with ample fertilizer but no compost or manure, it will deteriorate as all the existing humus is used up. In sandy soil, there will eventually be no organic matter to contain water or to hold the particles together. The soil will dry out rapidly and could be eroded seriously. Clay soil will become harder as the humus becomes depleted, because there will be nothing left to hold the minute particles apart.

Soil which is supplied only with the limited amount of manure available in cities, but no fertilizer, may lack the nutrients needed for intensive cropping and good flower formation.

Manure is bulky organic matter derived from animals or plants. It breaks down in the soil to become humus – a dark, gummy, fibrous substance which binds the soil particles into small groups, leaving gaps in between for air and water to circulate. The bacteria in the soil convert it into chemical salts, which in turn become dissolved in water and are taken up by the roots of the plants for food. Soil bacteria use a lot of nitrogen, which must be replenished.

Bulky organic manures for the garden are increasingly difficult to obtain, especially by town and city dwellers. The most convenient alternative is garden compost, which you can make yourself with vegetable waste matter from the garden or kitchen. (Do not confuse garden compost with potting soils which may also be referred to as composts.)

Making a compost heap

Unfortunately, the average suburban garden seldom yields enough material to produce the conditions necessary in a compost heap to produce rapid fermentation and decay. Consequently, compost heaps are frequently little more than neglected rubbish dumps. However, there are many ways to improve this situation and, in particular, the heap can be built up with extra material brought in from outside the garden, such as straw or fallen leaves.

The material in a compost heap is broken down by bacteria and other micro-organisms, which will thrive only if given air, water, nitrogen, non-acid conditions and a high temperature. And even under ideal conditions, there are limits to the rapid breakdown powers of the bacteria, so do not put woody material – not even Brussels sprout stems – on the heap. Chop any tough stems into small pieces before putting them on the compost heap.

Never use obviously diseased plant material in the compost heap, as the disease may be spread with the compost. Never use the roots of perennial weeds such as couch grass, oxalis or bindweed. Also avoid annual weeds which are carrying seeds.

The best compost is made from soft rubbish, such as dead leaves, lettuces which have bolted, pea

◄ PVC compost bins These proprietary bins provide a convenient means of containing garden compost while it is decomposing. Several weeks or months need to elapse before waste from the garden is fully converted by soil bacteria into a usable, dark brown, crumbly, manure-like substance. With this type of bin, the rotted compost can be extracted from the bottom while new waste is being added continually to the top.

MAKING GARDEN COMPOST

1 Build the compost heap layer by layer, beginning on bare garden soil to allow excess water to drain away freely. Spread the first layer about 30cm (1ft) deep and about 1.5 × 1.5m (5 × 5ft) wide.

2 Tread down the garden waste and soak it with water. Sprinkle sulphate of ammonia at the rate of one dessertspoon per sq m/yd to speed up the decomposition process, then cover with a 5cm (2in) layer of garden soil.

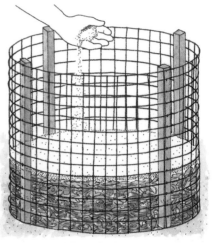

3 As you build up the heap, contain it within wire netting secured on wooden stakes. If your soil is acid, add a little lime to every alternate layer to keep the heap sweet. Cover the top with polythene or sacking.

4 As more garden waste becomes available, continue building the heap in 23-30cm (9-12in) layers up to a height of about 1.2m (4ft). Sprinkle each layer with compost activator. Cover the heap with a final layer of garden soil.

5 In very dry spells, moisten the heap with water every fortnight. Keep the compost covered with polythene or sacking. Heat will build up in the heap quite rapidly at first, but will die down in the last stages of decomposition.

6 After several weeks the heap will have shrunk to about one-third its original size. At this stage it's an advantage to turn the heap, so that the outer material, which is slower to rot, can be placed on the inside.

stalks and leaves, beetroot leaves, dead flowers, leafy hedge clippings, hay, straw and lawn mowings, along with the vegetable trimmings from the kitchen. Do not use cooked scraps or anything containing grease.

Build the compost heap into a neat, regular shape, so that it is less likely to become dry around the edges. A heap measuring approximately 2m × 2m × 1.5m high (7 × 7 × 5ft) is necessary for quick results. But in a small garden a sensible approach is to set up a neat enclosure of wire netting and posts. The best size must depend on the size of the garden, but 1.5 × 1.5m wide and 1.2m high

(5 × 5 × 4ft) is about right for the average garden.

The heap should be made directly on the soil, so that any excess water can drain away. The soil beneath, however, should be well drained.

You can also buy ready-made compost bins or make an open-topped wooden box, leaving spaces between the side boards to let air through. Brick constructions are equally suitable, as long as you leave a few bricks missing in the sides for aeration. If one side of the box is removable, it gives easier access to the compost.

Try to build the heap a layer at a time, each layer about 30cm (1ft)

thick. Tread down each layer and then give it a good soaking with a hose. To each layer add sulphate of ammonia at about 15g (½oz) – one dessertspoon – per sq m/yd to act as an accelerator for the decomposition process, and cover it with 5cm (2in) of ordinary garden soil. Cover the top of the heap with polythene or sacking to keep in the heat until the last layer has been added and covered with soil.

For a free-standing compost heap, build it up with gently sloping sides to the height you require. If your soil is naturally lime-rich there is no need to add more lime to the heap, but if the soil is acid sprinkle garden lime at the rate of 120g per sq m (4oz per sq yd) over every alternate layer and again over the finished heap before covering with a final layer of garden soil. The lime will keep the heap sweet. In a dry summer, hose the heap with water as soon as it shows signs of drying out.

Heat will build up rapidly when the heap is first made, but will die down after about a month, when the heap will have shrunk to about one-third its original size.

Decomposition is speeded up if the heap is turned after six weeks, moving the material on the outside of the pile into the centre. At the same time, water any dry areas. If you use compost bins, simply transfer the contents to a second bin, mixing the contents thoroughly as you do so.

However, turning is not essential, and in three months (or more if the pile was made at the beginning of the winter) the pile will turn into a crumbly, dark brown, manure-like material which can be dug into the vegetable garden or spread thickly around border plants, including perennials, shrubs and trees.

The normal application rate for garden compost is one 10 litre (two gallon) bucketful per sq m/yd. It can also be used as a top dressing or surface mulch.

If the heap is to remain undisturbed over winter, protect it by covering with polythene held down by bricks or stones, or tucked down between the compost and the rails of the bin.

Other sources of manure

Bulky farmyard manures are dug in during the winter or are used as mulches in summer. Some are rich in plant foods while others have little immediate food value, but all add to the soil's humus content and improve its condition.

In fact, any bulky organic waste is useful as a garden manure, provided it does not contain harmful industrial chemicals and provided it rots down reasonably quickly.

Bulky organic manures need to be used in large quantities. A good dressing would be a 15cm (6in) layer, or about a 10 litre (two gallon) bucket of manure per sq m/yd.
Farmyard/stable manure, which includes the animals' straw bedding, is one of the finest forms of organic manure.

The ammonia content of fresh farmyard manure may damage

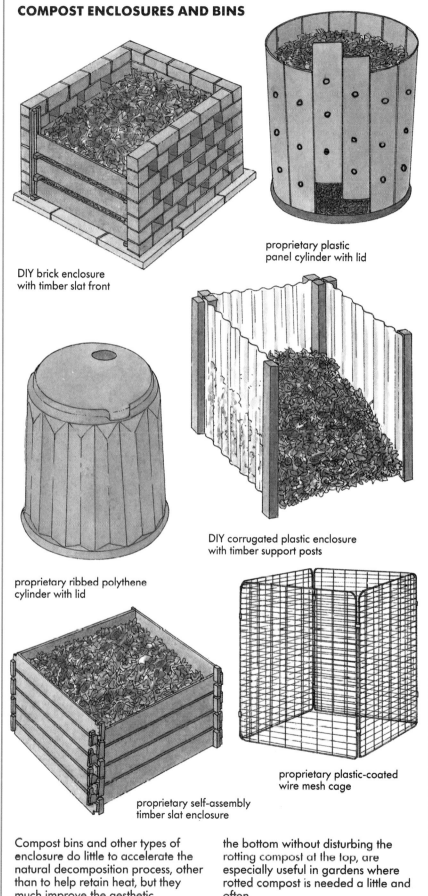

COMPOST ENCLOSURES AND BINS

DIY brick enclosure
with timber slat front

proprietary plastic
panel cylinder with lid

proprietary ribbed polythene
cylinder with lid

DIY corrugated plastic enclosure
with timber support posts

proprietary self-assembly
timber slat enclosure

proprietary plastic-coated
wire mesh cage

Compost bins and other types of enclosure do little to accelerate the natural decomposition process, other than to help retain heat, but they much improve the aesthetic appearance of the composting area — free-standing heaps can look very unsightly in a small garden.

Specially designed bins, which allow compost to be extracted from the bottom without disturbing the rotting compost at the top, are especially useful in gardens where rotted compost is needed a little and often.

With a little ingenuity, you can use bricks, corrugated plastic or iron, wire or plastic netting, chicken wire or timber to build an improvised compost enclosure.

plants, so it is usually best to use it after it has been stacked for a while and has partly decomposed. Stacking in the open means that the soluble nutrients are washed out by rain, and so well-rotted farmyard manure is low in plant nutrients. But it does provide the necessary humus, and soil rich in humus is usually very fertile.

Horse manure is 'hot' – that is, it ferments rapidly – and for this reason was at one time widely used to form hot-beds for raising early food crops. Nowadays, electric soil-warming cables are more likely to be used instead. It is one of the richest and driest manures, but often that sold by riding stables contains mainly urine-soaked straw and a few droppings. It decays rapidly into a disappointingly small heap.

Pig manure is slow to ferment and, when fresh, tends to be caustic and to burn the roots of young plants. It is best composted with straw and left for at least three months before use.

Cattle manure containing straw from the yards is wetter and lower in nutrients than horse manure, but it decomposes slowly into the soil, and is ideal for sandy soils.

Deep litter poultry manure may be bought by the load from poultry farmers. This partly rotted litter is usually dry and dusty and must be composted before use.

It takes some weeks for the wood shavings or straw on which the manure is based to break down. During this time the heap may develop an offensive smell so it should be placed as far away as possible from houses.

When composted with soil, deep litter poultry manure is rich in nitrogen but deficient in potash and phosphates.

Spent mushroom compost may be available from mushroom nurseries. Mushrooms are grown commercially on a compost based mainly on horse manure. When all the mushrooms have been harvested the compost is sold – either in bulk or in pre-packed bags.

This is a good garden manure or mulch, containing humus and plant foods. It also contains chalk, which makes it less suitable for soils that are already alkaline, though it won't do much harm unless applied every year.

Spent hops sold direct by breweries help to improve the physical condition of the soil, but they are

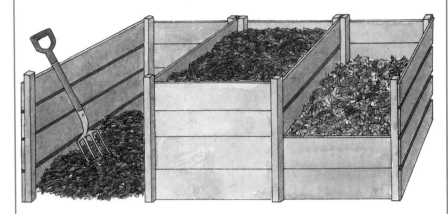

A THREE-COMPARTMENT BIN

If you have enough space, a three-compartment timber bin is ideal. Construct it so that the front boards can be slipped into position as the boxes are filled. The left box contains compost being used; the middle box is in the process of decomposing; and the right one is being filled. Fork the compost from one box to another to aerate it.

low in plant nutrients. This can be remedied by using them in conjunction with a general fertilizer.

Alternatively, buy treated hop waste which has had nutrients added to it from a fertilizer supplier. This is excellent manure, but expensive to use as a soil conditioner in large quantities.

Sewage sludge, processed by some local authorities, is a well-balanced manure. Despite its unpleasant origin, this material is generally inoffensive to handle. Inquire at the Engineer's Department of your council offices to check availability.

Seaweed is rich in plant foods, especially nitrogen and potash, and breaks down quickly into humus. Stack seaweed for a month or two to allow rain to wash out most of the salt, then dig it in at the rate of about 5.5kg per sq m (12lb per sq yd).

Leaf-mould may be made by composting any fallen leaves, though oak and beech leaves are the most satisfactory if somewhat acid. Do not use conifer needles.

Pile up alternate layers of leaves and soil, each about 5cm (2in) deep. A sprinkling of general fertilizer on each layer of leaves will assist decomposition. Do not make the heap more than 1m (3ft) high. Turn it at two or three-month intervals.

The compost will be ready in about a year. Apply at the rate of 2.5-3kg per sq m (5-6lb per sq yd).

Peat substitutes Nowadays many people prefer not to use peat in their garden since it is becom-

ing increasingly scarce. Alternatives such as coir fibre and composted bark are made from renewable natural resources.

Coir fibre compost, made from coconut fibre, actually holds more air and moisture than peat. Nutrients are added to give it a pH of 6.5, making it equivalent to sedge peat in acidity and use.

Composted bark is a by-product of the softwood timber industry, and can also be used in much the same way as peat to improve the condition of the soil. Bark products do, however, tend to trap nitrogen from the soil, so it is best to use composted bark for mulching and coir compost for planting seeds and cuttings.

Green manure crops are grown for the sole purpose of turning them into the soil to provide humus and plant nutrients. They are particularly valuable on heavy clay and light sandy soils. The overall effect is equivalent to digging in compost or manure, but the soil cannot be used while the cover crop is growing and, ideally, for several months after it has been dug in. Plants used for green manuring include clover, comfrey, fenugreek, lucerne, lupins, mustard, rape and rye-grass.

Wool shoddy is a waste product from the woollen industry. It is now uneconomic to use at any distance from the factories due to transport costs. Shoddy is rich in nitrogen, which is released slowly over three years. Without first decomposing it, dig it in at about ½kg per sq m (1lb per sq yd).

USING MULCHES

**A surface dressing of a bulky organic or inorganic
material reduces moisture loss from the soil, keeps roots
cool in summer and suppresses weed growth.**

Soil is a natural reservoir for water, which is needed to a greater or lesser extent by all plants. The only natural source of water in most gardens is rain – and to a lesser extent snow – though moisture can seep in from adjacent streams and permanently boggy soil, especially in low-lying sites.

Apart from surplus rain-water which drains away, soil loses moisture in two ways – by direct evaporation from the surface and through the action of plants, which take up water in their roots and keep cool by transpiring it through their leaves.

In hot, dry spells the moisture content of soil needs to be supplemented by watering, but it can also be conserved by mulching. This entails placing a physical barrier between the moisture-holding soil and the air.

Mulches can be made from many materials – both organic and inorganic – but wood bark chippings, garden compost, well-rotted stable manure and black polythene are the most commonly used types nowadays.

In some regions, other organic materials may be readily available for use as a mulch – such as spent mushroom compost from mushroom farms, spent hops and brewery waste, seaweed, straw, shoddy waste from woollen mills and sawdust or wood shavings from saw mills.

In the long term, mulches of organic material, such as manure or compost, have an additional value – they ultimately add to the humus content of the soil.

Advantages of mulching
In addition to moisture conservation, the addition of a good mulch to the soil surface has many useful functions in the garden, around both crop plants and ornamentals.
☐ Weed seedlings are suffocated and shaded from light, so they mostly die soon after germinating. Continual use of sheet material, such as polythene, prevents weed seeds from getting into the soil in the first place. Annual weeds in particular are suppressed by mulches.
☐ Surface capping of the soil is prevented and good soil structure is maintained.
☐ Excessive fluctuations in surface soil temperature – which can scorch delicate young roots – are reduced. Mulches also reduce the risk of the soil freezing in winter.
☐ The decorative value of the ground around ornamental plants is increased by the use of some mulches – such as wood bark chippings and gravel – especially where new beds or borders have a lot of space between young developing plants.
☐ Worms are attracted by the extra protection offered by surface mulches and these creatures in turn help to improve the aeration of the soil.
☐ Lawn mowings (provided they have not been treated with weed-killer) can be used as a moisture and nitrogen-retaining mulch around peas and bean beds.

◄ **Straw mulch** Stable manure makes a useful surface dressing around globe artichokes, helping to conserve soil moisture, keep roots cool and suffocate weed seedlings.

☐ Alkaline mulching materials, such as spent mushroom compost, composted seaweed or limestone chippings, help to prevent acid soils from becoming even more acid – they are unlikely to make an acid soil alkaline.

☐ Organic mulches such as well-rotted manure or garden compost add plant nutrients to the soil and increase its fertility.

☐ Sheet materials such as polythene, and straw, can be used to keep strawberries and other low-growing soft fruit crops clean – rain often splashes soil and other debris on to the fruits.

☐ With the improved soil conditions, vegetable crops often produce a higher yield, and ornamental plants grow faster with better foliage and flowers.

Disadvantages of mulching

As with all good things, mulching has its disadvantages in certain situations, though many of these can be overcome.

☐ The roots of perennial weeds left in the soil before the mulch is applied can grow into new plants. These are then difficult to eradicate by hand-weeding or hoeing without disturbing the mulch.

☐ Some mulching materials, such as wood bark chippings, can deplete the soil of nitrogen.

☐ It may be more difficult to apply fertilizers – especially granular forms – once the mulch is in place.

☐ Polythene sheeting and other water-tight materials prevent rain-water from reaching the plant roots under the mulch. Absorbent organic materials soak up light showers of water, keeping plant roots dry.

☐ All mulches can harbour pests, especially slugs, snails and wireworms. If moist organic mulches smother the bases of plant stems they can cause rotting.

Preparing the soil

The addition of a mulch to the surface of the soil will impede subsequent cultivation of the ground, so it is important to prepare the site thoroughly beforehand.

Dig over the soil and eliminate all perennial weeds, either by hand-weeding or with chemical herbicides, since even broken segments of root can often grow into new plants and penetrate the mulch. At the same time, remove as many annual weeds as possible.

Rake in a general purpose slow-

ORGANIC MULCHES

▲ **Wood bark chippings** make a decorative and long-lasting mulch. The large and relatively heavy particles don't blow around in the wind and they counteract rain splash on to low plants.

▲ **Garden compost,** provided it is well rotted, can be used as a combined mulch and soil conditioner – as it decomposes further, nutrients and humus are mixed into the soil. Renew it every year.

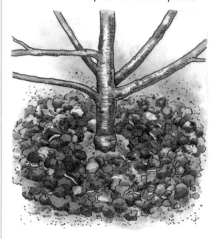

▲ **Stable manure** should be well decayed otherwise it will scorch delicate roots and smell unpleasant. Don't pile it up around the base of plants. Grass weed seeds may be mixed with the straw.

▲ **Composted bark** is used in much the same way as peat as a mulch and soil conditioner. It is good for acid-loving plants and its dark colour provides a good visual foil for decorative plants.

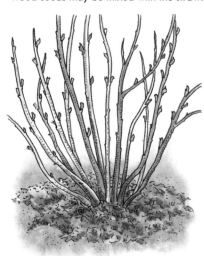

▲ **Grass clippings** can be used as a cheap mulch, but compost them first. Never use clippings from a lawn which has been treated with weedkiller and keep the mulch to a maximum 1cm (½in).

▲ **Straw** makes a soft open-textured mulch for strawberries and other low-growing soft fruit crops, helping to keep the ripening fruits clean. It is too obtrusive for use among ornamentals.

release fertilizer which will feed your plants for several months after laying the mulch. Later feeding can be achieved by using liquid fertilizers applied to the foliage or to the ground, but it will be impossible to mix granular types with the soil.

If you plan to use straw, wood bark, wood shavings or sawdust as a mulch – organic materials which have not been composted and will therefore use up nitrogen from the soil as they decompose – rake in an extra dressing of nitrogenous fertilizer at the rate of about a handful per sq m/yd before mulching.

If the reason for laying a mulch is to conserve moisture, ensure that the soil is saturated before covering it. Either wait for a heavy downpour of rain or water the site by hand. The water in the soil will still be depleted by the plants and by evaporation, and you will need to water during dry periods, but not as often as you would if the soil had no mulch.

Using mulches

The best time and method of applying mulches depend on your choice of material and the purpose for which it is mainly required.

Mid spring is generally the best time to apply mulches – at this time of year weeds are rarely established and the ground is moist. Don't mulch any earlier than this, because it is also important for the ground to be warmed up by the sun before mulching. Once applied, a mulch acts as an insulating blanket.

The plants that will benefit most from a regular yearly mulch are the garden's long-term residents – the shrubs, roses, fruit trees and bushes, especially the surface-rooting raspberries, and strawberries. In all these cases, the plants remain in the same place year after year and there is usually room to work around them. The herbaceous border and vegetable garden also benefit from a spring mulch.

INORGANIC MULCHES

▲ **Tree spats** can be bought from specialist suppliers. Made from bituminous felt, they are durable and easy to install.

▲ **Black polythene** is a good mulch for conserving soil moisture and suppressing weeds, especially around thirsty salad crops such as tomatoes.

▲ **Proprietary strawberry mats,** made from synthetic whalehide, keep the fruits clean and help to protect them from soil-borne pests.

▲ **Stone chippings** or coarse gravel make a natural-looking, free-draining mulch around alpines and keep the collars of the plants dry and rot-free.

GROUND COVER PLANTS

Certain shallow-rooted, low-growing plants can themselves be used as a living mulch around the roots of larger plants which like cool, moist roots. Here, golden creeping Jenny (*Lysimachia nummularia* 'Aurea') helps to provide the right cool soil conditions for a large-flowered clematis hybrid without competing significantly for water or nutrients, and is a very decorative feature in its own right.

LAYING A BLACK POLYTHENE MULCH

1 Prepare the planting bed as usual. Then lay the polythene sheeting over the entire area, allowing a little overhang at the edges. Using a hand trowel, make a shallow trench all round the perimeter of the bed.

2 Tuck the edges of the polythene into the trench, then anchor them by infilling with soil. The surface of the polythene should be flat but not too taut. Don't tread on the mulch — work at all times from the edges.

3 Using a sharp knife or scissors, cut crossed slits at the required spacings to act as planting and watering holes. Then dig planting holes in the soil below the slits using a hand trowel or bulb planter.

4 Insert young plants through the slits, firming them into the soil underneath the mulch. Water well through the slits and make sure that the polythene tongues are smoothed back around each plant stem.

As a general rule, leave a gap of 2.5-5cm (1-2in) around plant stems. Most young ornamentals and vegetable plants are liable to suffer if an organic mulch such as compost or manure is in direct contact with them. It may infect them with any disease the mulch contains. Incompletely rotted compost could also burn the stems and basal leaves.

Any plant that is grown as a grafted variety on a rootstock – most roses and fruit trees, for instance – runs an extra risk if any mulch is piled up against its stem. The covering can induce the grafted variety to develop roots of its own from above the union with the rootstock. These roots can change the nature of the plant – on a fruit tree, for instance, the new roots will overpower the dwarfing effect of the rootstock and encourage the tree to grow larger.

Thickness When using bulky organic or inorganic mulches around herbaceous plants, roses and other established plants, apply an evenly forked 5-7.5cm (2-3in) deep layer. Smaller plants and young plants require a thinner layer – 2.5cm (1in) is usually adequate.

Straw mulches around raspberry canes, currant bushes and gooseberries are most effective in a layer 7.5-10cm (3-4in) deep.

If possible, mulch all bare soil in your garden, except around annual seedlings or tiny, newly planted rock garden plants until they are well established. But cost – if you have to buy the mulching material – and difficulty of access to the ground around the plants may prevent you from doing this.

If you haven't got enough mulching material to go round, spread the appropriate depth around each individual plant. Leave the rest of the garden uncovered rather than applying too thin a layer over it.

At the other extreme, don't be too generous with the mulch. One that is too thick becomes just another rooting zone for weeds and will cut down on the amount of air and water able to get through to the soil and the roots beneath.

Special uses

Black or clear polythene sheeting can be used as a surface covering to keep a newly prepared bed in prime condition until sowing or planting – a heavy rainstorm can ruin your hard work. This is useful where you have only a day or two available per week and you are ruled by the weather. Keep the polythene in place with a few bricks or large stones.

A clear polythene mulch can be used to promote the germination of weed seeds in a seed bed. After initial preparations of the bed, anchor the polythene with a few bricks until weed seedlings appear. Then remove it and hoe off the weed seedlings. If you now sow your vegetable or flower seeds without disturbing the surface of the seed bed any further, subsequent weed problems will be reduced significantly.

Straw mulches can be used to protect the crowns of perennial plants which are not reliably frost-hardy. Cover the crowns with straw in late autumn or early winter and anchor it with a sheet of polythene and a few bricks or large stones. Remove the protective mulch in mid spring.

Use clear polythene sheeting as a surface mulch to warm up the soil in spring and early summer. Grow early crops – potatoes, tomatoes, courgettes and sweetcorn, for instance – through the polythene and their roots will be kept several degrees warmer than normal, speeding up growth.

Shallow-rooted ground-hugging plants, such as pachysandra and periwinkle, provide a decorative soil cover beneath taller growing plants. At the same time, they form a living, weed-smothering mulch for their partners.

Lawns and hedges

In terms of garden design, lawns are the carpets, and hedges are the walls, of an outdoor living space. As with interior design, careful thought should go into the choice and siting of lawns and hedges since they are both permanent features, and provide a constant, soothing green setting for short-lived seasonal displays of flower colour. The aim is usually to create a large, often flat surface which contrasts with the livelier shapes of flowers, trees and shrubs, garden furniture and ornaments.

Choosing the right lawn grasses and hedge plants for your garden depends largely on its intended use. Soil, aspect and exposure must also be considered, along with your taste, budget and the garden's style.

Hedges, for example, can create security, shelter and privacy or be purely decorative. They can be evergreen or deciduous; flowering or foliage only, formal or informal; and plain or ornate (even incorporating topiary and arches). Lawns can be started from turf or seed; be formal or informal; and range from bowling green perfect to all-purpose family lawns, and even rough wild meadows.

Site and soil preparation, levelling for lawns, and planting or sowing techniques are important, as is early care, while the young lawn or hedge becomes established. But the overall garden picture can only be perfected with regular maintenance. Feeding, watering and seasonal mowing or trimming keep lawns and hedges healthy and looking good. Any lawn troubles or areas needing repair should be dealt with quickly and effectively to minimize damage and maintain a consistently attractive appearance.

Green carpets Closely-mown, neatly trimmed lawns are the hallmark of good gardening.

GRASS IN THE GARDEN

**A beautiful lawn, as smooth and dense as
a bowling green, is many gardeners' dream. It can come true
if you create perfect conditions.**

Lawns are one of the most popular garden features, and for good reasons. A lawn can draw together a garden's flowerbeds and borders, focal points and ornaments into a harmonious whole. An established, well-tended lawn provides a background of green all year round. In the growing season it offers cool, restful relief next to the brighter colours of flowers, and provides textural contrast to the bolder forms of branches and foliage. In winter, a lawn may well be the only source of green colour in the garden.

An uninterrupted stretch of grass provides a marvellous surface for recreation, whether it is kicking a ball around or sunbathing. Lawns are also particularly suitable for toddlers, allowing them to be adventurous without suffering cuts or grazed knees from hard surfaces.

However, there are also some drawbacks. If you are starting a lawn from scratch, it takes lots of painstaking preparation – levelling, removing debris and weeds, fertilizing, then seeding or turfing. Unlike most trees and shrubs, which, once established, more or less look after themselves, lawns require careful watering, mowing and feeding to keep them looking good. A poorly kept lawn gives the garden a neglected appearance.

Siting a lawn

Some grasses are more tolerant of shade than others, but no lawn will thrive in deep shade, especially under trees, where roots and the overhanging canopy of leaves make the soil bone-dry and starved of nutrients. Nor will lawns thrive in waterlogged soil,

▼ **Lawn design** A well planned lawn is more than a stretch of grass – it draws together the various components of a garden, while providing year-round greenery and acting as a foil to foliage and brightly coloured flowers.

The addition of an elegant half-moon brick border has made this lawn a central feature.

▲ **Grassy banks** A slope can be used to link two different lawn levels as long as it doesn't take heavy use. Make sure that the slope isn't too steep or cutting the grass can be a problem.

◄ **In place of grass** Chamomile is less hard-wearing than lawn grass. Use stepping stones to save it from too much wear and tear.

although some grasses are more tolerant of damp soil than others.

Most lawns are flat or gently sloping, but, depending on the soil type, you can have one on a steeper slope – a grassy bank, for instance, can make an attractive feature.

Lawns can also be sunken, to form a sheltered seating area and create a feeling of intimacy. However, small sunken lawns can end up as water gardens unless the soil is very free draining or there is a soakaway.

Raised lawns can add interest to a flat garden, while providing informal seating on the retaining wall. Small raised lawns, however, look odd and dry out quickly in hot weather. With raised and sunken lawns, easy access for a mower is important.

Shaping a lawn

A formal square or rectangular lawn surrounded by borders is one of the most popular garden layouts. Such a lawn usually echoes the garden boundaries. But the shape of a lawn can also differ from that of the garden, such as a circular lawn in a square garden.

A curving lawn gives an informal, relaxed feel to a garden, and creates borders with interesting shapes – those that extend partway across the lawn can divide it into sections and add a sense of mystery as to what lies beyond.

As a general rule, though, the simpler the shape, the better a lawn looks and the easier it is to maintain. Avoid small hectic curves and lots of tiny island beds. Both of these work against a lawn's restful quality and make mowing difficult.

With an island flowerbed, make sure that there is at least a mower's width of lawn between this bed and any adjacent borders. Whatever a lawn's shape, a mowing strip, such as a single row of bricks or paving stones, between lawn and borders makes mowing much more convenient.

Types of lawn

A perfect-looking lawn might not be the best lawn for you and your family. It depends very much on what you want to use your lawn for and how much time and money you spend on its upkeep.

There are over 10,000 species of grass. However, most ordinary seed mixtures and turf are composed of just three or four species. These mixtures usually contain both tuft-forming grasses, such as the fescues (*Festuca*) and stoloniferous types, such as bents (*Agrostis*), which have leafy shoots that creep along the ground. How much of each is used in a mixture can vary according to the climate, soil type and water content, cost and amount of shade, wear and maintenance envisaged.

Beautiful velvety lawns are made up of fine-leaved grasses, such as fescues and bents. These are slow growing, especially when started from seed, and expensive to buy as turf. Fine-leaved grasses are relatively delicate, and do not stand up to heavy wear or periods of neglect. They are also vulnerable to invasion by stronger, coarser grasses, such as meadow

grass (*Poa*) – regular close mowing is needed to discourage them from gaining a foothold. Any coarse grasses or lawn weeds that do become established stick out like a sore thumb. Furthermore, any small bump, hollow or awkward level change is immediately noticeable because the lawn hugs the ground so closely.

Ordinary, hard-wearing lawns are made up of a careful mixture of broad-leaved grasses – meadow grasses, perennial rye grass (*Lolium perenne*), crested dog's tail (*Cynosurus cristatus*) and Timothy grasses (*Phleum*). They are relatively inexpensive in seed and turf form, and quick growing.

Unlike most of the fine-leaved grasses, broad-leaved types will tolerate heavy use, neglect and poor management without deteriorating too much. Any wild grasses that seed themselves quickly become part of the fabric of the lawn.

▼ **Formal layouts** In this split-level garden, the sharply trimmed lawn edges are as important to the formal geometric design as the flower borders and clipped hedges.

ing once established. But there are alternatives – these can be delightful if given the environment and care they need.

Chamomile (*Anthemis nobilis*) was a favourite lawn with the Elizabethans because of its sweet scent when bruised. There is no need to mow it and it is softer and springier to walk on than grass. However, it is short lived, can develop bare patches and often turns brown in winter. The non-flowering, dwarf 'Treneague' is best, but cannot be grown from seed.

Creeping thyme (*Thymus serpyllum*) is another possibility for small areas. It, too, is sweetly scented, but can also become thin and uneven. Both creeping thyme and chamomile need full sun and free-draining, sandy soil.

Paths of pennyroyal (*Mentha pulegium*) and Corsican mint (*M. requienii*) are lovely, but they tend to be invasive, sending rooting shoots into nearby beds.

▲ **Grass paths** Beneath pergolas and archways, grass paths can look highly attractive. Make sure to use a hard-wearing grass mixture and one which will also tolerate light shade.

▶ **Semi-wild corners** Rough grass cuts maintenance to a minimum as it needs mowing only twice a year. Wild and garden flowers can flourish undisturbed among the long grass.

However, broad-leaved grasses need frequent cutting, especially in spring and summer.

Rough grass areas create a rustic feel and are suitable for large gardens. They are ideal for naturalizing bulbs, such as daffodils and bluebells, and concealing their unsightly foliage as it fades.

Selected wild flowers, such as cow parsley and willow herb, poppies, cornflowers and foxgloves, can be encouraged, particularly those that attract butterflies.

Rough grass needs cutting only twice a year – once after the bulbs have died down completely and again in autumn. Weeding can be a problem, though, since ground elder, ragwort, thistles, docks and brambles quickly establish themselves. Apply a selective lawn weedkiller once the bulbs have completely died down.

Alternatives to grass

Grass tolerates heavier wear than any other plant, and is self renew-

LAWN MAKING

For a pleasing end result, plan your lawn first, if only in your mind's eye – and prepare the site thoroughly.

A prime-quality lawn, fine-textured, even and with a short pile, makes a wonderfully cooling and refreshing visual impact. Such perfection is achieved through sowing fine-leaved grasses of compact growth, mowing frequently to prevent coarser grasses becoming dominant, constant maintenance and minimum wear. But what most people need is a lawn that's hard wearing, long-lasting and easy to maintain.

A lawn that will stand up to reasonable wear and can tolerate a certain degree of neglect contains coarser and broader-leaved grasses than a prime quality lawn. It won't have a luxuriant close texture – although a good cylinder mower will help to improve the finish – but will present a pleasing contrast to the colour and leaf shapes of the borders while allowing you and your family to enjoy it as a main surface outside the house.

Preparing the site

The best time to sow is from late summer to early autumn or else in mid spring. Turf is best laid from mid autumn to late winter, but it can also be put down in early

▲ **Lawn stripes** Use a cylinder mower to maintain regular stripes in closely mown grass.

▼ **Stepping stones** Prime-quality lawns don't tolerate a lot of hard wear. Lay paths of paving or stepping stones or wooden logs on the routes most often followed round the garden.

PREPARING THE BED

1 Break down clods using a roller, or alternatively, trample systematically over the surface. Then rake the bed carefully, removing stones and debris.

2 Having made a level bed with an even, stone-free surface, roll over the area again to make sure it is quite firm. Work in two directions at right angles to each other.

3 A week later, firm the bed again by trampling across it, putting all your weight on your heels. Rake, then repeat both procedures until the bed is evenly firmed and absolutely level.

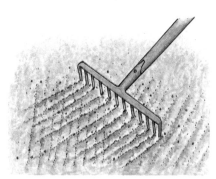

4 Lastly, rake in a general-purpose fertilizer and leave the bed untouched for a further week before sowing seed or laying turf. Take delivery of the turf as close to the laying time as possible.

spring. Whenever you plan to sow seed or lay turf, you must start preparing the ground at least three to four months in advance.

Levelling Begin by clearing the site of all rubbish, then you can set about adjusting levels and dealing with any drainage problems. A gentle slope can be an advantage and, on a large area, slight undulations are not a problem. But no lawn should have abrupt bumps and hollows.

Small-scale irregularities can easily be adjusted if you first establish a level by pegging out the area. You may need to bring in some topsoil to fill hollows, since even when you take soil from bumps you should leave an absolute minimum of 15cm (6in) of topsoil.

If a major levelling job is required, first take off the topsoil and store it on a piece of tarpaulin at one side, to be redistributed over the surface later.

Drainage On most sites, improving the soil texture by adding bulky organic matter or inorganic matter such as gritty sand will give the free drainage that a lawn needs. On heavy clay soils you may have to construct soakaways at the lower end of sloping sites. These are pits about 1m (3ft) deep, filled with rubble and a layer of small stones below the topsoil. Laying drainpipes bedded in gravel in the subsoil is an effective but costly solution that should only be considered if all other measures fail.

Weeding Dig the area or work over it with a mechanical cultivator about three months before sowing or turfing to allow weed seeds to germinate and the soil to be broken down by weathering. Avoid bringing subsoil to the

surface, and remove stones and the roots of perennial weeds as you go along.

Hoe out weeds that grow during the weathering process or treat with a chemical weedkiller. A final treatment is useful just before preparation of the surface.

Preparing the bed Success in establishing a lawn depends on having a well-levelled, firm bed. The worked surface or tilth should be finer for sowing seed than for turfing.

Break down clods using a roller if you have one, or trample over the surface. Choose a day when the soil is reasonably dry to do this. Next, rake across the bed, removing any stones or debris.

About a week later, firm the ground by working your way across it, treading very closely and putting your weight on your heels (work systematically). Rake, and then repeat both procedures, this time moving at right angles to the direction you first took.

Repeat until there are no soft patches and no bumps and depressions. The top layer of soil should have a crumbly texture. At this stage rake in a small handful of general fertilizer per sq m (sq yd) and leave the soil to settle for about a week before sowing seed or laying turf.

Buying turf

Buy from a reputable supplier and ask to see a sample. There should be uniform healthy growth with a high proportion of fine-leaved grasses and few, if any, weeds – something that can be hidden if the grass is not cut reasonably short. Check that it is of uniform depth, that the soil is of satisfactory quality and that there is good root growth, showing

TURF OR SEED?

Turf
- ☐ Gives instant cover and colour, and can be walked on quite soon.
- ☐ An expensive option, prime-quality and seeded turf especially so.
- ☐ Not prone to seedling troubles.
- ☐ Planting bed doesn't have to be so finely prepared as for seed-sowing, but turf is very heavy to lay.
- ☐ Best laid in mid-autumn to late winter – a period when the ground is in least demand, but difficult to work.
- ☐ Deteriorates quickly if not laid within a few days of delivery.
- ☐ May contain a high percentage of coarse grasses and weeds.

Seed
- ☐ Takes a year to reach maturity, during which time the lawn cannot be used and needs close attention.
- ☐ The cheapest option.
- ☐ Seed frequently eaten by birds.
- ☐ Seedlings prone to damping off disease and competition from weeds.
- ☐ Less physically demanding to 'lay', but requires a finely prepared bed.
- ☐ Best sown in late summer to early autumn – a period when there are many other garden jobs to do.
- ☐ Doesn't deteriorate quickly after purchase – you can wait for a fine day.
- ☐ No introduced weeds.

LAYING TURF

1 Lay the first row at one edge; adjust undulations as you go. Firm down well.

2 Standing on planks, lay the next row with turf staggered like brickwork.

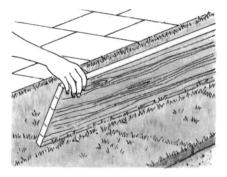

3 Roll over the planks on to the second row, then lay the third row, and so on.

4 Lightly roll the lawn twice, first in one direction, then the other.

5 Lift the flattened grass and remove any debris, using a stiff broom.

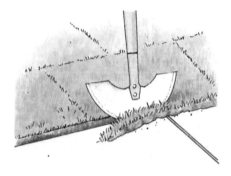

6 Once the lawn is fully laid, trim all the edges with a sloping cut.

no tendency to fall apart. The cheapest grade – and the most popular – is meadow turf, but it rarely contains many lawn-quality grasses, though it can produce a serviceable utility lawn. Downland turf is far more satisfactory – it contains a much higher percentage of fine-leaved grasses. The very best is known as parkland turf.

Turf is cut in various sizes but there is rarely a choice from any one supplier. Most are cut to a width of 40cm (16in). Lengths greater than 1m (3ft) can be difficult to handle.

A few suppliers now offer seeded turf – rolls of turf sown with a specified mixture of grass seed. You know what you are getting and, as with ordinary turf, you rapidly achieve the look of an established lawn. However, this is the most expensive method of all and needs a very well-levelled site.

Laying turf
When the turfs are delivered they can be left stacked for two to three days, but if there is a longer delay spread them out in a shady place. Avoid laying turf when the ground is frozen.

Lay the turf a row at a time, the first row slightly overhanging the edge of the lawn area. Remove weeds in the turf as you lay them and discard any that are very weedy. Any unevenness in level can be adjusted by the addition or removal of soil under the turf.

Firm down the first row before starting the next one. Work across the rows you have already laid, using a plank to stand on. Stagger rows like brickwork, but never have less than half-size pieces of turf at the end of a row. Do not try to bend them to fit curving edges; lay in straight lines and leave the excess to be trimmed off later.

When all are laid, fill any cracks with a top-dressing consisting of half sand and equal quantities of peat and loam. Using a half-moon turfing iron, or the edge of a flat-bladed spade, trim edges with an outward sloping cut. Go over the lawn with a stiff broom to lift flattened grass and to remove any debris and then use a sprinkler to water thoroughly.

Some experts recommend rolling a new lawn lightly about a week after turfs are laid. This is not essential, but, if you are going

To cut a curved edge mark out the desired curve using a piece of string firmly attached to a peg. Cut an arc with a large sharp knife held at the end of the taut string. Sever the turf with a sloping cut using a half-moon turfing iron or a flat-bladed spade.

to do it, roll first one way and then again at right angles.

Aftercare of newly laid turf
The new lawn may need watering to help it establish and to prevent shrinkage. If any cracks do open up, fill these with the top-dressing mixture. When growth starts in spring begin the mowing regime with the blades set high; they can be gradually lowered as the lawn becomes established.

SOWING SEED

1 Hoe out any weeds which have germinated on the prepared seed bed. Then rake over the surface for a final time to make sure it is free of lumps and very even.

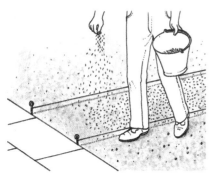

2 If hand-sowing, mark out strips about 1m (3ft) wide across the bed. Measure out the exact quantity of seed for a strip, then sow half this in one direction and half in the other.

Choosing a seed mixture

If you opt for seed, either buy a prepared seed mixture suitable for your particular requirements and conditions, or make up one with seed of several species. For most gardeners, particularly those with a relatively small lawn area, it's easier to buy a mixture.

Highest quality lawn-seed mixtures contain only the fine-leaved, compact grass types – generally browntop bent and Chewing's fescue in a proportion of 2:8 – which thrive with regular close mowing.

Mixtures for utility lawns show much more variation – a typical mixture might contain 10% browntop bent, 20% creeping red fescue, 30% Chewing's fescue and 40% smooth-stalked meadow grass. These are broader-leaved grasses with a coarser texture. They are hard wearing, withstand some neglect and camouflage the infiltration of native grasses which, on a high quality lawn, would stand out as 'weeds'.

Many cheaper mixtures include perennial rye grass, old varieties of which, although quick to establish, tended to grow too vigorously and to die out when close-mown. New fine-leaved rye grasses are a great improvement and can be a useful addition to a utility lawn mixture.

Each grass species has its own particular merits – some are good on light soils or shady positions, others resist dry conditions or extreme winter cold, for example.

Special seed mixtures are available for particular soil types – there are selections for sandy soils, clay soils, etc – and for better results than the standard grades when grown in shaded areas (though no lawn prospers under heavy shade). A shaded lawn, no matter which grass types it contains, should never be close-mown.

Sowing seed

Choose a dry, still day for sowing, ideally when the top of the soil is dry, but moist just beneath. Begin by raking over the surface again, making sure it's free of lumps.

Shake the seed and thoroughly mix it before dividing it up for sowing. Most seed should be sown at a rate of a small handful per sq m (sq yd), but check the supplier's instructions. Allow for additional seed that may be lost when sowing along the edges. Use a seed distributor to help spread the seed evenly; or, if sowing by hand, sow in marked-out strips about 1m (3ft) wide to get an even distribution and prevent double sowing. Always sow half the appropriate quantity in one direction and half in the other to reduce the risk of leaving patches unseeded. Lightly rake the seed into the soil.

Grass seed is generally treated with a bird-repellant, but dust-bathing birds can be as great a nuisance as those taking seed. Black cotton criss-crossed about 7.5cm (3in) above the ground is probably the most effective discouragement.

Aftercare of a new lawn

Lawn seed takes one to three weeks to germinate, depending on humidity and soil temperature. During dry spells it is essential to water newly seeded lawns. Ideally, use a lawn sprinkler that can be adjusted to give a fine spray which will not dislodge the seeds or emerging young seedlings.

Watch for damping off, which will show as yellowing of the young seedlings. Act promptly, watering the affected area and surroundings with Cheshunt Compound. Remove any weeds that appear at this stage by hand, taking care not to disturb the delicate young seedlings. It is important not to use weedkillers on newly-sown lawns.

When the grass is about 4cm (1½in) high sweep off worm casts, then roll it lightly – firming encourages better rooting and more vigorous growth.

A few days later, make the first cut. Again, sweep away worm casts and, with the blades set high, take off about 1.2cm (½in). In subsequent mowings the blades can be gradually lowered until they are set to about 1.2cm (½in). Avoid giving the new lawn hard wear for the first year.

AFTERCARE

1 When the grass reaches about 4cm (1½in) high, sweep off worm casts and any other debris. Take care not to scuff the surface.

2 Lightly roll the lawn – the back roller of a cylinder mower with the cutters held up is ideal. This firms the soil and encourages better rooting. About six weeks after sowing, the lawn can be mown for the first time.

ALL-YEAR LAWN CARE

**A lawn needs regular care – especially mowing
and feeding – if it is to become and remain first-class
turf in both appearance and texture.**

A lawn provides both a recreation area and a foil for the bright colours of flower borders and beds, and often forms the most prominent feature in the garden. The basis of a really good lawn is careful preparation of the site before sowing or turfing. Adequate drainage is essential, although the soil itself must be moisture-retentive and not shaded by a dense overhead tree canopy. By judicious feeding, elimination of weeds, and watering regularly in dry weather, the grass will soon become established. But even an established lawn can soon deteriorate if it does not receive careful and regular attention.

To maintain healthy growth, colour and texture, a lawn should be carefully mown and rolled, aerated regularly, brushed and raked, top-dressed, weeded, and kept free of fungi and pests.

Regular mowing is the most important requirement – an operation similar in effect to pruning. If it is carried out frequently in late spring, when growth is at its most vigorous, it will encourage a thick, firm but resilient turf to develop, which will be resistant to drought and invasion by weeds and moss.

If mown infrequently, the coarser grasses become dominant, and will sometimes smother the finer more desirable grasses completely. Feeding is another important spring activity. As the grass begins to grow again, its vigour must be maintained. A well-fed lawn will also recover quickly from any set-back such as drought or heavy use.

Nor should the lawn be forgotten in autumn. You must try to correct conditions which may have developed during the summer, such as compaction, wear, thin patches, fibre build-up in the turf or emerging fungal diseases.

Mowing

A lawn must be mown in order to maintain its attractive appearance, but a balance between visual charm and plant health must also be maintained. In general, the grass should be kept tall enough to prevent it from being starved of energy, but short enough to look neat and tidy.

The frequency of mowing depends on the amount of growth. This can be two or three times a week in the height of the growing season – late spring and early summer – but once a week should be adequate at other times. If the lawn is mown frequently, the job is neither very strenuous nor time consuming. The mowing season is from early spring to mid autumn, but an occasional light topping may be needed during mild winters when there can be late or early growth.

Do not mow when the grass is very wet, since you will damage the surface both with the mower and with your feet. You will also clog the mower with mud and clippings. Wheeled mowers should be used only when the soil immediately below the surface is fairly dry, otherwise the wheels will sink in leaving irreparable tracks.

◄ **Pleasing green** A neat lawn, rich green in colour with a fine, even texture and free of weeds and bare patches, is every gardener's dream. With regular maintenance — mowing, trimming, watering, feeding, raking and spiking — a quality lawn is not too difficult to obtain.

Before mowing the lawn, remove wormcasts and other debris with a stiff brush or besom. If casts are not removed they will form uneven humps, rot the grass and cake the mower blades.

Cutting the grass to a height of 1.2cm (½in) gives the best results for a luxury lawn – very close mowing weakens the growth. On lawns for rougher use, 2-2.5cm (¾-1in) is adequate. Leave the grass slightly longer in dry weather and in early spring and autumn when growth is slow.

Mowing in parallel strips gives the best appearance, but change direction at successive mowings so that the new mowing is made at right angles to the previous one. This prevents ridging. Push the mower at a constant speed in a forward direction, completing each strip in one non-stop pass – back and forth manoeuvres with a cylinder mower produce an uneven surface.

Creative mowing

You can achieve a striped finish on a lawn by mowing in alternately different directions. Cylinder mowers, with eight to twelve blades and fitted with a roller, are best for this.

Parallel-striped lawns, with alternating bands of light and dark grass, give a garden a formal, perfectly controlled look.

If a small lawn is striped lengthways, it makes a garden seem longer. Similarly, a long narrow lawn striped crossways takes on an additional feeling of width.

Lawnmower safety

When using an electric mower, ensure that the cable is kept well away from the cutting blades – never run over the cable. Shut pets indoors and don't allow children to play on the lawn while you are working. Do not leave electric mowers plugged in to the mains, or petrol-driven motor mowers running when unattended.

Hover mowers must be used with caution, especially on uneven sites. Do not run them over the edge of a lawn since the air cushion effect will be lost and the blades will scalp the surface. When cutting a grass bank, wear stout shoes with a good grip and work from the top of the bank in sweeping arcs from side to side, not up and down. During very dry periods, leave the grass cuttings

CHOOSING A LAWNMOWER

electric-powered 'hover' mower

hand-driven cylinder mower

electric-powered rotary mower

electric-powered cylinder mower

There are a multitude of lawnmowers on the market, ranging from hand-driven types, through electric-powered to petrol-driven. For small gardens, the first two types are adequate – petrol-driven cylinder mowers produce an excellent luxury-quality finish, but are expensive and require careful maintenance.

Hand and motorized cylinder mowers have spirally arranged blades which cut with a scissor-like action, producing a neat surface. The cutting height can be set to various measures, suitable for a luxury or utility lawn. Most models include a grass-collecting box. They are less suitable for rough grass since wiry flower stalks remain intact and tufts are often flattened rather than cut.

Rotary mowers cut with a slashing action – one or more blades rotate

horizontally at high speed. This makes them suitable for dealing with long grass or bumpy surfaces, but the quality of cut is coarser than that of a cylinder mower. The machine may be mounted on wheels – affording an easy means of adjusting the cutting height – or float on an air cushion.

Wheeled rotary models steer in a straight line whereas 'hover' types tend to glide – useful when cutting in awkward corners or on a slope. Hover mowers are more efficient than wheeled types on damp, long grass and are the easiest to store away and the cheapest to buy, but need the greatest operating care to avoid accidents. Wheeled rotary mowers may incorporate a grass box, but hover mowers generally do not. Remember also that the maximum safe length for an electricity cable is 60m (200ft).

on the surface, provided the lawn is free from weeds. This will help to conserve moisture. At all other times, use the grass box on the mower or sweep up the cuttings afterwards. A continual return of cuttings leads to soft, weak turf and encourages worms and fungi. Empty the grass box before it

spills over and, with rotary mowers fitted with a grass box, clear the guide slot occasionally to ensure free passage of cuttings, especially when the grass is damp. Always switch off the power before putting your fingers anywhere near electric cutting blades.

Thoroughly clean and dry all

mowers before putting them away – use a stiff brush or a rag to clean the blades. Finish by wiping an oily rag over all bare metal, especially the blades. Oil all moving parts regularly to ensure smooth operation. You will need to spend some time on this cleaning routine, but it takes much less effort than trying to operate a neglected machine. Check and adjust the cutting action of cylinder mowers several times a year. Sharpen or replace the blades as necessary. Blunt and maladjusted blades tear the grass rather than cut it, resulting in bruised, brown tips soon after you have mown.

Dealing with lawn edges

No lawnmower can cope with the edges of a lawn – these must be treated separately, usually after the lawn has been mown. There are a number of tools available which will help you, though for the average sized lawn the expense of some of the more elaborate models may outweigh their usefulness.

A neat edge contributes as much to the overall attractiveness of a lawn as does the quality of the surface. Attend to the edges after the first mowing in spring and repeat at frequent intervals throughout the growing season – preferably after each mowing.

The first edging treatment invariably involves some cutting back of the turf to get a straight or regular line. For a straight line, use a plank as a guide, or mark the edge with a taut string line. Standing on the plank, make clean cuts with a half-moon edging iron, sloping slightly away from the lawn so that the edge

SETTING THE CUTTING HEIGHT

1 To check the height of the blades of a cylinder mower, place a straight edge across the underside of the front and rear roller. The height of the cut is the distance from the straight edge to the bottom of the fixed blade. Make sure each side has the same setting.

Cut a utility lawn to 32mm (1¼in) in spring and autumn or during very dry spells

Cut a utility lawn to 25mm (1in) in summer

Cut a luxury lawn to 18mm (¾in) in spring and autumn or during very dry spells

Cut a luxury lawn to 12mm (½in) in summer

2 Adjust the cutting height to suit the quality of lawn, the time of year and the weather conditions according to the diagrams above.

does not crumble away. Alternatively, use a spade, but the slightly curving blade will not produce such a straight cut and it is harder to cut to a consistent depth.

During the rest of the year use long-handled edging shears or a mechanical edger to maintain the neat edge – never use a half-moon edging iron to trim an edge which is already straight, since this tool is designed for cutting turf, not blades of grass. Long-handled edging shears, if sharpened regularly, do a very good job. They are available with handles of various lengths – buy the right size for your height.

Mechanical edgers consist of a roller with a disc of sharp-edged spikes which rotate as you push the device along the edge of the lawn, cutting the grass against a fixed blade. Though slightly less

tiring to use than long-handled shears, these edgers generally do not make such a clean cut. Motor-powered edgers are also available and these can produce a good finish. They do take much of the back-ache out of edging a large expanse of lawn, but, whether battery powered or run from mains electricity, they are expensive and sometimes difficult to manoeuvre.

If your soil is crumbly or the lawn receives a lot of wear and tear, natural lawn edges may break away. To avoid this problem, lay an edging strip of aluminium, timber or plastic. Proprietary edging strip is available which gives a very clean finish, or you can make your own. Ensure that the edging strip lies slightly below the lawn surface so you can mow right to the edge.

Trimming around obstacles

Not all lawns are a perfect rectangle – many meander around trees, have island beds with overhanging plants or are edged with walls or steep banks, for instance. Lawnmowers can only deal with flat surfaces and cannot cut close to a vertical barrier.

Various tools are available for horizontal trimming of grass – the choice depends on how much you are prepared to spend and on whether you prefer to stand up or bend down to do the cutting. Simple garden shears do an adequate job – provided they are sharpened regularly – but are suitable only for small areas since you must crouch to use them.

THE CORRECT MOWING PATTERN

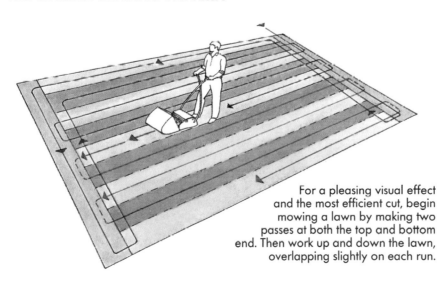

For a pleasing visual effect and the most efficient cut, begin mowing a lawn by making two passes at both the top and bottom end. Then work up and down the lawn, overlapping slightly on each run.

DEALING WITH EDGES

1 During the winter, lawn edges become ragged and often encroach on the flower borders. Cut them to shape in spring using a half-moon edging iron.

2 Throughout the rest of the growing season, use long-handled edging shears to trim the lawn edges after each mowing. Rake up all the clippings.

3 Mechanical edging tools take much of the physical effort out of edge trimming, but they don't produce quite such a good finish as shears.

4 Aluminium edging strips keep the lawn in check. Make a slot then firm it in place, keeping the top edge just below the surface of the lawn.

THE LAWN-CARE YEAR

Mid winter Brush off fallen leaves.
Late winter If wormcasts appear, remove, and apply a worm killer.
Early spring As soon as the ground is firm, brush off surface debris. Roll when dry to consolidate ground lifted by frost. Rake thoroughly to lift up grass and weeds and mow lightly. Two cuts are generally enough in early spring.
Mid spring Apply a fertilizer followed a week or two later by a selective lawn weedkiller or lawn sand. Mow often enough to keep the grass down, but not lower than 18mm (¾in).
Late spring Increase the frequency of mowing as necessary. Cut at 6mm (¼in) above the summer level. This is the best month to eradicate weeds.
Summer Mow to normal summer level, one to three times a week. Rake gently before mowing. Water well during prolonged dry periods. Destroy isolated weeds with spot weedkiller.
Early autumn Increase intervals between mowing, and raise the height of the cut by 6mm (¼in) above the summer level. Apply worm killer if necessary. Rake, spike and top-dress the lawn.
Mid autumn Regular mowing comes to an end. Use a high blade setting for the last cut or two.
Late autumn If the weather is not frosty or wet, and the surface is firm, mow once with the blades set high. Brush off any leaves.
Early winter Brush away the last of the autumn leaves, but keep off the lawn if it is very wet or frozen.

Applying the same cutting action as hedge trimmers, battery-operated grass trimmers provide a less energetic means of cutting grass around obstacles. With a single charge, the battery generally lasts long enough to cut up to 20 sq m/yd.

For use in a standing position, long-handled lawn shears give the neatest cut. As with ordinary shears, the blades must be sharpened regularly. Ensure that the handle length and cutting angle suits you when buying – various models are available.

The easiest of all to use, nylon cord electric or motorized trimmers have become very popular in recent years. These cut grass, weeds and even quite coarse undergrowth by the whipping action of a nylon cord which rotates at high speed within a safety shield. The cut surface is not very neat, however, and this type of machine is suitable only for informal lawns. Drawbacks include relatively high cost, a hazard from flying debris thrown up by the cord – wear goggles – and the rather piercing noise generated by the motor and cord.

Watering the lawn
If the lawn is not watered regularly during prolonged dry spells it loses vigour, allowing tougher grasses and weeds to take over. Symptoms of water shortage include loss of springiness in the grass and fading of colour from lush green to a rather greyish green. Severe water shortage results in yellowing of the grass. However, grass is surprisingly resilient and usually recovers once water is applied.

Use a sprinkler, preferably an oscillating one, to obtain maximum coverage. Soak the grass well at weekly intervals in hot, sunny weather – though wait until late afternoon or evening otherwise the water will evaporate as fast as you apply it. If the soil is sandy, water every four or five days.

The equivalent of about 2.5cm (1in) of rainfall is needed at each watering. Gauge this roughly by positioning a straight-sided can underneath the spray. Note the tap setting and then find the time taken to fill the bottom 2.5cm (1in) of the can. Use the same tap setting and time for all future watering. Droughts may bring a ban on watering. Stop mowing to prevent serious damage to the lawn.

If the lawn has been neglected – while you are away on holiday, for instance – and looks parched with a dry, cracked surface, it is best to prick the surface all over with a garden fork or aerator before applying water.

Feeding a lawn
The application of fertilizer to a lawn does not merely make the grass grow faster – something which few people would want – but encourages more compact and bright green growth which is better able to compete with weeds and coarser grasses. With constant mowing, the grass needs a

TRIMMING GRASS AROUND OBSTACLES

1 Use long-handled lawn shears to cut any grass which the lawnmower cannot reach. If you don't mind bending down, ordinary shears are equally good.

2 Nylon cord trimmers – 'strimmers' – require much less effort to use and can deal with even the roughest grass, though the cut is less neat.

3 Battery-operated cordless trimmers are easy and convenient to use in a small garden, making a quite clean cut with a scissor-like action.

regular supply of nutrients throughout the growing season if the lawn is to remain in the peak of health.

Apply a liquid or granular general-purpose fertilizer – such as Growmore at the rate of two tablespoons per sq m/yd – in mid spring when the soil is moist and the grass is dry.

Even distribution of fertilizers is important, so that the grass is not scorched and regular growth is obtained over the whole surface. Mix powdered fertilizer with four to eight times its weight of sand before spreading it on the lawn. Divide the mixture and apply half up and down the lawn and the

other half working across the lawn from side to side.

Granular fertilizer is much easier to spread. A wheeled mechanical spreader will spread it at the correct rate. If spread by hand, use pegs and string, or garden canes, to mark out the site into 1 sq m/yd sectors. Compound lawn fertilizers are available under many brand names – follow the manufacturer's instructions for application method and rate.

Water in solid fertilizers with a garden sprinkler to avoid any risk of scorching the grass and to feed the roots as quickly as possible.

Apply liquid fertilizers with a large watering can, using a rose or

dribble-bar attachment. Avoid overlapping and double application, which may scorch the grass.

Do not use nitrogenous fertilizers after late summer. Autumn feeding will be necessary only if the lawn has suffered compaction or drought. Use a fertilizer high in phosphates (but low in nitrogen) to redevelop a strong root system. A suitable mixture is 3kg (7lb) of sterilized bonemeal and 1.4kg (3lb) of sulphate of potash, applied at two tablespoons per sq m/yd.

Spiking and top-dressing
Spiking the lawn in early autumn is essential on heavy soils where drainage is poor. It is also neces-

APPLYING FERTILIZERS AND TOP-DRESSING

1 Fertilizers must be spread very evenly otherwise you will get random patches of untreated and over-treated (scorched) grass. Mark out 1 sq m/yd areas with canes or pegs and taut string, then treat them one at a time.

2 To ensure an even distribution of granular fertilizer, use a mechanical spreader. Work systematically in up and down strips as for lawnmowing, but don't overlap each run by more than the thickness of the wheels.

3 Apply a top-dressing – a mixture of sieved loam, leaf-mould, garden compost and sharp sand which has been left to mature for a year or more – by placing half a bucketful of dressing on each sq m/yd of lawn. Rake the heaps level.

AERATING A LAWN

1 To aerate a lawn in early autumn, spike it with a garden fork – making 7.5-10cm (3-4in) deep holes. This will assist drainage and relieve compaction caused by heavy wear.

2 Hollow tine spikers aerate the soil more efficiently than a garden fork since they remove entire plugs of soil. Sweep up the debris and brush a sandy top-dressing into the holes.

3 Wheeled mechanical spikers do the job more quickly and with much less effort – so are ideal for large lawns. As with the special hand spikers, interchangeable tines are available.

sary where soils have been compacted by heavy use and wear. Spiking also assists root growth.

On small areas and lighter soils use a garden fork. Push it in at 7.5-10cm (3-4in) intervals and 7.5-10cm (3-4in) deep. Use a straight, in-and-out action with the fork – do not pull back on the handle as this will make a ridge.

Specially designed spikers are made which have interchangeable tines. They are easier to use than a garden fork and give better aeration on all types of soils. The solid tines can be replaced by hollow ones, which remove a core of soil. These are best on heavy ground. Sweep up the cores after spiking

and brush a sandy top-dressing into the holes.

In autumn, after aerating the lawn, apply a light top-dressing to it. This will smooth out slight surface irregularities and, used annually, will form a layer of moisture-retaining material.

An ideal dressing can be formed of alternate layers of 15cm (6in) thick loamy soil and 10cm (4in) thick well-rotted manure left to stand for a year or more, after which it should be sieved. Mix sand with it for heavy clay soils, but leave it as it is for light sandy soils. Apply the dressing at about half a bucketful per sq m/yd. Do not exceed this rate of application.

Brushing and raking

In spring, lightly brush or rake the lawn with a wire-tined lawn rake to remove winter debris, particularly before mowing for the first time. Avoid dispersing any moss.

In late spring and summer, brush the lawn occasionally with a besom before mowing. This helps to clear wormcasts, remove dew or rainwater from the leaves and lift flattened grass and weed stems.

In early to mid autumn, scarify – rake thoroughly and vigorously – with the lawn rake to clear away all debris. Remove the rakings with a stiff brush or besom. Sweep all fallen leaves from the lawn once a week in autumn.

RAKING, ROLLING AND SWEEPING

1 A wire-tined lawn rake is the best implement for removing winter debris prior to the first spring mowing. It is also ideal for scarifying (raking thoroughly and vigorously) in autumn.

2 Use a roller to consolidate the turf in spring – winter frosts often lift the soil surface. Never use a roller to try to smooth out bumps in summer – you will merely accentuate them.

3 Use a besom to sweep leaves and other debris from the lawn in autumn. This type of brush can also be used in spring and summer to remove wormcasts and dew before mowing.

LAWN REPAIRS

**A patchy, uneven or badly worn lawn is
unattractive and difficult to mow. However, neglected
lawns can be repaired quite effectively.**

In most gardens, the lawn receives far more wear and tear than is good for it, and many types of damage can occur:

☐ Bumps and hollows caused by poor initial laying, or later heaving or subsidence.

☐ Bare patches caused by wear, poor drainage, shade, scorching by pet urine, excess fertilizer doses, weed removal or continuous drips from overhead foliage.

☐ Broken or dead edges caused by damage during cultivation of borders, or by overhanging plants.

☐ Shrub suckers and tree roots breaking up the surface.

Some are only minor and, if left alone, may repair themselves. Others, however, need careful treatment to restore the natural beauty of the lawn.

Levelling bumps and hollows
Bumps show up especially when the lawn is close-mown in summer. The raised areas tend to get scalped, leaving brown patches. Hollows, on the other hand, show as areas of much greener, lusher grass.

Simple levelling work is best carried out when the grass is dormant between mid autumn and early spring.

Level small hollows simply by scattering a thin layer of soil over the area and brushing it in. Make up a mixture of half finely sieved, loamy soil and half sand. Apply no more than 1.2cm (½in) at a time, repeating every couple of weeks from autumn until spring. The soil will settle in after each application and eventually level the site.

To reduce a small bump, prick it over with a special hollow-tine aerator. This tool removes small plugs of soil. As the remaining soil settles into the holes, the level drops slightly. Begin in autumn and repeat every month or so until the bump has levelled out.

Larger hollows and bumps need different treatment. Peel back the turf over the affected area and add or remove soil until the right level is reached.

▼ **Lawn discoloration** Unsightly yellow patches on an otherwise healthy lawn may be caused by urine scorching — especially that of a canine bitch. Re-seeding or re-turfing the patches can resolve the problem, but make sure the cause is eliminated in the future.

BUMPS AND HOLLOWS

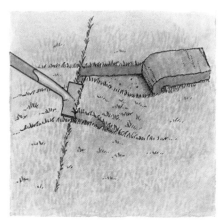

1 Using a spade or turfing iron, cut a cross through the centre of the bump or hollow, extending the cuts to the perimeter of the problem area. Make two or three parallel cuts each side of one line of the cross. Under-cut the turfs and peel them back.

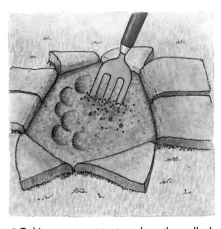

2 Taking care not to tread on the rolled back turfs, fork over the exposed soil to a depth of 8-10cm (3-4in) — it may be quite solid, so break it up well. If the surface was too high, remove some soil, then firm and rake level. If the surface was too low, add fresh soil before firming and levelling.

3 Finally, fold the turfs back over the levelled soil, and firm them down well using a roller or by treading systematically over the area. Fill any cracks with sieved loamy soil — sprinkle it by hand then brush in lightly. Water in gently and keep the area moist.

Filling bare patches

First try to determine why the grass has died out. Some causes, such as weed removal, oil spillage or pet urine scorching, may not recur on the same spot. Others, such as poor drainage or wear, are likely to be long-term recurring problems. Learn to recognize the symptoms:

☐ Excessive wear – muddy, compacted tracks.
☐ Drought – yellow and eventually dead, brown grass.
☐ Weed/moss removal – irregular areas of dead or depleted grass.
☐ Pet urine – regular, circular, brown patches surrounded by a narrow ring of unusually deep green grass.
☐ Chemical/oil/petrol spillage – brown patches, often irregular in outline.
☐ Buried builder's rubble – brown or yellow patches on a new site.

Before starting the repair, remedy the cause if possible. Worn patches generally reflect routes of maximum use. Consider replacing these areas with a path or stepping stones. Train pets – especially female dogs – to use a pet toilet away from the lawn. Repair and maintain the lawnmower in the garage, not on the grass.

Re-seeding This is the easiest method of repairing a bare patch. The best time is spring or autumn during reasonably fine weather, but wait at least six weeks after applying a hormone weedkiller to the lawn. First loosen the surface with a hand fork. Work in a sprinkling of granular fertilizer and then rake the soil to a fine, even tilth. (Add a little fresh, sieved soil if the site isn't level or the soil is poor.)

Select a seed mixture which matches the existing lawn. Some seedsmen offer special re-seeding mixtures which are said to germinate very quickly and produce an excellent finish within just a few weeks.

Sow general-purpose grass seed – containing ryegrass – at a rate of 25g per sq m (1oz per sq yd). Sow fine-quality lawn seed a little thicker at about 40g per sq m (1½oz per sq yd). Rake the seed in and firm down lightly.

Water gently, but frequently in warm, dry weather. If you have a sprinkler, leave it running for about 15 minutes each day.

Also protect seed from birds – though many seed mixtures contain a bird repellant chemical, it's a good idea nonetheless to take precautions. A network of black cotton stretched over the area can be effective. Alternatively, lay a sheet of clear polythene over the patch and secure it with pegs. This method will also conserve some moisture, but remove the polythene as soon as seedlings appear.

Re-turfing may be more appropriate where quite deep digging is necessary to eliminate the cause of the problem – to remove buried rubble, or improve drainage, for example. If the bare patch lies in a prominent spot, replace it with turf taken from a less noticeable part of the lawn. Re-seed this patch later. Alternatively, if you have quite a few bare patches, buy new turfs.

Begin by digging out the dead patch, using a hand fork. If deep

---

TREE ROOTS AND SUCKERS

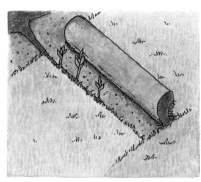

As trees and shrubs age, their roots swell and may lift grass into a hump. Many also produce suckers – a hazard when mowing. Treat as for bumps. Cut and peel back the turf, then chop off the offending root.

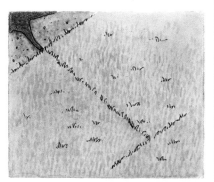

Fork over the soil and re-level. Roll the turf back and firm it down. Where bulky tree roots break through it may be best to re-shape the lawn around the root and grow ground cover plants instead.

RE-TURFING A BARE PATCH

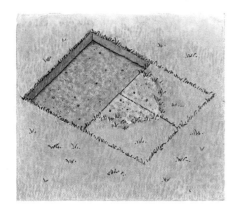  

1 Cut out any dead or diseased grass, together with any other debris from the bare patch. Where chemical or oil spillage has occurred, dig out all the polluted soil and replace with new. Square off the area with a spade.

2 If you intend to replace with bought turf, cut out a patch equal in size to one or more new pieces. Otherwise, make the patch as small as possible. Fork the soil and level it over, removing any polluted soil or debris.

3 Lay the replacement turfs in position, making sure they are level with the lawn. If not, take them aside and add more soil or remove some as necessary. Firm in the turfs, then fill cracks with sieved soil.

RE-SEEDING A BARE PATCH

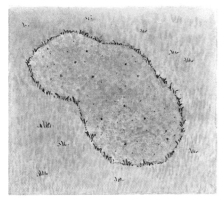 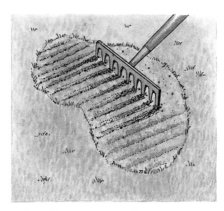 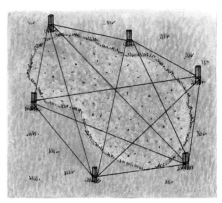

1 Prepare the patch by forking up any dead or diseased grass, together with any weeds or other debris. Gently loosen the soil to a depth of about 7.5cm (3in), using a hand fork, but don't loosen the surrounding grass.

2 Sprinkle some general-purpose fertilizer — about a handful per sq m/yd — and rake in, leaving a level, even surface. Scatter grass seed and rake in. Firm down with the back of the rake or tread in lightly.

3 Keep animals off until new grass is well established. Black cotton stretched between pegs deters most birds. Or, lay clear polythene over the patch — secured with pegs — until the seedlings are through. Keep well watered.

digging is necessary, use a garden fork or spade. Remove all polluted soil and debris. Once the full extent of the problem has been exposed, square off the area by making shallow cuts with a spade or half-moon turfing iron. If you intend to replace with bought turf, cut out an area equivalent in size to one or more pieces. Otherwise, cut out as small an area of lawn as is possible.

Loosen and re-level the exposed soil, adding fresh soil if necessary, before bedding the replacement turf. Lastly, firm down the new turf, fill in the cracks with a 50:50 mix of sieved, loamy soil and sand, and water in well.

Water re-seeded and re-turfed areas if they show signs of drying out. Remove any weeds by hand and delay mowing until the re-paired patches are properly integrated in the established lawn.

Renovating a sparse lawn
A lawn badly infected with weeds which has been treated with weedkiller may end up rather sparse. If growing conditions are perfect, the lawn may fill in on its own, but you can speed up the process. The best time is spring or autumn.

Once the weedkiller is inactive — generally allow at least six weeks — mow the grass and then rake it over to loosen the soil surface. Sprinkle grass seed evenly over the entire area at a rate of 15g per sq m (½oz per sq yd). Sieve a fine layer of good garden soil over the seed. Lightly roll the surface or use the back of a spade to pat the soil down. Keep the lawn well watered, especially in dry spells.

Repairing broken edges
Lawn edges can be damaged in a variety of ways. Overhanging plants often smother the grass and it soon dies out. When the offending plants are cut back, the lawn must be repaired. Certain lawnmowers can also damage the edge — particularly the hover type — or you can break the edge with your heel while cultivating an adjoining plant border.

Begin by cutting out a rectangle of turf around the broken edge, using a spade or turfing iron. Cut sections small enough to lift out without breaking into pieces. You may need to make several cuts along a badly damaged edge. Trim away any dead roots or bare soil from the broken edge.

Lift the turf with a spade and reverse it so that the undamaged inner edge forms the new outer edge. You are now left with an irregular hole. Fill this with sieved loamy soil before firming down the whole area. Lastly re-seed or re-turf the bare patch as described previously.

Aerating stagnant areas
Poor drainage, especially under an old or neglected lawn, is a common cause of poor grass growth. The surface may become very compacted with constant wear, yet soil just below remains constantly wet. Using a hollow-tine cultivator or aerator, take out small plugs of soil all across the stagnant area. Sprinkle coarse sand over and brush it into the holes. In this way, dozens of tiny drains will be made which will allow the trapped water to seep away.

A drought-stricken lawn
Grass is surprisingly resilient to drought – there have only been a couple of long, hot summers in living memory in Britain when lawns have died completely, though both were fairly recent.

When moisture is low, grass does, however, become almost dormant, allowing certain weeds, such as yarrow and clover, which are better adapted to dry conditions, to take over. Also, annual meadow grass may die out more quickly than coarser grasses.

If the surface is baked and hard, first spike with a fork or aerator. Turn on a sprinkler for an hour or so during early evening or morning – watering in hot sun is a waste of time as it evaporates faster than it soaks in. (If the use of hose-pipes and sprinklers has been banned by your local authority, bath water applied with a watering can be of some value.) Repeat two or three times per week during very hot spells, but never water more than once a week during normal summer weather – you will encourage weeds and reduce the vigour of grass roots.

Sandy, free-draining soils are most susceptible to drought damage. Incorporate plenty of bulky organic matter to increase water retention before making a lawn.

REPAIRING A DAMAGED EDGE

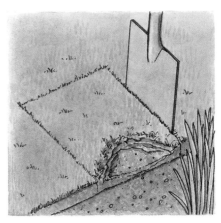

1 Using a spade or half-moon turfing iron, cut a rectangular section behind the damaged edge — large enough to incorporate a good chunk of healthy grass, but small enough to lift with the spade without breaking. If the damaged area is large, you may have to cut out more than one section of turf.

2 Under-cut the severed section with a spade and lift it carefully. Remove loose old soil and any dead grass — you can do this before lifting if you prefer. Turn the turf round and re-lay it with the ragged edge innermost. You can now appreciate the importance of cutting a perfect rectangle or square.

3 Firm the turf well in. Fill the remaining hole with sieved, loamy soil, then sow with grass seed as shown for re-seeding a bare patch. Keep well watered and deter birds and pets with black cotton as before.

RENOVATING A NEGLECTED LAWN

Begin by examining the grass and weeds covering the lawn. If the dominant plants are coarse grasses, mosses and persistent weeds, the best solution is to lay a new lawn. If, however, good quality grasses make up the main part of the lawn, carry out the following programme of work. With care, the good quality grass can be made to re-colonize the whole lawn area.

Start renovating in spring before the grass begins to grow actively. Cut down tall grass and weeds to 5cm (2in) above ground. Use a rotary lawnmower, a scythe or a pair of shears, depending on the area to be cleared. Rake off all the clippings.

Remove all dead vegetation and debris — including any large stones — using a rake and brush. Mow the grass with the blades set as high as possible. Subsequent mowings should be carried out regularly, each time with the blades set a little lower. In summer, mow at least twice a week. Fit the grass box to the lawnmower, or rake off the clippings.

Feed and weed the lawn in late spring or summer, using a general lawn fertilizer first, and then a selective weedkiller about a fortnight later. Some manufacturers supply a mixed fertilizer and weedkiller which does the job quicker and easier. Also apply a proprietary moss killer or lawn sand to get rid of moss if necessary. If, after six weeks, some persistent weeds remain, apply a liquid weedkiller containing mecoprop and 2,4-D.

Apply another feed of lawn fertilizer in early autumn, together with a worm killer and a fungicide. Again, certain manufacturers combine all three ingredients in one. Remove coarse grass by hand.

A week or two later, spike the surface all over with a garden fork to a depth of about 7.5cm (3in). This will improve drainage and aeration. Apply a good top-dressing of loam and sand; or well-rotted manure, garden compost or leaf-mould. Scatter this dressing over the surface at a rate of about ten handfuls per sq m/yd, and work it well into the surface using the back of a rake. If the lawn is thin, mix in grass seed with the top-dressing at a rate of 15g per sq m (½oz per sq yd). Rake off fallen leaves which can spread disease.

Re-seed or re-turf any bare patches which appear after the weedkiller applications have taken effect. The lawn should be in a satisfactory condition by the following spring, when normal lawn maintenance can begin.

LAWN TROUBLES

The best way to achieve a weed-free, trouble-free lawn is by frequent mowing and feeding. A neglected lawn can still be restored.

Prevention is better than cure where lawn weeds, pests and diseases are concerned, since a thick covering of healthy grass with few bare patches will resist the onset of such infestations. It is also more resistant to prolonged drought. If your lawn looks more like a roadside verge, however, with weeds, toadstools, mole hills and moss patches, there are still many ways of renovating it to a bowling-green finish.

Controlling lawn weeds

Check surface-creeping weeds such as clover and yarrow by raking or brushing them upright before each mowing. This ensures that their leaves and stems are cut off by the mower blades. Some annual weeds, such as trefoil and mouse-ear chickweed, may also be controlled to some extent by this treatment.

Use the grass box when mowing, and destroy the clippings – they invariably contain weed seeds and fungal spores. Isolated weeds can be removed by hand before they develop into a serious infestation. Use a daisy grubber or small hand fork and try to remove as much of the root system as possible intact, since broken sections of root often regrow, especially those of dandelions and thistles.

Selective weedkillers, in the form of powders or liquids, are effective against most weeds. They are best applied in late spring to mid summer, but can be used up to early autumn.

Apply a lawn fertilizer a fortnight before the weedkiller to give the grass an extra boost. Mow the lawn two or three days before applying the weedkiller and try to pick a warm, still day for application, when the grass is dry and the soil below it is moist. Follow closely the manufacturer's recommendations for application rates and timing.

Chemicals frequently used for lawn weedkillers include 2,4-D, dicamba, dichlorprop and mecoprop. Often two or more of these chemicals are combined as 'cocktails', giving a more thorough weed-killing action. They may be formulated as concentrated liquids, soluble powders, granules or foams.

Selective weedkillers are based on a hormone substance which over-stimulates weed growth, causing the leaves to twist and curl. Finally, the weeds die and rot away. The amount of hormone absorbed by the grass is not enough to do any harm – grass leaves are narrow with a waxy surface and a longitudinal channel-like mid-vein, so liquids tend

▼ **Lawn weeds** Daisies and dandelions frequently infest lawns. While they have individual charms – and look attractive in a wild sward – such weeds destroy the appearance of the lawn and compete with the grass for light, water and nutrients.

Once established, such weeds may spread with ever increasing speed by means of seeds or runners; they should be eradicated as soon as possible.

ELIMINATING LAWN WEEDS

1 Isolated weeds can be removed by hand, taking care to remove as much of the root system as possible. Use a daisy grubber to lift daisies and other rosette-forming weeds. Alternatively, use a small hand fork.

2 Individual weeds may be killed by applying a lawn weedkiller aerosol. These consist of a foam which makes it easy to see which weeds have been treated — useful on a large lawn where some weeds could be missed.

3 'Gun-type' ready-mixed sprays are convenient for treating moss patches in a lawn or on pathways and walls. Mosskillers are also available in liquid-concentrate form combined with a 'green-up' grass fertilizer.

4 Liquid weedkillers are best for treating heavily infested lawns where spot-treatment would be impracticable. Follow the maker's instructions for dilution and application rates and apply as evenly as possible.

to run off the surface before they are absorbed.

Do not mow the lawn for at least three days after using the weedkiller. Compost the clippings for at least six months before using them to allow time for the weedkiller to decompose completely.

Weedkillers can be bought as combined formulations with lawn fertilizers, though the weedkiller may be slightly less effective than when applied after a fertilizer.

Spot weedkillers can be used to treat isolated weeds in a lawn. Nowadays, the most popular spot weedkillers are formulated as foams and are sold in aerosol cans. Spray the chemical directly on to the crown of each weed. The active ingredient is usually 2,4-D with dicamba.

Lawn sand preparations are also available as alternatives to hormone weedkillers for controlling daisies and other broad-leaved weeds. Lawn sand is also an effective moss killer, though special moss killers give more long-lasting control.

The chemical ingredients of lawn sand are sulphate of ammonia and sulphate of iron. Mixed with sand, these have a corrosive effect on broad leaves, but are absorbed to a much lesser extent by the narrow-leaved grasses.

Apply lawn sand in spring or early summer. Follow the manufacturer's instructions and do not overdose. The best time is when the grass is moist with dew and the soil damp.

Water the lawn if rain has not fallen after two days. After three weeks, rake up dead undergrowth.

Apply a further dressing of lawn sand if necessary.

Temporary blackening of the older grass often occurs. However, once the chemicals have been washed down, the grass will recover rapidly.

Other lawn troubles
Broad-leaved weeds are by no means the only causes of lawn problems. Certain pests and diseases attack even the best-kept lawns.

Algae may appear in damp turf. These simple plants are usually black, slippery and jelly-like. Spike the lawn to improve drainage, then apply a mercurized lawn sand, sulphate of iron or copper sulphate. Top-dress and feed the lawn to build up the grass's strength.

Ants make small hills of soil as part of their nest-building activities. These are most frequent on sandy soils and generally appear in summer. Brush off the soil hills before mowing. Dust the affected area with a proprietary ant destroyer or place gel-type ant baits around the nests.

Chafer grubs may kill small patches of turf by gnawing at the roots in spring and summer. The grass turns brown in colour and breaks away from the surface. Roll the lawn in spring to crush the grubs. Earthworm and leatherjacket control measures also destroy chafer grubs.

Dogs, especially bitches, urinate on lawns causing scorching — grass turns yellow, then brown. Once killed, the grass must be dug out and replaced, but isolated troubles can be avoided by flooding with water immediately to dilute the urine.

Earthworms push small, irregular mounds — casts — of soil to the surface. On heavy soils, and when flattened down hard by walking or by the mower roller, these can stifle the smaller grasses and make an uneven surface.

Remove worm casts by regular sweeping. Fewer large cast-forming worms are found in acid soil, so dressing the lawn with sulphate of ammonia, sulphate of iron and organic substances such as leafmould will help to prevent this trouble. In severe cases, apply a worm killer, such as chlordane, according to the manufacturer's instructions.

Leatherjackets cause yellowish

IDENTIFYING MAJOR LAWN WEEDS

SPECIES	FEATURES
Annual meadow grass (*Poa annua*)	Low-growing, broad-leaved annual grass forming unsightly clumps in close-mown turf
Bird's-foot trefoil (*Lotus corniculatus*)	Creeping plant, often forming large clumps; each leaf made up of three oval, pointed leaflets with two leaf-like growths at the base of their stalk; clusters of red-marked bright yellow pea flowers in late spring to late summer
Buttercup, bulbous (*Ranunculus bulbosus*)	Bulbous-rooted plant; deeply toothed and finely hairy, 3-lobed, rich green leaves; golden-yellow, cup-shaped flowers in early spring to early summer
Buttercup, creeping (*Ranunculus repens*)	Creeping stems rooting frequently; deeply toothed and finely hairy, 3-lobed, dark green leaves; golden-yellow, cup-shaped flowers in late spring to late summer
Cat's-ear (*Hypochoeris radicata*)	Similar to dandelion, but leaves hairy with less jagged teeth; flower stalks branched
Chickweed, mouse-ear (*Cerastium holosteoides*)	Creeping stems; small oval leaves covered with silvery hairs; tiny white starry flowers in mid spring to early autumn
Clover, white (*Trifolium repens*)	Creeping plant rooting frequently; each leaf made up of three rounded leaflets; white or pinkish globular flower heads from late spring to autumn
Crowfoot (*Ranunculus acris*)	Clump-forming plant of the buttercup family; deeply lobed, rich green leaves with coarse teeth; golden-yellow, cup-shaped flowers in late spring to late summer
Daisy (*Bellis perennis*)	Rosette-forming plant with a very spreading habit; spoon-shaped leaves with scalloped edges; prominent yellow-centred white flowers from early spring to autumn
Medick, black (*Medicago lupulina*)	Creeping plant; clover-like leaves; small, yellowish, clover-like flowers from mid spring to late summer
Dandelion (*Taraxacum officinale*)	Rosette-forming plant; lance-shaped leaves with deep, jagged teeth; stems and leaves exude a milky sap when broken; many-petalled bright yellow flowers
Parsley piert (*Aphanes arvensis*)	Creeping plant; tiny fan-like leaves; minute insignificant green flowers in spring to autumn
Pearlwort (*Sagina procumbens*)	Tufted plant with radiating, creeping stems, often forming a dense mat; tiny, narrowly lance-shaped leaves; tiny white flowers in late spring to early autumn
Plantain, greater (*Plantago major*), hoary plantain (*P. media*)	Rosette-forming plants; large, coarse-textured leaves with prominent parallel ribs; greenish flowers from late spring onwards, in slender upright spikes in *P. major*, and compact, oval heads in *P. media*
Ribwort (*Plantago*) (*lanceolata*)	Rosette-forming plant; quite large, lance-shaped leaves with prominent parallel ribs; flowers similar to those of hoary plantain
Selfheal (*Prunella vulgaris*)	Creeping plant rooting at intervals; oval, pointed leaves; clusters of purple, hooded flowers in early summer to early autumn
Sheep's sorrel (*Rumex acetosella*)	Slender, wiry plant with somewhat creeping stems; deep green, narrow, arrow-shaped leaves, turning reddish with age; spikes of green to red flowers in late spring to late summer
Speedwell, slender (*Veronica filiformis*)	Slender trailing stems rooting frequently; small rounded leaves with scalloped edges; tiny mauve-blue flowers in mid spring to summer
Thistle, stemless (*Cirsium acaule*)	Rosette-forming plant; very prickly, incut leaves; reddish-purple thistle flowers growing directly from the leaf rosette in early summer to early autumn
Trefoil, lesser (*Trifolium dubium*)	Similar to white clover, but with smaller flowers which are yellow to brownish
Woodrush (*Luzula campestris*)	Tufted grass-like plant; narrow leaf blades fringed with fine hairs; brown grass-like flowers in mid to late spring
Yarrow (*Achillea millefolium*)	Creeping plant rooting at intervals; long feathery leaves; flattish clusters of small cream-white flowers in summer
Yorkshire fog (*Holcus lanatus*)	Rather broad-leaved but soft-textured grass forming unsightly clumps in close-mown lawns

creeping buttercup

mouse-ear chickweed

white clover

cat's-ear

daisy

dandelion

parsley piert

pearlwort

self-heal

greater plantain

sheep's sorrel

slender speedwell

yarrow

woodrush

SPECIAL LAWN DISORDERS

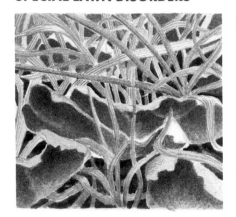

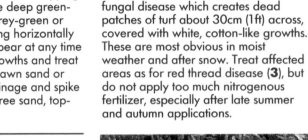

1 Lichens are composed of overlapping leafy structures. They are deep green-black when moist and grey-green or brown when dry, growing horizontally in the turf. They may appear at any time of year. Rake out the growths and treat the affected areas with lawn sand or moss killer. Improve drainage and spike the lawn. Brush in lime-free sand, top-dress and feed.

2 Snow mould or fusarium patch is a fungal disease which creates dead patches of turf about 30cm (1ft) across, covered with white, cotton-like growths. These are most obvious in moist weather and after snow. Treat affected areas as for red thread disease (**3**), but do not apply too much nitrogenous fertilizer, especially after late summer and autumn applications.

3 Red thread or corticium disease shows as dead patches of turf bearing red, thread-like fungus growths. The danger period is autumn after rain. Apply a complete lawn-care compound containing weedkiller and fertilizer in autumn. Or, apply lawn sand or any other proprietary fungicide. Spike to aerate the soil, and use a nitrogenous fertilizer in spring.

patches in a lawn, and damage may be more extensive after a wet autumn. These pests are the grubs of crane flies – daddy-long-legs. Improve the drainage of the soil and dust with HCH.

Moles can ruin a lawn by excavating large heaps of loose soil. These are joined just under the turf by long, interlinking tunnels. The tunnels, leading to the nest chambers, sometimes collapse, causing sunken channels across the lawn.

Eradication of moles is rarely successful unless carried out by a professional mole catcher. Traps and poisons are the most effective means, but smoke pellets placed in the runs may deter some moles.

Moss is a common enemy. It is a symptom of run-down turf, primarily associated with over-compacted soil, poor drainage, excess shade and under-feeding. Dichlorophen is the most effective chemical for moss control and may be bought as a liquid concentrate or ready-to-use spray.

Apply moss killers in spring and autumn. Rake out the dead moss a few weeks later and re-seed any bare patches – moss infestations often take over entire areas of the lawn. Keep the remaining grass in good condition by feeding in spring. Avoid cutting the lawn too closely since this weakens the grass, allowing low-growing mosses to thrive. Lawn sand also burns out moss at the same time as boosting the grass.

▲ **Grass invasion** Fairy rings of small toadstools can appear at any time of year. The grass around the ring may become darker green and look unsightly, though the toadstools themselves do no harm. Conceal this effect by applying a 'green-up' fertilizer to the rest of the lawn. There is no effective chemical treatment for fairy rings. In serious cases, dig up and burn diseased turf to a depth of 30cm (1ft) and at least 30cm (1ft) either side of the ring. Remove all the soil, ensuring that it does not fall onto the healthy turf alongside. Replace with fresh topsoil and re-seed.

CHOOSING HEDGES

**Hedges provide shelter and privacy, and – with
their foliage, flowers or berries – they can be beautiful
as well as practical garden features.**

Hedges are as much a part of garden layout as flower borders and lawns, and can range in size from huge walls of greenery made of yew or beech to decorative edgings of lavender or dwarf box. They demarcate the boundaries and can also make a garden private and sheltered, create a series of separate spaces within a design, or form a backdrop for focal points.

Boundary hedges

Hedges are a traditional way of defining land ownership. Large, thick and thorny types, such as hawthorn, physically deter intruders and stray animals. (For more thorough protection, reinforce hedging with chain-link fencing through the centre.)

Smaller hedges can act as boundary markers, though dwarf hedges are liable to be trampled, especially in corners or by short cuts. Some people prefer low boundary hedges, so that their homes are visible from the street to discourage burglars.

If you are considering a shared boundary hedge, it is courteous to discuss your plans with the appropriate neighbours. Legally, you must plant the hedge within your garden, so that it doesn't encroach on neighbouring property. However, a cooperative neighbour might allow the hedge to be planted on the boundary, and may even be willing to share the cost. It is also polite to discuss the hedge's height and shape.

Hedges for shelter

Hedges act as windbreaks and, because they filter wind rather than block it, they can cause less turbulence on their leeward side than more solid walls. Plants benefit from the shelter created by a hedge. Fierce winds have a drying effect on plants, especially newly planted evergreens, and can prove fatal.

On sloping land, hedges can be

▼ **Boundary hedges** A beech hedge forms a near impenetrable barrier and can be maintained at the desired height with a light annual trimming. The brown leaves remain attractive through autumn and winter and complement the berries of the wall-trained *Cotoneaster horizontalis*.

Within the garden, hedges can be used to screen eyesores, such as a dustbin area or shed. Hedges give little actual protection against noise, although they are psychologically soothing and also cut down the glare of car headlights at night.

Hedges as features

Ornamental dwarf hedges can be used to create pretty, interlocking geometric patterns with the spaces between filled with colourful flowers. These old-fashioned knot and parterre patterns are particularly effective when seen from a raised patio or a first-floor window.

Large hedges can be combined with topiary, with shrubs allowed to grow out at regular intervals, then clipped into geometric or animal shapes. Arches, buttresses and alcoves for seats or statues can

◄ **Flowering hedges** Compact growth and even shape are the main considerations in choosing an informal hedge. The yellow-flowered shrub *Hypericum* 'Hidcote' grows to a maximum height of 1.5m (5ft) and flowers throughout summer and autumn.

used to redirect frost, which flows like water, away from the garden. Hedges also offer shelter from dust and their roots help to check soil erosion.

The higher the hedge, the more shelter it creates, but it also produces more shade and a greater rain shadow. The larger the hedge, the more water and nutrients it takes from the soil.

Hedges for privacy

Hedges for general privacy should be at least 1.5m (5ft) high, although hedges 1.2m (4ft) high will provide privacy for a seating area. Enormously tall hedges, especially in small gardens, can be overbearing and not worth the extra privacy provided. Hedges planted next to a level change, such as along the top of a retaining wall, seem much higher than they really are when seen from the lower level.

► **Formal hedging** The small-leaved evergreen box (*Buxus sempervirens*) is a superb hedging plant that comes in a number of varieties. Dwarf varieties can be planted as formal borders; large varieties can be used in topiary or for a boundary hedge.

be formed out of hedging, given time, space and patience.

Formal or informal?

In old-fashioned, formal hedges, each plant's individual character is sacrificed to create an overall geometric shape. Traditional hedges can look as attractive in informal gardens as in formal ones. The straight lines of a formal hedge can complement the 'rough-and-tumble' of a mixed border, or an area of long grass and spring bulbs. Formal hedges are particularly suitable for edging small, square or rectangular-shaped gardens, but they require regular pruning, up to four times a year. As a result, they tend to be dense and non-flowering, as the young, flowering wood is constantly removed.

In informal hedges, a plant's natural shape and habit of growth are the main features to consider. Plants grown in such hedges tend to produce more flowers and berries than rigorously clipped hedges, since less new wood is removed. Escallonia, hydrangea, spiraea and shrub roses make excellent informal hedges. Infor-

mal hedging of mixed shrubs can lose its 'architectural' quality, and look more like a shrub border, which may be exactly what you would prefer.

Dwarf hedges, ideal for edging flower beds or dividing up areas within a garden, can be formal or informal, depending on the choice of plant and pruning treatment. Box, for example, makes a formal dwarf edging; lightly pruned cotton lavender, an informal one.

Evergreen versus deciduous

Evergreen hedging offers year-round colour and more privacy than deciduous hedging, but apart from a few examples they are insignificant in flower. Deciduous hedging plants, on the other hand, not only produce flowers in season, but many also have coloured spring foliage, handsome autumn tints and berries, and several, like the hornbeams, beeches and hawthorns, are effective visual screens even in winter when their foliage is brown.

Formal hedges are usually composed of a single species, and are most restful looking this way, but you can combine two or three

▲ **Conifer screens** The vigorous Leyland cypress (× *Cupressocyparis leylandii*) is ideal for screening. A fast-growing conifer of dense columnar form, it withstands high winds.

▼ **Colour and protection** The firethorn (*Pyracantha* 'Buisson Ardent') makes an impenetrable hedge, its thorny branches deterring intruders. Colourful, with cream-white flowers in spring and berries in autumn, it grows to a height of some 1.8m (6ft).

types of plants for an interesting tapestry effect. Try variegated and green-leaved forms of holly or privet, or purple and green-leaved forms of beech. Combining deciduous and evergreen plants makes for winter interest. The proportions can vary, but if the plants vary in vigour or growth rate, be prepared to give the weaker a helping hand. Too many different plant types in one hedge, however, may result in an uneven barrier lacking visual effect.

If you want a flowering or berrying hedge, keep in mind the amount of time it is out of flower or berry, and try to choose a plant that has attractive foliage or form as well. *Rosa rugosa* varieties make excellent flowering hedges, and are dog and child-proof. The flowers, which range from white in 'Blanc Double de Coubert' to rose-pink in 'Fru Dagmar Hastrup' and wine-red in 'Roseraie de l'Hay', can be single, semi-double or double, and are freely produced in summer and autumn, often followed by attractive hips. *Cotoneaster simonsii* produces brilliant berries and richly coloured autumn foliage, and stands hard pruning. Fragrance can come from foliage – rosemary or lavender, for example – as well as from flowers.

Practicalities

Quick-growing evergreen hedging, such as Leyland cypress, is tempting, but it can grow too tall unless cut back vigorously and single plants sometimes die off, creating unattractive gaps. The quicker growing a formal hedge, the more often it needs pruning – three times a year for privet and shrubby honeysuckle (*Lonicera nitida*), for example. Yew is often thought of as slow, but makes 23-30cm (9-12in) annual growth, and only needs clipping once a year.

When buying hedging plants, small shrubs are cheaper, less risky to establish and grow more strongly than larger specimens. Always choose plants that are well furnished with branches down to ground level. Make sure you choose the right species or variety for the desired height. For example, *Buxus sempervirens* 'Suffruticosa' is a dwarf edging box while *B.s.* 'Handsworthensis' grows to a height of 3.5m (12ft). Some garden centres have available bare-rooted hornbeam, hawthorn and beech, which are per-

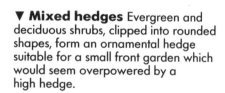

▲ Hedge tapestry The deciduous cherry plum (*Prunus cerasifera*) makes a dense windbreak and is highly decorative when mixed with the purple-leaved variety 'Atropurpurea'.

► Informal hedges Yellow and red-flowered varieties of broom (*Cytisus*) create vivid splashes of late-spring colour on the edge of a lawn.

▼ Mixed hedges Evergreen and deciduous shrubs, clipped into rounded shapes, form an ornamental hedge suitable for a small front garden which would seem overpowered by a high hedge.

fectly acceptable if planted when dormant and much less expensive than container-grown specimens.

Hedges can be planted in single or double rows. Single rows are cheaper, and considered better for the ultimate health of the plants, which are less crowded. Against this, it takes longer to make effective screening. Double rows are more expensive and crowd the plants, but are more quickly effective. Space plants 30cm-1m (1-3ft) apart, according to size and growth rate; leave about 45cm (18in) between double rows, staggering the plants.

Pruning regimes vary, but formal hedging must be pruned back hard in the first year after planting, by up to half, to encourage compact growth. Get the rough shape and proportions first, even though it means a temporary loss of height. Formal hedges should be narrower at the top than at the bottom to allow light to reach the lower branches and prevent bare bases. Large-leaved hedging plants, such as Portugal laurel

▶ **Hedge decoration** Privet is one of the most popular hedging plants. A quick-growing evergreen, it responds well to trimming and is ideal for ornamental topiary work and unusual decoration.

◀ **Internal hedges** Foliage shrubs don't have to be confined to the boundaries but can be ornamental features in their own right. This meandering design of low-growing prunus attracts the eye without inhibiting the view.

(*Prunus lusitanica*), look best pruned branch by branch; a once-over with electric hedge clippers or shears is fine for the others. Established formal hedges should be pruned as often as necessary, usually between late spring and late summer.

Informal hedges need light pruning to remove old, dead or diseased wood, to keep the hedge within bounds and to encourage flowering. As a general rule, prune flowering shrubs, such as potentilla, which flower on new wood, in winter or early spring; prune those that flower on one-year old wood, such as cherry plum and berberis, immediately after flowering; and prune those that flower on old wood very lightly.

HEDGING PLANTS

NAME	DESCRIPTION	HEIGHT & SPREAD	FOLIAGE	GROWTH RATE
FORMAL HEDGES Beech (*Fagus sylvatica* 'Dawyck's Purple')	Purple leaves; foliage turns golden-brown over winter	2.4 × 1m (8 × 3ft)	Deciduous	Moderate
Box (*Buxus sempervirens* 'Handsworthinsis')	Large, dark green leaves; erect and robust	2.4 × 1m (8 × 3ft)	Evergreen	Slow
Cotoneaster (*Cotoneaster simonsii*)	Rounded, dark green leaves, scarlet berries	1.8 × 1m (6 × 3ft)	Semi-evergreen	Moderate
Hawthorn (*Crataegus monogyna*)	Tough; thorny, white flowers, red haws	2.4 × 1m (8 × 3ft)	Deciduous	Moderate
Holly (*Ilex × altaclarensis* 'Hodginsii')	Dark green moderately spiny leaves; purple stems	2.4 × 1m (8 × 3ft)	Evergreen	Moderate
(*Ilex aquifolium* 'Golden Van Tol')	Dark, glossy almost spineless leaves with gold edges, red berries	2.4 × 1m (8 × 3ft)	Evergreen	Moderate
Hornbeam (*Carpinus betulus*)	Pointed leaves gold-brown in autumn/winter	2.4 × 1m (8 × 3ft)	Deciduous	Moderate
Laurel (*Prunus laurocerasus*)	Dark green leathery leaves; purple-black berries	2.4 × 1.2m (8 × 4ft)	Evergreen	Moderate
Leyland cypress (x *Cupressocyparis leylandii*)	Drooping sprays of grey-green leaves	3 × 1.2m (10 × 4ft)	Evergreen	Very fast
Portugal laurel (*Prunus lusitanica*)	Bushy, dark glossy green leaves; reddish stalks	2.4 × 1.2m (8 × 4ft)	Evergreen	Slow
Privet (*Ligustrum ovalifolium* 'Aureum')	Glossy mid-green oval leaves edged with wide yellow borders	1 × 1.2m (3 × 4ft)	Evergreen	Fast
Yew (*Taxus baccata*)	Densely bushy with narrow green leaves	2.4 × 1m (8 × 3ft)	Evergreen	Slow
INFORMAL HEDGES Berberis (*Berberis × stenophylla*)	Narrow leaves; profuse orange-yellow flowers, sparse purple fruits	2 × 1.2m (6 × 4ft)	Evergreen	Moderate
Escallonia (*Escallonia macrantha*)	Dense and luxuriant growth with glossy leaves; rosy-red flowers	2 × 1.2m (6 × 4ft)	Evergreen	Moderate
Firethorn (*Pyracantha rogersiana*)	Bright green leaves; golden-yellow to reddish-orange berries	2.4 × 2m (8 × 6ft)	Evergreen	Moderate
Laurustinus (*Viburnum tinus*)	Dark glossy green leaves; white flowers in winter, black-blue fruits	2.4 × 2m (8 × 6ft)	Evergreen	Moderate
Mock orange (*Philadelphus* 'Manteau d'Hermine')	Double creamy flowers; oval green leaves	1.2 × 1m (4 × 3ft)	Deciduous	Moderate
Potentilla (*Potentilla fruticosa* 'Katherine Dykes')	Bushy with lobed mid-green leaves and bright yellow flowers	1.2 × 1.2m (4 × 4ft)	Deciduous	Moderate
Rose (*Rosa rugosa*)	White, pink or red flowers; red hips	1.2 × 1.2m (4 × 4ft)	Deciduous	Moderate
Rosemary (*Rosmarinus officinalis*)	Bushy and spreading; narrow aromatic leaves and lilac-blue flowers	1.2 × 1m (4 × 3ft)	Evergreen	Moderate
Spiraea (*Spiraea × vanhouttei*)	Arching habit; profuse white flowers in early summer	2 × 1.2m (6 × 4ft)	Deciduous	Moderate
DWARF HEDGES Berberis (*Berberis thunbergii* 'Atropurpurea Nana')	Oval red-purple leaves redder in autumn; red berries	45 × 30cm (1.5 × 1ft)	Deciduous	Moderate
Box (*Buxus sempervirens* 'Suffruticosa')	Dense; glossy and leathery bright green leaves	60 × 30cm (2 × 1ft)	Evergreen	Slow
Cotton lavender (*Santolina chamaecyparissus*)	Silver-grey leaves with button-sized yellow flowers	60cm × 1m (2 × 3ft)	Evergreen	Fast
Lavender (*Lavandula angustifolia*)	Aromatic; narrow grey-green leaves, mauve to purple flowers	1 × 1m (3 × 3ft)	Evergreen	Moderate
Sand cherry (*Prunus × cistena*)	Bushy, with reddish-purple leaves, white flowers and black-purple fruits	1 × 1m (3 × 3ft)	Deciduous	Moderate

PLANTING HEDGES

**Thorough preparation of the site and regular
aftercare are essential if a new hedge is to remain healthy
and attractive for many years to come.**

Apart from being attractive features in themselves, hedges are used to mark out boundaries, provide privacy and conceal unattractive views. They can also form windbreaks and screens against damaging prevailing winds. In exposed regions, hedges are preferable to solid walls which are less effective in deflecting and filtering potentially destructive gales.

All hedges, whether formal or informal, should be even and compact in growth so that they retain their shape over a long period. For a formal effect, they must be able to withstand regular trimming. In particular, hedges should not die out at the bottom or develop patches with age.

To be really successful, you must pay great attention to site preparation and planning, since a hedge is a permanent feature and it will be difficult to attend to soil conditions in later years.

Planning

A hedge must be tended regularly and so access to both sides is essential. If it is to form a boundary between neighbours, you may leave half the job to them. Elsewhere, you should be able to walk freely around both sides. A tall hedge may need trimming from a stepladder, so firm, level ground to a width of at least 1m (3ft) on either side is required. For safety, electric trimming tools should not be used in confined spaces – never get involved in a balancing act.

Ideally, the site should be consistent from end to end in terms of sun/shade, soil drainage, soil type and wind exposure – uneven conditions invariably produce an uneven hedge.

Preparing the site

For best results, the planting strip should be about 1m (3ft) wide. Narrow sites encourage competition from weeds, neighbouring plants or grass during the hedge's early years which results in poor or erratic establishment.

For spring planting, which is best for most evergreens, prepare the ground in autumn and winter. Sites for deciduous hedges to be planted in autumn are best prepared in spring and kept weed-free during the summer.

Soil condition along an old boundary is often poor, especially where a wall or fence has been removed. If there is a lot of rubble, poor soil or drainage problems, dig out the site to at least one spade's depth and replace with new topsoil – bought or transferred from elsewhere in the garden.

▼ **Ubiquitous privet** The golden-leaved *Ligustrum ovalifolium* is a common hedging plant. It is cheap, tolerates polluted air and can be clipped to almost any shape.

PREPARING THE SITE

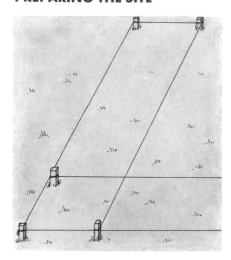

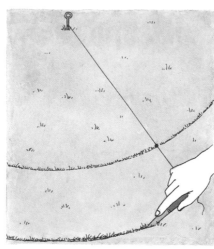

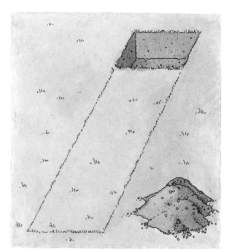

1 Plan and mark out the planting site using wooden pegs and strings. A mature hedge will have a root run of 1m (3ft) or more in all directions and so a planting area of at least 1m (3ft) across should be well prepared.

2 To mark out a curved site, insert a peg at the centre of the area and knot string around it. Make two guide knots 1m (3ft) apart corresponding to the position of the hedge. Pull the string taut and cut against the knots.

3 Begin preparing a turfed site by digging out one spade's depth of soil from one end. Pile this soil at the other end of the site — it will be used to fill in the last hole. Fork over the bottom of the hole.

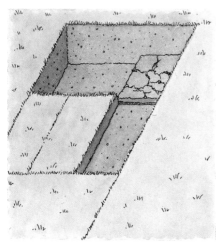

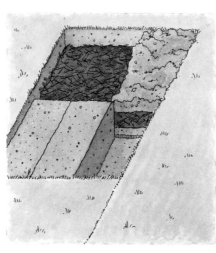

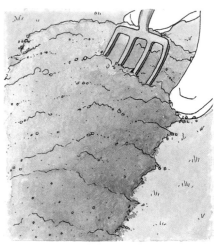

4 Skim off the turf from the next 30cm (1ft) or so of the site, using a spade, and turn it upside-down into the bottom of the previous hole. If the soil is heavy, break it up slightly with a garden fork and remove any tough roots.

5 Add a layer of well-rotted manure or compost, then turn in the soil from the newly exposed area. You have now another hole adjacent to the first. Fill it as before. Repeat the procedure until the site is complete.

6 Keep the site weed-free until ready for planting. Shortly before planting, fork over the soil again, at the same time incorporating a complete fertilizer. If the site is very wet, raise the soil into a slight ridge.

Other sites may be grassed or occupied by weeds or ornamental plants, which must be cleared. A rotary cultivator provides a quick means of turning over the soil, but the roots of perennials will be sliced up and turned in, creating a persistent weed problem. Manual cultivation, using a hand fork or spade, gives better results. Alternatively, apply a total, but non-persistent weedkiller, allowing plenty of time for the chemical to disintegrate in the soil before planting the hedge.

If no perennial weeds are present, turf can be turned upside-down and buried one spade's depth in the bottom of the planting trench. This preserves the valuable top-soil and improves the organic content of the soil.

Begin by marking out the site with pegs and string lines. Regular arcs and semi-circles can be plotted using string pulled taut from a peg inserted at the centre of the curve. Gauge the desired radius by knotting the string, slicing the curve with a knife held against the knot.

Turn over the soil throughout the site to one spade's depth and fork in a layer of well-rotted manure at the rate of a barrowful for every 2m/yd run. Shortly before planting, fork a complete fertilizer, such as Growmore, at one handful per m/yd run, into the soil over a 30cm (1ft) wide area along the hedge line.

Planting the hedge
Deciduous hedges can be planted when weather and soil conditions permit, between mid autumn and early spring, but preferably in autumn. Evergreen hedges are best planted in spring when transpiration loss will be smallest. Set the plants 45-60cm (1½-2ft) apart, depending on vigour, with only 25-30cm (10-12in) between dwarf types.

The ideal age of hedging specimens for planting varies, but as a general rule they should be small enough to make handling easy and staking unnecessary. Plant in a single row against a garden line to ensure a straight hedge. When planting around a curve, use a length of wood marked or notched as a gauge to determine the exact centre of the planting area.

Set the plants to the same depth as in the nursery, indicated by a dark soil mark at the base of the stem. Ease soil around the roots, and firm in well – more hedging plants die from loose planting than any other cause.

Trim all plants to a standard height using a string stretched between two canes as a guide. This ensures that they all have the same start. If plants aren't very bushy, cut back all growths by half or two-thirds, either at planting time or in spring.

Water young plants during dry spells in spring and early summer. Allow at least 10 litres (2 gallons) to soak in around each plant daily until established. Sprinkling, preferably with rainwater in a fine-rose watering can, is also beneficial.

Aftercare

Keep the hedge bottom free of weeds, and do not allow any other plants to grow within 30cm (1ft) on either side of a new hedge.

Regular applications of fertilizer are unnecessary, but all young hedges benefit from a dressing of complete fertilizer in late winter, one year after spring planting or 18 months after an

HEELING-IN

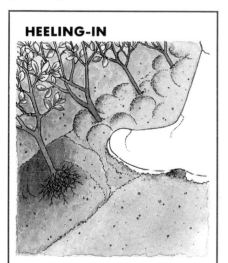

If hedging plants are delivered too early, heel them in temporarily in spare ground. Lay them close together in a trench, angling away from prevailing winds. Lightly firm soil over the roots.

PLANTING THE HEDGE

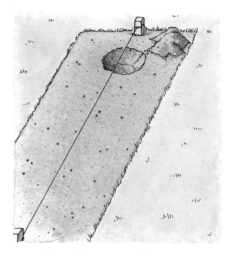

1 Mark out the centre of the planting area using pegs and string. Keep the string in place throughout the planting operation, making sure it remains taut – it's essential to plant in a perfectly straight line.

2 Use a length of wood with a notch cut at its centre to gauge the planting position when making a curved hedge. If the edges of the site are tidy and parallel, this method can be used also for straight plantings.

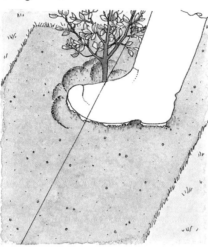

3 Dig the first planting hole, making it slightly larger than the plant's spread out roots. Bury roots to the same depth as they were in the nursery – the stem is darker at soil level.

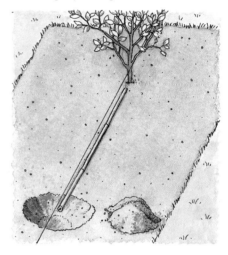

4 Having firmed in the first plant very securely with heel and toe, mark the position of the next one. Use a cane cut to the required length as a gauge. Plant as before.

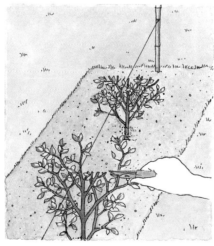

5 Trim the plants to a standard height. Insert canes and stretch string between at a height equal to that of the strongest growth on the shortest plant. Prune to string level.

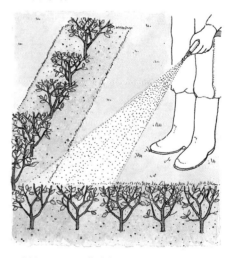

6 Water in well if the soil is dry and repeat daily as necessary. Give enough water to soak the soil thoroughly over the whole planting area – at least 10 litres (2 gallons) per plant.

MAKING A SPIRAL CONE

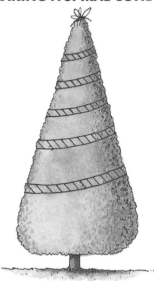

1 To make a spiral from a mature cone-shaped bush or small tree, begin by marking out the spiral with strings, attaching them to branch tips at regular intervals. Step back to check the pattern.

2 Using shears or secateurs, cut into the plant following the string lines. Remove all stems and leaves back to the main stem or trunk. With time, foliage will grow in to hide the bare surfaces (as below).

autumn planting. Apply a small handful per m/yd run on each side of the hedge. Repeat every year if growth is poor.

Staking is usually not required, but on exposed sites a new hedge may need the shelter of a temporary fence or screen until established. Alternatively, support each plant individually, or erect a line of stakes with wires or strings stretched between, tying in as required with garden string.

For all hedges, early training is important. To promote a thick, bushy habit from the base to the top, side branching must be encouraged. Never allow a hedge to reach the desired height before pruning – it will become thin and straggly at the base.

Informal, flowering hedges may be left to grow freely after the initial tipping at planting time, but if branching is poor sacrifice the second year's flowers in favour of a second pruning. Allow formal hedges to reach the desired height only in stages. Prune the leading shoots regularly when they are 23-30cm (9-12in) long.

Aim to make the hedge widest at the bottom, with a rounded or broadly sloping top. This promotes better growth of the low branches and gives the best wind shelter.

Decorative hedge trimming

Many free-standing hedging plants can be trimmed into decorative shapes when they are mature or they can be trained to shape from young plants. The former method is suitable for simple topiary designs, such as cones, globes and pyramids.

Make use of a shrub's natural growth shape – for example, a naturally conical shrub is much easier to train into a cone than a spreading species. Privet, yew and the accommodating box lend themselves to topiary designs.

Ensure that the plant is well-staked and securely tied so that wind action cannot separate and disfigure the branches. Bind the branches with string or thin rope over winter to prevent snow loads from breaking them.

Specimen topiary shrubs can look effective in large tubs. Choose a container to complement the shape of the topiary, ensuring that it is large enough to accommodate a large root ball – the shrub will be growing for many years, ideally without disturbance.

HEDGE MAINTENANCE

**All hedges need regular trimming to
promote a dense, impenetrable screen and to
maintain their shape and beauty.**

The first few years of a hedge's life are very important. Most hedging plants will develop into a bushy or upright shape without any assistance, but these characteristics alone do not ensure a good hedge. What is needed of each plant is a dense, uniform growth habit with a shape to suit the desired height and width of hedge. Regular and careful pruning and trimming from the year of planting onwards is the only way to achieve this – a neglected hedge is very difficult to restore. In general, formal hedges should be trimmed two or three times during the growing season, and informal ones after flowering.

Trimming and pruning tools
For a couple of years after planting the only tool you will need for hedge trimming is a sharp pair of secateurs. In subsequent years, hand shears or some form of mechanical hedge trimmer will be essential for all small-leaved, formal hedges.

Species with large leaves, however, such as laurel, should be trimmed throughout their life with secateurs – shears and mechanical trimmers slice leaves as well as stems and the damaged edges later turn yellow and brown, creating a very unsightly effect. Secateurs are also best for trimming all types of informal hedge.

Choose and use mechanical hedge trimmers with care – though they can save much time and labour, many are potentially quite hazardous. Look for models with as many safety features as possible. Blade extensions, which prevent any object larger than about 1cm (⅜in) in diameter – equivalent to the size of the largest stems of most hedging plants – from coming into contact with the cutting blades, are extremely useful. The blades should also be fitted with a brake which comes into operation within a fraction of a second of the power switch being released.

Since most accidents occur with mechanical trimmers when the operator lets go of the handle with one hand to clear debris or move the power cable, two-handled machines which have a power switch on each handle, together with an efficient brake, are especially safe – the blades are inoperable until you grip both handles

---

▼ **Garden shears** The traditional implement for trimming small-leaved hedges has handles offset to the blades. This gives a good cutting angle for both the sides and top of a hedge according to how they are held.

TRIMMING UPRIGHT HEDGING PLANTS

1 In the second winter after planting — preferably in late winter — prune back the previous year's stems by half and trim any remaining lateral shoots to within a few centimetres of the structural framework stems.

2 During the following summer, trim back all lateral shoots to maintain the desired hedge shape whenever they reach about 20-30cm (8-12in) in length. Ensure that the sides taper towards the top of the hedge.

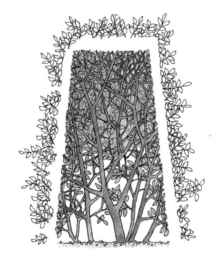

3 In the next winter, cut back any leaders which are developing an uneven height. This procedure must be repeated yearly until the desired height is reached — never let a new hedge gain height too quickly.

4 Once the hedge is established, summer trimming is all that's necessary. Using shears or mechanical trimmers, trim the side and top growth to maintain the desired shape, repeating every six to eight weeks.

TRIMMING CONIFER HEDGES

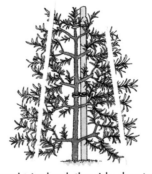

1 Securely tie all conifers to stakes or canes at planting time. Trim all straggly side shoots to encourage even branch development.
2 In the following summer, tie in the

leaders and trim back the side shoots, maintaining tapering sides.
3 Pinch out the leaders when they reach the desired height. Trim back side and top growth every summer.

and activate both switches.

Always use a residual current circuit breaker when operating an electric hedge trimmer. These ensure that the power is switched off immediately if the cable is cut or if a leakage of current occurs — they will save you from serious electric shock or burns in an accident. The safest place to keep the extension cable while working with an electric trimmer is across your shoulder where it is least likely to come into contact with the blades.

Ultimate aims

Formal hedges are grown to provide a physical barrier against noise and wind, or simply to give a degree of privacy. Provided the growth is dense enough, there is no need for any hedge to exceed 60cm (2ft) in width. All hedges should taper towards their top — that is, be slightly wider at their base — to be most stable and resistant to wind and snow damage.

Informal hedges are used more for screens and divisions between two separate parts of the garden and for concealing unwanted views from the garden. They do not need to be so dense or regular in outline, and require no more pruning or maintenance than free-standing shrubs.

Pruning and trimming

Hedging plants fall into three categories: those with a naturally upright growth habit which must be encouraged to thicken up at their base; those with a naturally low and bushy growth habit which must be encouraged to gain height and density at their top; and the conifers which need only minimal training to establish their shape.
Upright hedging plants, such as privet, hawthorn, snowberry and blackthorn, must be cut back hard throughout their early years to promote strong basal growth. Left inadequately pruned, these plants become bare at their base.

At planting time they should be cut back to about 15cm (6in) from the ground. During the following summer lightly trim all branches to encourage active growth of as many new shoots as possible. The cutting pattern must reflect the desired final shape of the hedge. Cut back new growths again by half during the second winter to make them bush still further. At the same time, prune back all other branches close to the main structural stems. Above all, discourage the leaders from reaching their final height too quickly.

Pruning during the next year will depend on how dense the hedge has become. If further thickening is desired, repeat the winter pruning once more as for year two. If the density is satisfactory, trimming in subsequent years can be restricted to the growing season. The frequency of trimming during any one year will depend on the cultural conditions and on the species concerned, but every six to eight weeks from mid to late spring through to about early autumn is the usual requirement. Aim to keep the plants neat and within the confines of the desired overall hedge shape, and ensure that the sides of the hedge taper.

Bushy hedging plants, such as beech, hazel and hornbeam, need less severe pruning in the early formative years.

At planting time, trim back the major side branches and the leader by about one-third. Allow the plants to develop naturally during the first summer. During the second winter, repeat the pruning as for year one. Eliminate all straggly growth.

As with upright hedge plants, trim only during the growing season in every subsequent year, maintaining a tapered outline. Preferably, trim twice in each season – in early summer, then again in late summer or very early

NEGLECTED HEDGES

Overgrown hedges can be renovated, though replanting may be better. Cut all branches back to the main stems – in winter for deciduous hedges; in spring for evergreens. Prune one side hard back, doing the other side the next year.

TRIMMING TECHNIQUES

1 To ensure a perfectly straight top edge when trimming a small-leaved hedge, always work to a taut string line stretched between a stout stake inserted at each end of the hedge. For a patterned top edge you will need to construct a template made from timber or rope. A regular wavy top can be gauged by draping rope from a tensioned line positioned across the top of the hedge.

2 Never use shears or mechanical trimmers to cut a large-leaved hedge such as laurel – you will slice many of the remaining leaves and these will later turn yellow and brown, creating an unattractive effect. Instead, use a pair of secateurs and prune in the same way as for a free-standing shrub. Though more laborious and time-consuming, this is the only satisfactory method.

3 Using secateurs or long-handled pruners, cut out dead wood from a hedge in summer when healthy wood is clearly visible. Make a clean, downward-sloping cut through healthy wood a little below the dead material. To avoid damaging surrounding healthy stems, cut large dead branches into several pieces before extracting them from the hedge. Train surrounding stems into the bare patch.

autumn. The early summer trim can be ignored if you wish.

Coniferous hedging plants, such as Lawson and Leyland cypresses, and Western red cedar, need rather different treatment. The leader must not be removed at planting time. Slightly trim only the straggly side branches to promote the formation of well-balanced laterals.

The main stem of most young conifers is not rigid enough to withstand strong winds or snow loads and must therefore be staked and tied loosely but securely. As the conifers get older

and stronger, remove the stakes.

Allow the leader to develop unhindered until it reaches the desired final height. During the second and subsequent years after planting, trim only the side branches during the growing season. Most species require only one trim in late summer. If vigorous species become too overgrown by mid summer you can overcome this in subsequent years by giving an extra trim in early summer.

Flowering formal hedges, such as forsythia, should be trimmed during the growing season immediately after the flowers have

AVOIDING SNOW DAMAGE

Heavy accumulations of snow can cause considerable physical damage to all hedges, especially those with lax stems, such as conifers, or those with large leaves, such as laurel. Using the head of a soft broom, gently shake the branches after each snow fall to dislodge it – once branches have been allowed to sag for more than a few hours it is usually difficult to train them back into position. Where heavy snowfalls are common, bind hedges with string or rope throughout winter to prevent snow-laden branches from breaking.

HEDGE TRIMMING TIMES

Beech (*Fagus sylvatica*): mid summer to late summer

Berberis × *stenophylla*: late spring to early summer

Berberis *thunbergii* 'Atropurpurea Nana': late summer

Box (*Buxus sempervirens*): early summer

Cherry plum (*Prunus cerasifera*): mid summer

Shrubby honeysuckle (*Lonicera nitida*): mid spring to early autumn

Cotoneaster simonsii: mid summer

Cotton lavender (*Santolina chamaecyparissus*): spring

Escallonia macrantha: early summer

Firethorn (*Pyracantha rogersiana*): early summer

Forsythia × intermedia: immediately after flowering and late summer

Hawthorn (*Crataegus monogyna*): early summer to late summer

Holly (*Ilex* species): mid summer

Hornbeam (*Carpinus betulus*): mid summer to late summer

Hydrangea macrophylla: late spring

Laurel (*Prunus laurocerasus*): mid summer to late summer

Laurustinus (*Viburnum tinus*): after flowering

Lavender (*Lavandula angustifolia*): early autumn

Lawson cypress (*Chamaecyparis lawsoniana*): early summer and early autumn

Leyland cypress (× *Cupressocyparis leylandii*): late spring to early summer

Mock orange (*Philadelphus* hybrids): immediately after flowering

Portugal laurel (*Prunus lusitanica*): early to mid summer

Potentilla fruticosa 'Katherine Dykes': after flowering

Privet (*Ligustrum ovalifolium*): late spring to early summer, and mid summer to late summer

Rose (*Rosa rugosa* varieties): early spring or autumn

Rosemary (*Rosmarinus officinalis*): mid summer to late summer

Sand cherry (*Prunus × cistena*): mid summer to late summer

Spiraea × vanhouttei: immediately after flowering

Western red cedar/arbor-vitae (*Thuja plicata*): early summer to mid summer

Yew (*Taxus baccata*): early summer to mid summer

faded. A second trim in late summer may be necessary to maintain a neat shape, but do not remove too much growth or next year's developing flower buds will be lost.

Flowering informal hedges, such as berberis, should be pruned according to the age of wood on which they flower. If they flower on old wood, trim to shape immediately after flowering; if they flower on the current season's wood, trim in early spring.

Fruiting hedging plants, which develop attractive fruits after the flowers have faded, such as pyracantha and berberis, should have their young growth trimmed in mid to late summer, leaving most of the fruiting wood intact. This selective trimming must be done with secateurs. Alternatively, leave trimming until the fruits have gone.

Other routine care

Hedges need more than just annual trimming – you must pay attention to watering and feeding, and to the control of pests, diseases and disorders if they are to remain healthy and attractive.

Watering is necessary during dry spells in the growing season – hedging plants are generally spaced much closer than other garden plants and so their roots compete heavily for water. You can use a garden hose or sprinkler, but the most effective method is to lay a seep hose along the base of the hedge. Apply enough water to saturate the top 15cm (6in) of soil – equivalent to 2.5cm (1in) of rainfall – at each application and repeat whenever the top 2.5cm (1in) of soil is dry.

Mulching annually with forest bark around the roots of a hedge will help to prevent undue water loss from the soil.

Feeding should be carried out regularly. Apply a general-purpose fertilizer, such as bonemeal, at the rate of a generous handful per sq m/yd in spring as a soil dressing. Treat a strip up to 90cm (3ft) wide from the base of the hedge and hoe the fertilizer into the surface 2.5cm (1in). Water it in if the soil is dry.

If the root run of the hedge is under turf or paving, then apply nutrients as a foliar feed from a pressure sprayer. Use a liquid fertilizer which is rich in nitrogen for leaf growth. Repeat whenever the foliage appears dull and lacking vigour. Foliar sprays can also be applied as a mid to late season back-up to the main spring soil dressing.

Weeding Eliminate weeds from the base of a hedge using a draw hoe, by hand or with chemical sprays. Weeds compete with the hedge for nutrients, water and light so remove them before they begin to accumulate.

Water-soluble diquat and paraquat weedkillers are effective against most weeds under a hedge, but avoid wetting the leaves of the hedge. Glyphosate in liquid or gel form is ideal for killing persistent perennial and annual weeds.

Cutting out dead wood is another vital task. Branches often die out in the centre of an established hedge. These should be pruned away since they can harbour diseases such as coral spot which soon spread through the entire hedge. Make clean cuts with secateurs back to healthy wood. This is best done during the growing season when live wood is clearly visible.

If a whole plant dies out within a hedge, grub it out and replace with a young specimen after first preparing and conditioning the soil as for planting a new hedge.

Pests and diseases should be treated as for other garden shrubs and trees. Healthy plants are resistant; use chemicals with care and discretion.

Planting
and sowing

Buying plants is one of the most pleasurable aspects of gardening. A thoughtful choice, based on sound knowledge of the conditions in your garden, the space available and the plant in question, is far better than impulse buys, which rarely work out well. Doing your homework beforehand, so you know exactly what you want and what a healthy specimen should look like, helps to prevent disappointment or problems since garden centre staff may not be as knowledgeable or helpful as you might wish, and labels may be inadequate or misplaced.

Knowing where to buy is also important. It is often best to buy your plants from reputable garden centres and nurseries, which usually have access to the most reliable sources.

To give new plants a healthy start, they must be planted in the right position, at the right depth and at the right distance apart. Annuals, bulbs, shrubs and trees should all be planted in a slightly different way – and, of course, planting in containers demands an entirely different technique. Since new plants are vulnerable until they have become established, aftercare such as watering, weeding and staking is vital. With shrubs and trees – the most permanent and expensive plants – this initial care is doubly important.

Plants grown from seed are the cheapest option, and seed catalogues offer greater choice, especially of annuals, than garden centres. Using the right techniques for preparing your seed trays, for sowing, and for caring for the seedlings after germination can make the difference between success and failure. Home-saved seed, especially of hybrids, however, doesn't always breed true to type and fresh replacement seed is best.

Balled-root shrubs Newly lifted shrubs have their root balls wrapped in loose-weave sacking for sale at garden centres.

BUYING THE BEST PLANTS

**Start gardening with young, healthy and
vigorous plants and you're well on the way to success.
Knowing how to select the top quality means you won't be wasting
money on weak plants, and it also avoids the risk
of spreading disease and pests.**

It is sometimes difficult to imagine how gardeners managed before there were garden centres. However, they are far from being the only source of plants and you may do just as well – or sometimes better – to look elsewhere. There are, for instance, many general and specialized nurseries, most of which sell direct to the public on site as well as by mail order. Large supermarkets and department stores often sell plants, too. Always put quality before economy, and make sure that the plants you buy are clearly labelled so you know exactly what they are. Even when your stock comes to you through a network of gardening friends, be choosy about the plants you accept.

Bedding plants
Since annual plants complete their life cycle in just one year, and biennials in two, they can easily be grown from seed. There are, however, good reasons for buying young plants.

One packet contains a large quantity of seeds, and you may need only a few plants for window-boxes or growing bags; alternatively, you may want just a small sample of a new line of vegetables. Or the plants you choose may be half-hardy – such as marigolds, petunias, tobacco plants and tomatoes – and need protection from frost as seedlings. It is an easy short cut to let the garden centre deal with the delicate early stages of such a plant's life, and

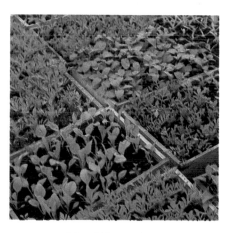

▲ **Annual bedding plants** These are strong, healthy, disease-free specimens.

▼ **Garden centres** A wide selection of plants can be bewildering. Follow the guidelines suggested here to help you choose.

just buy stock when it is ready for planting in the garden.

Space is another factor, since biennials, such as wallflowers and sweet Williams, take two years to produce flowers and they need to be sown outdoors in late spring the year before flowering. For the small garden at least, it makes sense to occupy that space with other plants and buy already growing biennials in autumn for flowering the following year.

Strips and small pots

The most common containers in which small bedding plants are sold are trays or polystyrene strips. When buying, look at the overall appearance of the plant, and in particular its leaves, soil and flowers (if any).

Plants should be compact and sturdy. Uneven, lanky growth is a sign of badly lit and perhaps over-heated conditions, or of a plant that has outgrown its container and compost. No matter how good the conditions are that you give the plant in later life, it will never recover completely.

If the plants are in strips, they should be fairly uniform in size. Where seed has been distributed unevenly, you may get one or two robust specimens and many straggly ones which have been defeated by the competition.

Check that the leaves are a good healthy colour and that there is evidence of strong growth coming on. Yellowing and discoloured leaves or, worse still, the presence of pests, are a sign of disease, inadequate food or water and general neglect. Remember to look at the undersides, too.

Test that the compost is moist. Plants allowed to dry out suffer checks to growth that they never make up. Make sure that plants growing in polystyrene strips have not outgrown their container (with roots growing right through the polystyrene) and avoid specimens with roots growing through the bottoms of pots and trays, as these have been in their containers too long.

Ornamentals in full flower have almost certainly exhausted the nutrients in their compost. In the case of plants growing in individual containers, a few open flowers are not serious, but avoid plants with dead flowerheads or any where it is obvious that dead heads have been removed.

▲ **Healthy bedding plants** Select plants with bushy, well-proportioned growth and healthy, fresh green leaves (left). Discoloured foliage, lank stems and full-flowering (right) are signs that plants in polystyrene strips have exhausted the soil.

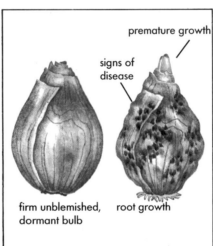

premature growth

signs of disease

firm unblemished, dormant bulb

root growth

◄ **Dormant bulbs** Best buys are rounded and firm without premature development (left); avoid any with shrivelled, mouldy skins, which are an indication of disease (right).

Bulbs and corms

Bulbs and corms are available at different times of the year, according to when they flower. Most benefit from early planting, so the sooner you buy supplies after they come in, the better.

Some corms and tubers, like those of cyclamen and winter aconites, are naturally hard and woody. But most dry bulbs should be plump and firm and show no sign of grey or blackish moulds, which indicate pest damage or fungal attack.

Others – lilies, for example – do not settle down well if the bulbs are allowed to dry out when they are lifted. They are therefore often kept in damp compost. Look for fleshy bulbs that show no sign of shrivelling. Take extra care to buy

lilies from a reliable nursery or supplier as virus diseases are a major problem and difficult to detect in lily bulbs.

A few bulbs, most commonly snowdrops, are sometimes sold immediately after flowering, with the leaves still attached. They settle more quickly if bought and planted 'in the green', rather than as dry bulbs later in the season.

Container plants

Shrubs, roses and conifers are often sold in plastic pots or flexible plastic sleeves. This allows much greater freedom with planting times, particularly for trees and shrubs – in the past, the general pattern was to plant deciduous specimens in autumn and evergreens in spring.

Look for young stock of well balanced growth. Large, older shrubs are often slow to establish and are quickly overtaken by younger, much more vigorous

WHY BUY READY-GROWN PLANTS?
Sowing seed is the cheapest and easiest method of creating bedding plants while perennials are easily propagated by division, and cuttings are the most economical way of propagating trees and shrubs. So what are the pros and cons of buying ready-grown plants?

Bulbs
☐ Seeds of bulbous plants take a long time to grow and develop a bulb that will produce flowers.
☐ Seeds of some bulbous plants are not readily available.

Bedding plants
☐ Only a few plants needed.
☐ Early start is gained for half-hardy annuals and biennials.
☐ Space is saved on biennials that will not flower for a year.

Perennials
☐ Much better result is achieved if a mature plant is bought.
☐ Cuttings and division take up time and space that can be saved.
☐ Provides 'instant' garden.

Container shrubs and trees
☐ More flexibility for planting times.
☐ Best chance of healthy specimens.
☐ Cuttings take long time to mature.
☐ Disadvantage is that container-grown plants are expensive.

Bare and balled-root trees and shrubs
☐ Cheaper than container types.
☐ Restricted to planting in late autumn and winter only.
☐ Packaged plants difficult to check for health – prone to being damaged or started into premature growth.
☐ Convenient for mail order but sometimes delayed or damaged.
☐ Cuttings take several years to grow.

ones. Check that grafted plants (where the stem or bud of one plant is united to the root of another) have a sound join, and that leaves, branches and roots are healthy. The join should not be so high – above 30cm (12in) – that a strong wind could snap off the new stem, nor so low that suckers grow from the rootstock.

Large bedding plants and perennials – such as delphiniums, dicentras and hostas – are also good container buys, saving several years of waiting. Perennials are slow to mature if raised from seed, which is frustrating when you are longing for the yearly display of beautiful flowers and foliage. Some perennials, too, need to be reared from cuttings or by division – again, a slow process best left to the nursery if you are after instant effects.

If you are buying container plants in full growth, select ones that are well proportioned and vigorous, with no straggly or wilting stems. The foliage should show no sign of disease or pest infection – black spot is a particular problem with roses.

Some weed growth on the surface of the compost is a good sign – an indication that the plant has not simply been dug out of the ground and dropped into a container shortly before sale. (Plants loose in pots are another giveaway

▲ Container-grown roses
Choose plants with robust growth from the base (left). Reject weak specimens or any that have dried out (right).

▲ Signs of good health A
compact shape (left) is proof of a strong root system and overall health. Avoid plants with thin, straggly growth (right), as these have had a poor start in life.

▶ Container-grown shrubs
Choose young and vigorous specimens (left). Wilting foliage or damaged branches (right) are a bad sign.

▲ **Balled-root evergreens** When selecting, ensure that the ball has not broken (right), although a light growth of weeds is a healthy sign. The ideal stock has balanced growth and plenty of flourishing leaves (left).

▲ **Balled-root trees**
These have spent their formative years in open ground, as proved in this case by the abundance of annual seedlings. On lifting, the soil ball is wrapped in sacking or a similar material.

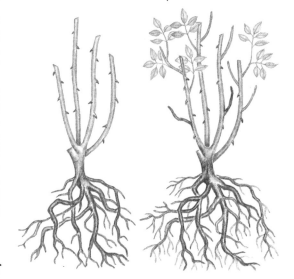

◀ **Bare-root roses**
Healthy plants should have a well-developed root system spreading in all directions (left). Opening leaf buds are a sign of too much growth too soon (right); steer clear of white roots and damaged stems.

that they have only recently been lifted from open ground.) Strong weed growth means, however, that the plant has had to fight for water and nutrients.

The plant should have a strong root system, growing in moist compost, but discard any specimens with thick roots escaping through the base of the container or with matted roots at the surface. In the case of hardy perennials bought in spring and autumn, you should be able to see healthy growth buds.

Balled-root plants
Evergreen trees and a variety of shrubs are often sold in balled-root form – when they are lifted from the ground the soil around the roots is retained and held by a wrapping of sacking.

Choose well-proportioned specimens with a good framework of stems and healthy foliage. Feel through the sacking to make sure that no roots have developed around the ball, indicating that the plant has been balled for too long. Discard any stock with the ball broken, as this probably means that the soil has been allowed to dry out.

Bare-root plants
Many deciduous shrubs, roses and biennials, such as sweet Williams

and wallflowers, are sold as bare-root plants. These are lifted in the autumn or during the winter months for planting before growth begins again.

As well as being sold through nurseries and garden centres, bare-root plants are also specially packaged for supermarkets and department stores in a box or polythene bag, with moist compost around the roots. The packaging often obscures the condition of the plant so that it is difficult to tell whether the shop's central heating has caused drying out, shrivelling or premature development. As a general rule, therefore, buy stocks as soon after they

become available as possible.

Any bare-root stock delivered through the mail should be moist but not soggy when opened. It should show no bruising of roots, stems and leaves. Reputable nurseries will usually replace plants that have arrived in a damaged or unhealthy condition.

All plants should be completely dormant when bought, showing no premature growth of rootlets and no sign of leaf buds opening. But they must have sturdy, well ripened stems (at least two in the case of roses), and an evenly developed, fibrous root system, showing no sign of damage from pests or distortion by disease.

PLANTING IN BEDS AND BORDERS

Annuals and herbaceous perennials give the best performance of colour if planted with minimum root disturbance in well-prepared beds and borders.

A garden can be filled quickly with colour from annuals and biennials – they flower longer than most other plants and are ideal for filling gaps in a border or for an entire summer bed. Herbaceous perennials, which spring up afresh year after year, can be grown exclusively in a border or island bed, but do equally well as attractive companions to mixed shrub planting.

An attractive border or bed depends much on how the plants are arranged. Later-flowering or foliage plants should conceal gaps left by earlier flowers – colours should blend and everything should be in scale. Seed and nursery catalogues provide inspiration and are available in good time for you to plan a selection and design the layout.

Preparing for annuals

Begin soil preparations in early to mid autumn. Pull this season's faded and dead plants from the soil, using a fork to loosen stubborn ones. Once all the old vegetation has been removed, apply a 2.5-5cm (1-2in) layer of well-rotted manure or garden compost to the surface of the soil. This gives body to light, dry soil and helps to retain moisture; it also improves aeration and drainage of heavy soils and adds nutrients.

Turn over the soil and compost together with a garden fork. Leave it lumpy since a better soil surface is produced if winter frosts are allowed to penetrate deeply and break it down naturally. It is easier to turn over soil when it's moist – if the ground is hard, water it thoroughly the day be-

fore. If the soil is too sticky after rain, leave it for a few days before you start digging.

In spring, as soon as the soil is dry enough, loosen up the top 15-20cm (6-8in) – slightly deeper if it was a severe winter – with a fork. While doing this look out for leatherjackets (leathery, slate-grey larvae, rather like legless caterpillars) and wireworms (segmented yellow-brown, worm-like creatures). Both pests feed on the roots of plants. If you see either, sprinkle some bromophos or HCH powder on to the soil. One

---

▼ **Planting annuals** Before setting bedding plants in the ground, space them out within the planting plan, then step back and assess the overall balance – adjust the spacing if you feel it is necessary.

MARKING OUT THE SITE

1 If your plan has a regular design, use a board to mark out the planting positions, setting plants inside the squares or at intersections.

2 For less regular designs, mark the planting areas with a cane or stick, varying their size and shape.

treatment should be enough to eradicate these pests.

Just before planting, add some general-purpose fertilizer, such as Growmore, to the soil. Scatter the fertilizer evenly at the rate of two handfuls per sq m/yd, then rake it lightly into the top 2.5cm (1in) of soil to produce a fine tilth.

Planting annuals

If you have raised plants under glass from seed, harden them off before planting out in a sheltered outdoor site. The best time for planting is between late spring and very early summer. Planting of half-hardy annuals can begin as soon as the risk of local frost has passed. The soil should be moist – if not, water thoroughly the day before planting.

Annuals can be grown in various containers – expanded polystyrene trays or strips, rigid plastic or wooden seed trays or in individual plastic or clay pots. The growing system adopted will influence the best planting technique. Certain hardy annuals get off to a better start if they are sown *in situ* the previous autumn.

Water bedding strips and trays an hour or two before planting – this ensures that the compost adheres to the root ball and so reduces root damage during planting out. Before removing plants from their container, mark out the planting site, according to your plan, using a garden cane, a stick, the edge of a board or trails of sand.

Plants grown on in individual pots or compartmented trays can be planted out with almost no root disturbance, but with other types you will have to separate individual plants and so some root damage is inevitable. With care, however, all newly planted annuals recover well and soon produce a fine show of flowers.

Remove plants from wooden or plastic trays with as much root as possible. Ideally remove the whole mass of seedlings, roots and compost intact. Loosen the soil and root mass by bumping the tray gently, then with the tray on the ground, tilt it to almost 90° until the root mass begins to flop out of the tray. Quickly insert the palm of one hand under the root mass, let go of the tray with the other hand and manoeuvre the plants gently on to the ground – this is less difficult than it sounds provided the compost is moist and the plants are well rooted.

Remove plants from bedding strips in a similar way, though you will have to turn the strip right over and take the root mass into the palm of the other hand. Many of these strips are flimsy and not re-usable, so it is often easier simply to break the container away from the root ball.

Separate the plants by cutting them apart with a knife or the edge of a hand trowel. Less root damage may be caused by easing the plants apart with your fingers, but be careful not to squash and break up the soil around the roots in so doing. Ensure that each plant has a good root system.

Spacing The correct spacing between plants will depend on the species. A good general rule is to space plants half their eventual height apart, except for those with a spreading growth habit, which should be spaced the equivalent of their full height apart.

Dig a planting hole with a hand trowel, making it wide and deep enough to accommodate the plant's entire root system but not so deep that air spaces are left beneath the roots. Remove any stones or other obstacles that may impede root penetration. Insert the plant so that the base of its stem is level with the surface of

◄ **Planting beds** Mark out the site with trails of sand if there is a chance of rain before planting is begun – they will remain visible whereas scratched lines may get washed away.

the soil. Fill the hole and firm in the plant with your fingers. When you have finished a bed, water in well using a fine-rose watering can – apply a fair amount of water since a light sprinkling will not penetrate to the roots and instead will merely encourage roots to grow near the surface, where they will be vulnerable to hoeing and dry weather.

Alternatively, insert the plant, then wash the soil into the hole and around the roots by 'puddling' with water from an open-spouted watering can. Leave while the water soaks in, then fill in any remaining small holes around the plant by hand. Level the surface after you have finished planting the bed.

When planting a lot of annuals, work in batches. Cut only as many plants from a box as you can plant in a couple of minutes, especially when working on a warm day. Avoid planting during hot sunshine when plants quickly wilt – a dull day or cool, damp evening is preferable.

Soon after planting, encourage plants that are not normally bushy to develop branching side shoots and more blooms by pinching out their growing tips.

Planting biennials

It is essential for biennials to be planted out in their flowering positions by mid autumn – whether from a nursery bed, greenhouse or cold frame – otherwise they may not have a chance to establish themselves before the onset of severe weather.

Before planting, dig over the soil and work in a light dressing of well-rotted manure or garden compost, together with a generous handful of bonemeal or a small handful of superphosphate for each sq m/yd.

Lift the biennials from their nursery bed, easing them out with a hand fork, with as many roots attached as possible. If the soil is very dry, water it first to ease lifting and lessen damage to the roots.

After lifting, put them into their permanent positions as soon as possible, before their roots can dry out. Wallflowers, however, tolerate being left unplanted for a day or two – they are often sold bare-rooted, wrapped in newspaper. Firm in the plants and water well.

In cold areas, plants put out in

PLANTING ANNUALS

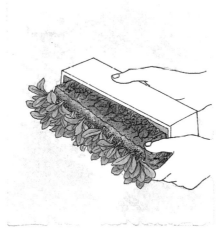

1 It is easier to separate plants if the whole mass of soil and roots is first removed. Having loosened the roots by bumping the tray on the ground, hold the tray at an angle and ease the entire plant mass out.

2 Separate the plants by slicing through the root mass with the edge of a hand trowel or with a knife. Or, ease the plants apart with your fingers, but do not break away too much soil from around the roots.

3 After laying the plants in position to get a balanced layout, dig holes sufficiently deep for the roots and set the plants in place. Ease soil around the roots until filled in.

4 Instead of firming in by hand, plants can be settled in by 'puddling' with an open-spouted watering can — wash soil from the sides of the holes on to the roots and leave to drain.

exposed positions may need winter protection – lay light evergreen branches or straw around them.

To replace plants lost through winter cold, it is wise to retain a few plants in the first bed. In spring they can be used to fill in any gaps caused by plants dying.

Preparing for perennials

The best time for planting perennials is early to mid autumn when the soil is still warm. Alternatively, plant perennials during spring – container-grown plants are widely available from nurseries in spring and can, in fact, be planted at any time of year during fine weather.

▲ Firming in All annuals, biennials and perennials should be firmed in, by hand or by 'puddling' with water, to ensure that no air spaces are left and that roots make contact with the soil.

Several weeks before planting make a plan for the bed or border, ensuring that ultimate plant heights and flower colour are correctly balanced.

For autumn planting, dig the bed thoroughly in early autumn to give the soil a week or two to settle, adding a bucketful of manure or garden compost per sq m/yd. Just before planting, break up any large clods of soil and tread the surface of the bed. Finally, sprinkle a couple of handfuls of general-purpose fertilizer, such as Growmore, to each sq m/yd and rake it into the top 2.5cm (1in).

For spring planting, use the same technique, digging in early autumn, but leave final preparations until spring.

Planting perennials

Perennials are best planted on a dull day. Begin by marking out the planting area as for annuals. Working from the centre of the bed outwards, lay the plants out one section at a time. Space them evenly, allowing room for the eventual spread of the foliage.

For plants with a small root system, use a trowel to take out circular planting holes; for larger ones, use a spade. The hole should be large enough to take the spread out roots of bare-root plants, or the entire root ball of container-grown plants.

Insert the plant upright and fill in around the roots with fine soil until levelled off. Firm the soil well, with your fingers if the soil is moist and lumpy, or with your heel if it is fairly loose and dry. Make sure that the plant when firmed is no more than 2.5cm (1in) deeper than it was before being dug up.

When planting container-grown plants, check that the root ball is not tight and spirally congested – tease away long roots by hand and spread them out in the planting hole before infilling with soil. Pot-bound plants not treated in this way won't grow well and may show leaf browning a month or so after planting. If these symptoms do appear, lift the plant, loosen the soil around the roots and replant immediately.

Plant prostrate perennials, such as artemisia and thyme, which are intended for spreading ground-cover, in groups of three or four plants. Bunch the roots and stems together to form one plant and

PLANTING PERENNIALS

1 For small perennial plants, dig the hole with a hand trowel. Use a spade to dig holes for larger plants. Make the hole deep and wide enough to take the spread-out roots. Try not to step on the planting area – work off a plank if the site is large.

2 Hold the plant upright and set it in the centre of the hole, spread out the roots, and replace the soil between and over the roots until the hole is filled. Prostrate perennials can be inserted in clumps of three or four to give rapid and more even ground cover.

3 When planting container-grown perennials, make the hole large enough for the root ball to sit level with or slightly lower than the surrounding soil. If roots are coiled around the ball, gently ease away the largest ones and spread them out in the hole.

4 After planting, firm the soil well around the roots so that no pockets of air are trapped – use your fingers if the soil is moist or lumpy. Loose plants won't be able to take up water or nutrients from the surrounding soil fast enough and may wither or die.

insert them as a clump. This will encourage the stems to grow out in all directions and so produce a very much more even coverage of the soil surface.

After the bed has been planted, prick the soil with a fork – using only the tips of the prongs – to aerate trodden areas.

Some autumn-planted perennials will show no signs of growth until well into the following spring. If you have not made a plan showing the position and name of each plant, label them clearly. Use metal or wooden labels and write names in pencil or indelible ink. Special plant labels are available on which the name can be scratched or etched.

5 On soil that is loose or dry, firm in plants with your foot, or 'puddle' in using an open-spouted watering can. Label all plants, especially when planted in autumn – they may be almost invisible until the spring.

PLANTING BULBS OUTDOORS

**To get the best results from hardy bulbs,
they need careful and correct planting
at the right time of year.**

Bulbs provide some of the most attractive and undemanding of garden plants. They vary tremendously in size, colour and scent, and also in flowering season – so with a little planning you can have bulbs in bloom from early spring to late autumn.

The term 'bulb' is generally used loosely to describe not only true bulbs, such as daffodils and tulips, but also the corms of crocus and gladioli and the tubers of dahlias and begonias. Rhizomatous plants like lilies-of-the-valley are also often included together with true bulbs.

When to plant
Planting times depend on the hardiness and flowering time of the particular bulb.
Hardy spring-flowering types such as crocus corms are planted in autumn. Snowdrops are an exception, however. You can plant them in autumn, but they generally do better planted 'in the

▶ **Planting bulbs** Clumps of flowers look better than straight rows.

▼ **Spring bulbs** An autumn planting of anemones, daffodils and tulips bursts into glorious spring colour.

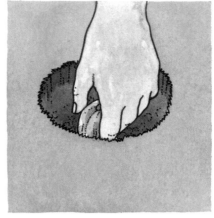

PLANTING IN GROUPS
1 Place the bulbs, growing point uppermost, over the planting area, spacing them at regular intervals.

2 Using a narrow trowel, dig a hole twice the depth of the bulb (or use a bulb planter or dibber). Put the bulb in firmly – don't trap air beneath it.

3 Cover the bulb with soil and firm it down with your foot. Water the area thoroughly after planting to encourage immediate growth.

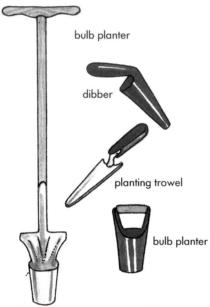

▲ **Planting equipment** Bulb planters (particularly waist-high ones) save you time and effort when naturalizing large numbers of bulbs. They take out and hold the plug of turf while you plant.

green' – immediately after flowering in early spring, with the leaves still attached.

Plant daffodil bulbs as soon as they become available – late summer if possible – so that they have the chance to develop a good root system before sending up shoots.

Delay planting hyacinth and tulip bulbs until late autumn or the beginning of winter. This reduces the risk of tulip fire disease and avoids frost damage to hyacinths.
Summer-flowering hardy bulbs, such as lilies, can be planted in good weather between autumn and early spring. *(Lilium condidum,* however, *must* be planted in autumn.) But wait until early or mid spring to plant

the more tender ones – gladioli corms, for example – or frost may damage growing shoots. A good plan is to stagger gladioli planting over several weeks so that you extend their display.
Autumn and winter-flowering bulbs Don't forget the value of bulbs that provide colour when it's most wanted. Colchicum corms, with their crocus-like blooms, settle down well if planted in late summer, even when they're on the point of flowering.

Planting depth
As a general guideline, plant bulbs in a hole twice their depth – for example, a 5cm (2in) high bulb should be planted 10cm (4in) deep. Lessen this depth on heavy soils but plant more deeply on light sandy soils or where you want bulbs naturalized in grass.

There are, of course, exceptions – namely lilies and cyclamen.
Lilies Many lilies produce roots on the stem above the bulb and so need to be planted to a depth about three times the height of the bulb. If you are not sure whether the lilies are stem rooting, cover them with 7.5cm (3in) of soil and add a 5cm (2in) layer of leaf-mould on top. However, plant the Madonna lily *(Lilium candidum)* just below the soil surface.
Cyclamen corms should also be planted just below the surface – *Cyclamen hederifolium* should be set so that the tips are just above the soil level.

Tops and bottoms
Always plant bulbs growing point up, and base (where the roots grow from) down. It is usually easy to

distinguish between the two – if not, it will not matter a great deal. The woody tuberous roots of anemones and winter aconites, for instance, have no obvious top and bottom, but they pull themselves around in the soil to face the right way. Cyclamen corms can present a problem: if you are not sure which end is which, look carefully for signs of old or new roots from the base.

With all bulbs, make sure that the base is firmly bedded in the ground, taking particular care when planting bulbs for naturalization that there is no air pocket left between bulb and soil. Specially designed tools – a narrow bulb trowel, dibber or bulb planter – make the job easier.

Spacing bulbs
Spacing depends on the effect you want. In containers, place bulbs as close together as you can without actually touching. In beds or borders, natural-looking groups or boldly planted clumps are most striking – don't dot bulbs about. Small bulbs, such as miniature daffodils, are best planted quite close together, about 5cm (2in) apart. Larger bulbs, for example daffodils and tulips, need about 15cm (6in) between plants and lilies even more – about 25cm (10in). For naturalized planting, space bulbs randomly.

Massed bulbs
The stunning effects of massed spring bedding schemes – a familiar sight in public parks – rely on bulbs flowering at more or less the same time. Even in a relatively small garden you can achieve a

similar scaled-down result.

Tulips and hyacinths are among the best spring-flowering bulbs for this purpose. They make an attractive show combined with other plants, for example tulips with dwarf wallflowers or forget-me-nots.

For large schemes like this, prepare a sunny bed well in advance, adding a layer of compost if the soil is poor. Allow the bed to settle for at least a week before planting. If you're mixing the bulbs with other plants, put the other plants in beforehand. As a further boost to growth, apply a light sprinkling of bonemeal at planting time.

Planting in borders

Smaller bulb plantings make an appealing feature in borders, rock gardens and raised beds, giving life and colour before annuals and perennials come out, and touches of splendour in summer.

Bulbs grow best in borders containing a mixture of shrubs and perennials – the rich manuring in pure herbaceous borders can be too much for them. Prepare the ground as for massed bulbs, and plant in clusters of at least five.

Bulbs in containers

Window-boxes, patio tubs and

▼ **Container planting** Plant bulbs close together in containers, but do not allow them to touch. They can be mixed with other plants such as pansies and azaleas (right); in shallow containers it is better to use small bulbs, such as crocuses (below).

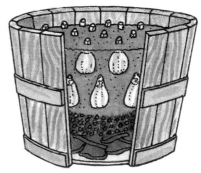

▲ **Bulb layers** For a spectacular effect, plant bulbs in two layers in a deep container. Plant the first layer not less than 10cm (4in) deep and add compost, leaving the tips exposed; set the second layer above the gaps in the lower layer. Cover with compost. Three tier planting is also possible – try daffodils at the bottom, tulips second and grape hyacinths on top.

▲ **Naturalized planting** Daffodils and grape hyacinths are ideal for rough grass. Scatter the bulbs at random; they will soon form colonies.

earthenware pots are all excellent containers for outdoor bulbs.

All outdoor containers need adequate drainage holes. A layer of crocks – broken crockery, stones or gravel – at the bottom also helps. The best soil mixture to use is a loam-peat-sand one such as John Innes No. 1.

Space the bulbs evenly at the right depth (twice their height) on a layer of compost. Cover them to within about 2.5cm (1in) of the top of the pot. If you are growing a large number of small bulbs, a shallow layer of grit on top of the compost reduces weed growth.

Naturalized bulbs
For an informal display of flowers, few effects can match a colony of bulbs growing in grass or under trees. Crocuses and daffodils are the outstanding choices for naturalizing, but many others are equally suitable. Whichever bulbs you choose, grouping colours separately usually looks best.

Most bulbs suitable for naturalization like some sun. Many flower before the foliage of deciduous trees is fully developed, while others enjoy the dappled sunlight of woodland fringes or glades. Yet others, such as cyclamen and lilies-of-the-valley, will thrive only in shade. One or two deciduous trees at the bottom of the garden are enough to suggest a woodland environment.

To achieve a truly natural effect, throw down a handful of bulbs and plant them where they fall. If you are naturalizing a fair number, a bulb planter is useful. For very large areas, cut and peel back the turf with a spade; fork over the soil before placing the bulbs, filling in with compost and folding back the turf.

Lifting and storing
Although many bulbs can be left in the ground from year to year, lift tender bulbs – freesias, gladioli, acidanthera, ranunculus, sprekelia and tigridia – at the end of the season. Bulbs removed after flowering and replanted in spare ground to leave room for other plants must also be lifted once their leaves have died down.

When leaves and stems have shrivelled, use a fork to lift the bulbs, taking care not to pierce them. Remove dead leaves, stems and old roots and detach bulblets, which you can use for starting new stock for the next season. Make sure that the bulbs are thoroughly dry before storing them in a cool, dry, frost-free place until it is time to plant them out again next year.

BULBS FOR NATURALIZING

Daffodils
'Actaea'
  white with small orange-red cup
'Carlton'
  golden, large-cupped
'Fortune'
  yellow with large orange-red cup
'King Alfred'
  golden, large trumpet
'Mount Hood'
  ivory, large trumpet
'Van Sion'
  golden, double

Bulbs under trees
Anemone
  (*Anemone blanda*)
Bluebell
  (*Scilla non-scriptus*)
Colchicum
  (*Colchicum speciosum*)
Crocus
  (*Crocus tomasinianus*)
Cyclamen
  (*Cyclamen hederifolium*)
Dog's-tooth violet
  (*Erythronium dens-canis*)
Glory-of-the-snow
  (*Chionodoxa luciliae*)
Lily
  (*Lilium martagon*)
Scilla
  (*Scilla sibirica*)
Snowdrop
  (*Galanthus nivalis*)
Snowflake
  (*Leucojum aestivum* 'Gravetye Giant')
Winter aconite
  (*Eranthis hyemalis*)

PLANTING SHRUBS AND TREES

**Shrubs and trees form the backbone of the garden.
Many create stunning focal points and if planted correctly
they will flourish for years.**

Shrubs are long-lived and prefer to stay in one position, so take time to consider where they will look their best – then plant them with care to give the maximum chance of survival. They'll form the permanent planting around which other plants, such as annuals and bulbs, are arranged.

You can buy shrubs in three different ways:
☐ Growing in a container
☐ Roots wrapped in hessian – known as balled
☐ Pre-packaged with bare roots

Pre-planting care and methods of planting differ according to the type of shrub.

Container-grown shrubs are established plants growing in plastic or whalehide pots of compost. These are the most expensive, but can be planted at any time of year, so long as the ground is workable.

Balled-root shrubs have some soil around the roots, kept in place by a wrapping of hessian. Plants which may have difficulty establishing themselves after being lifted from the nursery bed are treated this way to keep the root system intact, as are evergreens, including conifers, when their root systems are too big for containers. This system is also cheaper than the container type.

Bare-rooted shrubs are sold without any soil – a system reserved for shrubs such as roses

▼ **Mixed shrub border** With container-grown shrubs a border can be created in an instant. Keep it moist until the plants are established.

Container-grown shrub

Balled-root shrub

Bare-root shrub

Container-grown shrubs These are clean and easy to handle and can be kept until planting conditions are perfect.

Balled-root shrubs Large shrubs and conifers with long roots resent root disturbance and are sold with the roots wrapped in hessian; they can be heavy and need careful handling to keep the root ball intact.

Bare-rooted shrubs Dormant deciduous shrubs are sold with bare roots in late autumn and winter. Care is needed as the roots are easily broken.

and hedging plants that transport easily. Damp compost is sometimes packed round the roots to prevent them drying out. They are much cheaper than container-grown types, but may occasionally be difficult to establish – particularly if the roots have dried out.

Timing and preparation
Timing is crucial for success in planting shrubs. So is the condition of the soil – it must not be frozen or waterlogged, and must be well dug and fertilized.

Container-grown shrubs can be planted at any time of the year, but if you choose summer keep the soil moist until autumn. Newly planted shrubs will die if their soil dries out. If you cannot plant a container-grown shrub for several weeks after purchase, keep the soil moist (but not waterlogged) until you're ready to plant. Never remove the container until you have the hole dug and ready to take the plant. Also, protect the plant from high winds, staking the stem if necessary.

Balled-root shrubs Plant evergreen shrubs and conifers in mid spring and deciduous shrubs during the dormant season from autumn until spring. Balled-root shrubs can be left unplanted for several weeks as long as the soil ball is kept moist. Do not remove the hessian covering until the plant is set in the planting hole.
Bare-root shrubs are planted during the dormant season, and must be in the ground before their leaf buds burst. Plant from late autumn to early spring.

PLANTING CONTAINER-GROWN AND BALLED-ROOT SHRUBS

1 Check that the stem base of the shrub will be at or just below soil level when planted.

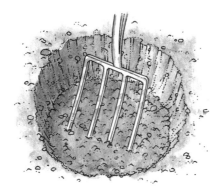

2 Break up the soil at the base of the hole, then add a layer of the prepared planting mixture.

3 Remove damaged or diseased wood, cutting the stem just above a healthy bud. Also remove stumps of old wood.

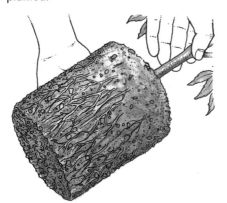

4 Check that there is a good root system. Cut away any tangled or encircling roots.

5 Place the plant in the hole, fill in with the soil mixture and firm in well, checking that it remains upright.

6 After planting, leave a shallow basin around the shrub for water retention. Water thoroughly, but gently.

Ideally, bare-root shrubs should be planted as soon as they arrive. If necessary, they can be stored for a couple of days in a frost-free place, with the roots kept moist. Alternatively, heel them in outdoors in a trench and keep them covered and firmed with soil until they can be planted out.

Preparing for planting

Dig over the soil thoroughly to one spade's depth, removing perennial weeds such as bindweed. Fork bonemeal into the topsoil at the rate of 130g per sq m (4 oz per sq yd), then allow the soil to settle for about two weeks. Just before planting, firm the bed thoroughly by treading the soil down.

Mark out with sticks where the shrubs are to go. The space between two shrubs should be at least half the sum of their ultimate spreads.

Next, remove one of the markers and dig a hole as deep as, and slightly wider than, the shrub's container or root-ball; it mustn't be too deep or too narrow.

Make up a planting soil mixture in a wheelbarrow by mixing the soil from the hole with organic material such as well-rotted garden compost or manure. An ideal mixture is two parts soil to one part organic material. Finally, water container-grown plants thoroughly just before planting.

Planting shrubs

Check the hole for depth by inserting the container or root ball. With a container shrub, the surface of the compost should be level with that of the surrounding soil, or just below it. With a balled-root or bare-root shrub the mark indicating the old soil level on the stem should be level with the surface of the surrounding soil; set a board or cane across the top of the hole to gauge the correct planting depth. Check that the hole is wide enough to allow the roots to spread out evenly. Break up the soil at the base of the hole with a fork, then add 7.5-10cm (3-4in) of the prepared soil mixture.

Check the plant for damaged or diseased top growth. Trim back any such stems, cutting just above a bud with secateurs.

Remove the container or hessian wrapping from the shrub and check the root system – be very careful not to break up the soil ball. If the container-grown shrub has a poor root system, return it to the nursery; if the roots are tangled or encircle the soil, carefully cut them away, but do not break up the soil ball. With a bare-root shrub, cut back any damaged or diseased roots with secateurs to healthy growth.

Hold the plant by the base of its stem and put it into the hole. With a balled-root or container shrub, fill in the hole with the prepared soil mixture. Tread it in firmly, top up with more soil, and tread again. After planting, leave a shallow basin round the plant for water retention.

With a bare-root shrub, put the plant in the hole and work in a couple of trowels of prepared soil mixture around the roots. Shake the roots gently so that the soil settles around them. Add a little more planting mixture and firm the soil around the plant. Fill up with more soil and firm again to eliminate air pockets. Lastly, dome the soil slightly around the stem and leave a shallow water-retaining basin.

Water the soil around the new plant thoroughly. In summer, water regularly and liberally during dry weather to prevent the roots drying out.

Planting between shrubs

Avoid the unattractive bare patches left between correctly-spaced new shrub plants by filling in with annuals. They can then be moved when the shrubs grow and spread.

PLANTING DO'S AND DON'TS

☐ Do choose shrubs carefully, noting eventual maximum height and width.
☐ Do handle plants with care.
☐ Do check planting times.
☐ Do mix a good soil/compost to encourage roots to establish.
☐ Do dig a big enough hole – condemning a plant to live in a tiny hole is a recipe for disaster.
☐ Do make sure the shrub sits at the correct level in the soil.
☐ Do water container-grown plants thoroughly before planting, and soak all shrubs well after planting.

☐ Don't buy diseased or damaged shrubs.
☐ Don't damage plants when handling/planting.
☐ Don't rely on existing soil.
☐ Don't allow shrubs to dry out at any time during their first season.

PLANTING BARE-ROOT SHRUBS

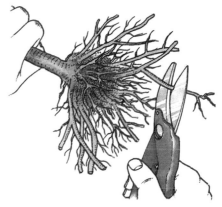

1 Dig and prepare the hole as for container-grown shrubs. Cut back damaged roots to healthy growth.

2 The old soil mark on the stem should be level with the new soil surface.

3 Once the hole is dug to size, set the shrub in place and work soil between the roots; shake it gently to settle the soil, then add more soil and firm.

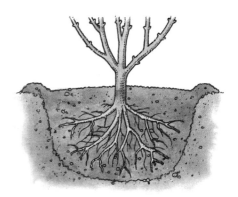

4 Build a shallow ring of soil around the area. Water thoroughly, but gently.

PLANTING TREES IN GRASS

1 For a lawn specimen tree, mark out a 90cm (3ft) circle with a 45cm (18in) piece of string stretched taut between two pegs. Cut through the grass.

2 Cut out sections of the grass with a sharp spade and set the turfs aside, then dig out the hole within the marked area 45cm (18in) deep.

3 Drive a stout stake, treated with a wood preservative, into the centre of the hole. On clay soils, fill the bottom with rubble to aid drainage.

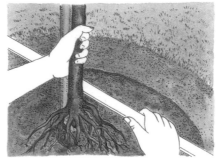

4 Chop the turfs into 10cm (4in) pieces and put in the hole, grass down. Top with manure and excavated soil until the hole is half filled.

5 Tread the soil firmly, then line up the tree against the stake, using a piece of wood to ensure that the old soil mark is level with the surface.

6 Fill in the hole, treading firmly and adding fertilizer when the roots are completely covered. Level the top and tie the tree to the stake.

Planting trees

Most ornamental trees are sold at three to four years old. The ideal planting season is late autumn to spring for deciduous types, mid spring for evergreens including conifers. Container-grown trees can be planted at any time.

Follow the planting procedures outlined for shrubs, but make the planting hole at least 45cm (18in) deep and some 90cm (3ft) across. If the tree is intended as a lawn specimen, use the turfs to fill in the hole; keep the surface area free of grass for a few years.

A young tree needs staking until the roots take firm hold. With a mallet, hammer a stout wooden stake in the hole before planting. When the hole has been filled in, tie the tree to the stake using a tree strap made from plastic or webbing and with rubber buffers that act as a cushion between tree and stake. Fasten the strap against the stake.

▶ **Tree ties** A stake should reach just below the first branches of the tree. Secure the new tree to the stake with a proprietary strap or hessian wound first round the stake then the stem and the stake together.

PLANTING IN CONTAINERS

**Plant-filled containers will brighten up any
part of your garden, and with careful preparation and
selection they can provide year-round interest.**

There are so many different plant containers – from heavily ornate to starkly plain – that one can always be found that is suitable for any site in the garden. Containers are chiefly thought of as additions to patios and terraces, but they can be placed in any part of the garden. They make a welcome sight alongside a front door or can be positioned to conceal an ugly drain cover. Both pots and hanging baskets can break up the vertical plane of a blank house wall and, even if you don't have a garden, outdoor plants can be used to great effect in a window-box – even in winter.

Pots and containers come in a range of types and sizes, from plastic tubs, baskets and troughs to wood and stone containers.

Preparing the container

Whatever the type of container, it must have adequate drainage holes in the base – waterlogging is the most common cause of plant ill-health in containers, especially where they are exposed to rain.

Most manufactured pots have drainage holes already made. Timber, glass fibre, plastic and even concrete containers – half barrels, tubs, troughs and window-boxes, for instance – that do not have drainage holes can be drilled quite easily. Use a 6mm (¼in) drill bit, or larger – be sure to select a masonry bit for concrete – and drill at a slow speed to avoid cracking fragile materials.

When attempting to drill a smooth surface, first stick masking tape in a criss-cross over the spot – this will help to prevent the drill bit slipping and splintering the surface.

Before filling with soil, ensure that the container is thoroughly clean and free from pests and diseases. Scrub old pots and troughs with a mild detergent, then wash with a strong general-purpose disinfectant before rinsing well with water – pieces of dead roots clinging to the sides, in particular, can harbour disease.

To increase the life of wooden containers – especially expensive oak half-barrels – treat them with a wood preservative recommended for horticultural use before planting. Never use creosote where plants are nearby – it gives off harmful fumes.

The interior of a wooden container can also be treated with a proprietary wood preservative, or it can be charred to destroy fungal spores. To do this, paint the inside with a liberal coat of paraffin and

---

▼ **Potted annuals** Begonias, petunias, small-flowered tagetes and trailing lobelia provide a riot of colour throughout the summer months. They flourish in the confines of containers as long as they are given good compost, adequate watering and regular feeding.

HANGING BASKET LINERS

By using a modern liner, planting a hanging basket is easy and clean. Pre-formed liners – made from compressed wood pulp, peat and textile fibre – are the simplest of all and give a natural effect. Just lower the liner into the basket, fill with soil, plant up and water well – no drainage material is required since the liner is porous.

Synthetic whalehide liners, which are sold flat but gather up into a bowl shape, are equally easy to use. Some incorporate a capillary matting pad in the bottom which acts as a water reservoir.

Plant trailing and cascading plants around the edge of the basket and add a single upright plant, such as a pelargonium or fuchsia, in the centre.

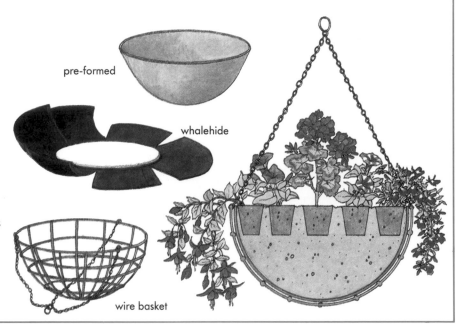

pre-formed

whalehide

wire basket

set it alight. Allow it to burn for a few minutes, then turn the container upside down to extinguish the flames. Treat the metal straps around half-barrels with rust-proofing paint.

Before filling a window-box, ensure that it is standing firmly or is fastened securely to the wall by metal stays. Use wooden wedges to prop a window-box level on a sloping sill, and to raise it off the sill to allow free drainage from the bottom. A drip tray can be positioned under the box to prevent waterlogging and water from running down the wall.

Similarly, with a hanging basket check that the supporting bracket is very secure – if it is at all corroded, replace it.

Filling the container

John Innes potting compost No. 2 suits most plants, as do proprietary loam-based potting composts. (Choose John Innes No. 3 for permanent subjects such as trees and shrubs.) Ordinary garden soil is not recommended; it is not sterilized and may harbour weed spores, pests and diseases that can quickly demolish the contents of a pot. Renew compost in shallow containers annually.

If you wish to grow lime-hating plants such as rhododendrons, azaleas, camellias and some heathers, use a lime-free compost such as John Innes acid compost or a proprietary peat-based compost.

When filling containers with soil, first make sure that the drainage holes are not clogged.

Place crocks over the holes to ensure that they remain open, followed by a thick layer of washed pebbles or coarse gravel. This drainage layer should, ideally, occupy about one quarter of the container's depth, but if you don't want too much weight, a 5cm (2in) layer is usually adequate for a short-term planting.

To prevent soil being washed into the drainage layer, cover it with a sheet of hessian sacking or rag. Or, place a thin layer of turfs – grass side down – on top. Finally, fill with the potting compost to within about 2.5-5cm (1-2in) below the rim; firm gently.

▲ **Wall displays** Iron mangers or half baskets make ideal wall planters. Line with black polythene to retain soil and prevent water soaking the wall, but perforate the front for drainage.

Hanging baskets of the rigid plastic type are planted like any other container, but open wire baskets need different treatment and should be lined before planting.

The choice of plants

Window-boxes 15-20cm (6-8in) deep are suitable for growing a large variety of plants. In spring they can come alive with bulbs planted the previous autumn –

snowdrops (*Galanthus*), crocuses, dwarf daffodils, narcissi and tulips, hyacinths, scillas and dwarf irises, for example.

Many summer bedding plants grow well in window-boxes, but avoid tall-growing kinds which spoil the proportions of the box. A charming effect can be created by mixing trailing plants – helichrysums, ivy-leaved pelargoniums, lobelias (*Lobelia erinus*), nasturtiums (*Tropaeolum majus*) and verbenas, for instance – with petunias, marigolds (*Calendula* and *Tagetes*), fibrous and tuberous begonias, pansies (*Viola* × *wittrockiana*) and salvias (*Salvia splendens*). Do not overlook dwarf shrubs and conifers which add form and permanency to a box – shrubby cinquefoils (*Potentilla* hybrids), fuchsias, hebes and dwarf conifers, such as the upright types of juniper.

In winter, dwarf conifers, especially the golden and blue forms, are excellent in window-boxes. They can be grown with winter-flowering heathers (*Erica carnea*) and ivies (*Hedera helix* varieties), while a few winter-flowering hardy cyclamen (*Cyclamen coum*) add a delicate touch.

Free-standing stone, concrete and plastic tubs and troughs can be filled with the same plants as window-boxes – the choice being wider for very large containers. Keep a good balance by planting tall plants with low-growing and trailing ones. The evergreen foliage of variegated ivy and periwinkle makes a good foil for the bright colours of busy Lizzies (*Impatiens*), pelargoniums, sweet Williams (*Dianthus barbatus*) and marigolds (*Calendula* and *Tagetes*), as well as calceolarias and heliotropes.

Many house plants are also effective with summer bedding plants. The arching leaves of spider plants (*Chlorophytum comosum*) complement agapanthus, while a cordyline set at the rear of a low container with bedding plants adds height and form. Also, the flaming colours of coleus mix well with silver-leaved cineraria (*Senecio maritima*) and either silver-grey or lemon-grey helichrysums.

Large tubs make ideal containers for lilies, hydrangeas and standard fuchsias, both in sun and light shade. Bay trees (*Laurus nobilis*), trained as standards, are

▶ **Moss liners** Hanging baskets look more natural with a sphagnum moss liner, obtainable from most garden centres. Choose a basket with a fairly close-woven framework so that the moss does not fall through.

Flowers tend to be produced more profusely if the plants are packed in quite tightly. Use a mixture of trailing and upright plants, such as fuchsias, pelargoniums, petunias and pansies. Trailing lobelia looks good through the base and sides of the basket.

MOSS-LINED HANGING BASKETS

1 Make a 'nest' of fresh, moist moss inside the basket to a thickness of about 2.5cm (1in). Work on a bench – not with the basket hanging up.

2 Line with a sheet of polythene to retain water, but perforate it heavily to prevent waterlogging and also to keep the moss moist.

3 Infill with John Innes potting compost No. 2 or an equivalent loam-based potting compost to within 2.5cm (1in) of the top.

4 Insert trailing plants into the side after puncturing the lining with the tip of a small trowel or with a knife. Put upright plants in the centre.

favourites beside the front door. And for a less formal effect plant winter jasmine (*Jasminum nudiflorum*) or forsythia. Roses, clematis, azaleas, camellias and Japanese maples (*Acer palmatum* varieties) are also good tub plants. For deep shade, plant tubs with pieris, mahonias, hostas, brunneras and hellebores.

Hanging baskets are usually viewed from below and should

consist mainly of trailing plants – nasturtiums, tradescantias, fuchsias, creeping Jenny (*Lysimachia nummularia*), petunias, ivy-leaved pelargoniums, lobelias and pendulous begonias, for instance.

Planting containers
Water all plants a few hours before planting. Organize the planting scheme by arranging the chosen plants on the surface of the

PLANTING A TUB

1 Cover the drainage holes with crocks – broken clay pots – to prevent them from becoming clogged, then add a thick layer of washed pebbles or coarse gravel for drainage.

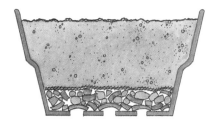

2 Put hessian sacking or rag over the drainage layer to prevent soil from washing into it, then fill the tub with potting compost.

3 Having planned the layout, begin by planting the tallest, upright plants at the centre or towards the back, depending on the view-point.

4 Fill in with several low, bushy plants and finish off by adding some trailing plants around the edges. Water in well immediately.

▲ **Summer window-boxes** Bright colours provide a marvellous spectacle from both indoors and outdoors. The attractive foliage of zonal pelargoniums offers a lush foil for deep blue and brilliant white petunias. Ferny leaved marguerites add a delicate touch among the bold array, and yellow creeping Jenny softens the hard edges of the box.

soil. Put the largest in the centre or towards the back of the container, finishing off with dwarf or trailing types around the edges.

Once satisfied that the design is correct, set the plants to one side. Using a hand trowel, dig holes for the largest ones first. Knock them out of their pots one at a time and plant them slightly deeper than in the original pot. Firm in well and water gently once all the plants are in place.

Where the planting is permanent or semi-permanent, a top layer of wood bark chippings, gravel or rock chippings can be sprinkled around the plants to improve the overall appearance and reduce moisture loss from the compost. A top layer of this kind also prevents soil surface capping where hard tap water is applied regularly. For temporary planting, mulching is unnecessary.

Aftercare

Containers dry out quickly, so frequent watering is essential, especially when they are standing in full sun. Apply water to the soil – not over the leaves and flowers – preferably in the evening or early morning. Give enough water to moisten the soil thoroughly, then leave until the soil is almost dry before watering again – overwatering a container is as harmful as too little water. In hot spells, water may be needed twice a day.

For additional plant vigour, give a regular liquid feed every two weeks – never apply fertilizer to dry soil. Dead-head all plants regularly and stake and tie tall species as necessary.

Watch out for pests and diseases – dense plantings often encourage fungal diseases and many insect pests. Spray with a general-purpose insecticide and fungicide regularly. Sprinkle slug bait to control slugs and snails – also check around the rim of a tub for snails hiding during the daytime. Clear away fallen leaves and other debris from the soil to discourage fungal growth.

With permanent plantings, scrape off the top 5-7.5cm (2-3in) of soil every spring and replace with fresh potting compost. Check the securing brackets of window-boxes and hanging baskets at the same time, replacing if necessary.

SOWING SEEDS

**Sowing seeds is the simplest and cheapest
way of raising large numbers of plants, especially
annual bedding plants and vegetables.**

Seeds are small embryo plants. Most produce plants of uniform appearance, virtually identical to their parents – these are said to be 'true to type'. They arise from natural self-pollination or by plant breeders always crossing plants with similar features.

Nowadays, you will often find F_1 hybrid seeds offered. These are the result of crossing two pure-bred strains under controlled conditions. They show improved vigour and uniformity, and often make better garden plants. But breeding and production costs increase the retail price.

Annual plants grow rapidly from seed and this is the only successful means of propagation. Most perennials also grow well from seed, though cuttings or division are often quicker methods of getting flowering plants.

Shrubs and trees *can* be grown from seed, but you may have to wait many years for a good-sized plant – for instance, a magnolia grown from seed may be just 1.5m (5ft) high after 10 years. Cuttings will often be a faster method, or you could buy semi-mature plants from a nursery. Bulbs, corms and tubers, too, produce seeds, but offsets or bought bulbs are easier means of increasing your stock.

House plants are often increased by cuttings, layering or division, but seed-sowing is a perfectly good alternative. Many seedsmen supply house plant seeds nowadays – even some quite exotic types. Cacti in particular are successful grown from seed.

Types of seed Seeds vary greatly in shape and size. They may be as big as a brazil nut or as fine as pepper; some have very hard coats, while others have soft fleshy coats. A few have wings or barbed hooks, which, under natural conditions, assist distribution. These differences largely determine their cultural needs.

Pelleted seeds are also available. Each seed is coated with a decomposable material, making it larger and easier to handle. With precise spacing possible, there's no need to thin seedlings – but the pellet does not improve germination, and can even slow it down.

For yet simpler sowing, buy a seed strip which consists of a roll of tape with seeds stuck to it at precise intervals – bury the whole tape in the seed drill. You can even buy small containers with ready-sown seed in a soil-less compost such as vermiculite – you just add water and quite soon seedlings will emerge.

◄ **Plastic seed trays** Standard trays are ideal for germinating herb, flower and vegetable seeds and for pricking out seedlings. They are strong, and stackable after use.

PEAT PELLETS

Jiffy-7s are perfect for raising species which dislike root disturbance during planting out. Bought as dehydrated, compressed pellets, they consist of peat wrapped in a mesh bag. After soaking in water, they swell up ready for sowing. Just pop in a seed and firm down. Plant out the whole thing – roots grow through the mesh.

SOWING IN A SEED TRAY

1 Fill the tray with seed compost and firm it down evenly to 1cm (½in) from the top. A wooden tamper cut the same size as the inside of the tray, with a handle attached, will help you to get a perfect surface.

2 Scatter seeds thinly and evenly. Large ones can be placed individually, but tap smaller seeds directly from the packet. Mix dust-like seed with a little sand to make it more visible and thus easier to get an even spread.

3 Cover the seeds with finely sieved compost – not much deeper than the thickness of each seed. You can sieve directly into the tray or sprinkle by hand. Fine seeds may need no covering – follow advice on the packet.

4 Water the compost, then cover the tray with a sheet of glass or polythene. An additional sheet of newspaper reduces condensation and shades tiny seeds which are not buried.

Sowing depth Generally, seeds should be sown at a depth equal to their thickness, although very large seeds can go deeper. Small seeds, such as petunias, need only a fine covering of soil. A few, such as begonias and celery, are best left uncovered since light is essential to germination – most seed packets give guidance.

Raising seedlings indoors

Half-hardy annuals can be raised easily indoors, and, with earlier sowing than is possible outdoors, plants can be brought to flower a few weeks earlier. Sow between late winter and mid spring, according to advice given on the seed packet.

If you use old trays or pots, first scrub them in soapy water or detergent, then rinse thoroughly. Fill them with seed compost, such as John Innes seed/cutting type. (Never use potting composts – they contain fertilizer which burns delicate seedling roots. Multi-purpose composts are suitable, however.) Firm the compost down to 1-1.5cm (¼-½in) from the top of the container.

Sow seeds thinly on the compost – open up the seed packet to make a spout, then, holding it over the compost, tap it on a fingernail of the other hand to produce a slow but steady flow of seeds.

Many suppliers seal seeds in plastic-lined foil sachets for freshness. Tear these open and tip the seeds into your hand, then either tap them off with a finger of the other hand or pinch a few between finger and thumb. If seed is very fine, mix it up with a little sand in a saucer before sowing – this makes it easier to see, and so get an even sowing.

Cover large seeds with sieved compost, using a coarse flour sieve, or sprinkle carefully with your hand. Small seeds are best covered with fine silver sand.

Water the compost by standing the tray in water halfway up its sides in a sink or bowl. Remove from the water when the surface of the compost appears wet – most composts darken when moist.

Label the container, using a pencil rather than ink so it doesn't wash off or fade. Cover with glass or polythene, which must be wiped daily to remove excess condensation. You can also cover with newspaper to prevent a build-up of high temperatures and reduce the

amount of condensation.

Stand the container in a warm place at 15-24°C (60-75°F). From a couple of days to three weeks after sowing, seedlings appear – at first generally consisting of a pair of round or oval seed leaves. Remove the cover and move the container to a bright window-sill. As soon as the first true leaves have developed, the seedlings are ready for pricking out.

If you use a propagating frame, there's no need to cover the seed tray with glass or polythene. Once seedlings appear, remove the top of the propagator during the day to allow a flow of fresh air over the tray – damp, stagnant air promotes damping-off disease.

Pricking out seedlings

Fill a seed tray with moist John Innes potting compost No. 1 or a proprietary potting compost. Firm it in as for seed sowing. Mark out the planting holes with a small dibber or pencil, spacing them 2.5-3.5cm (1-1½in) apart each way.

Gently lever a small clump of seedlings, with some of their compost, from the container – a plastic plant label makes a useful tool. Hold each seedling by one of its leaves and tease it away from the others. Never handle them by the stem – a damaged collar is invariably fatal.

Lower seedlings into their planting holes and firm in the compost around each, again using a dibber or blunt pencil. Don't damage the roots. Label the tray and water with a fine-rosed can or mist sprayer. Place the tray on a

DAMPING OFF

This common disease turns the base of the seedling brown and kills it. Avoid sowing too thickly and don't overwater. Remove dead seedlings immediately. Treat with thiram or benomyl as routine, and immediately the disease strikes.

PRICKING OUT

1 Pricking out should be done as soon as the seedlings have produced their first true leaves — the time for this varies according to species. Gently ease up a small clump of seedlings with some compost intact, using a plant label or small dibber.

2 Make spaced holes in the potting compost with a pencil or dibber. Gently tease away seedlings from the lifted clump and place them singly in each hole, holding a seed leaf, never the stem — damaged stems invariably result in death. Firm in lightly and water.

window-sill out of direct sun.

A couple of days later, move the tray to a sunny spot. Keep the compost moist, but not wet.

Hardening off

Once established — four to eight weeks after pricking out — harden off young plants. Begin by moving the tray to a sheltered spot outdoors in fine weather, bringing it back indoors at night. After a week or so, leave outside permanently, but protect from harsh weather and shelter at night.

A cold frame is an ideal place to harden off plants. For the first few days, open the frame slightly, during the day only. Increase ventilation gradually, until by late spring the cold frame is completely open.

Sowing seeds outdoors

All hardy annuals and many half-hardy annuals, as well as biennials and certain perennials, shrubs and trees, can be propagated from seed sown in the open ground — whether in a seedbed for later transfer, or directly in their flowering/cropping site.

Where soil-borne pests and diseases are a problem, shake seeds up with a proprietary seed dressing before sowing.

Soil preparation Dig the soil in autumn, allowing frosts to break up the clods. For vegetables — except root crops — work in some

---

◄ **Young seedlings** Prick out seedlings as soon as they are large enough to handle. Crowded in a seed tray (far left) they become spindly and are starved of essential nutrients.

SOWING IN POTS

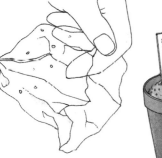   

1 Small quantities of seeds can be sown in a 7.5cm (3in) pot. (Larger half pots or margarine tubs are also suitable, but deep pots waste compost.) Fill with seed compost and sow as for trays. Label it and keep the compost moist by putting the pot into a transparent polythene bag.

2 Prick a few holes in the bag for ventilation and secure it with a rubber band. Stand the pot in a warm, shady place such as an airing cupboard or shaded window-sill until the seeds have germinated. Look at the pot every day — some species germinate very quickly, others take some time.

3 If a lot of moisture forms on the inside of the bag, turn it inside out daily. After seedlings have emerged, remove the polythene bag and put the pot in a brighter position. If they are left in the dark seedlings will grow very straggly and soon die. Watch out for damping-off disease.

MAKING A SEED DRILL

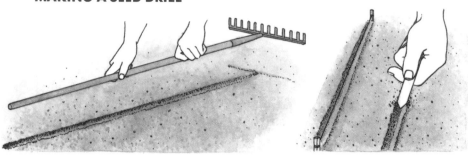

1 On light soils, make short drills by pressing the handle of a rake or hoe into the surface. (Do not use this technique on heavy soils.) Rows of vegetables get more even sunshine if you run the drill from north to south.

2 Short drills can also be scratched out using the pointed end of a plant label or a piece of stick. Mark out the rows with a peg at each end and make them as straight as possible. Avoid standing on the sowing area.

3 For longer drills, use the corner of a draw hoe or the edge of a rake. Keeping the blade against a taut line stretched between two pegs as a guide, pull the hoe or rake towards you in short, gentle strokes.

SOWING SEEDS OUTDOORS

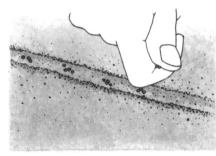

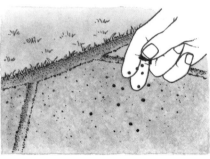

1 Sow seeds thinly to avoid the need for too much thinning later on. Tip a small quantity into the palm of your hand then, taking some between the finger and thumb of your other hand, dribble them evenly into the drill.

2 Another method is to sow three or four seeds at regular intervals – known as station sowing. The only thinning then needed is to remove all but the strongest seedling plant at each of the stations.

3 Informal drifts of hardy annuals can be broadcast-sown. Mark out the planting layout with shallow furrows or trails of sand, then simply scatter seeds thinly over each of the patches and rake in lightly.

compost or well-rotted manure.

In spring, as soon as the soil is dry enough not to stick to your shoes, loosen the top 15-20cm (6-8in) with a fork. Apply a good handful of general-purpose fertilizer per sq m/yd, then rake it in. Just before sowing, rake the soil again to get a fine, crumbly tilth.

Sowing in a border Prepare a sketch plan of the desired layout in advance – grouping colours and heights according to your own preferences. Mark out the sowing areas with the edge of a hoe or a stick, or with a trail of sand.

Within each sowing area, either sow seeds in grooves – drills – or scatter over the whole surface and rake into the soil – broadcast sowing. With broadcast sowing, though, it's harder to ensure correct sowing depth and to weed between seedlings later on.

Sowing in drills Make shallow drills 1-1.5cm (¼-½in) deep. Sow thinly to avoid too much thinning later. Space drills for upright species half the height of the plant apart. Space drills for dwarf or

bushy types the full height of the plant apart.

Cover seeds by running the tip of the hoe along the ridge of the drill. Or, lightly draw a rake along the length of the drill. Then tamp down with the flat side of the hoe or rake, or firm the drill lightly with your feet.

When sowing in spring and in well-prepared soil, watering is generally unnecessary at first. In dry weather, in exposed sites or where the soil is light and dusty, moisten the soil a day or so before sowing, then again two or three days after sowing. Repeat a week later if still dry.

Thinning In general, thin spring-sown seedlings once to 10-15cm (4-6in) apart; autumn-sown seedlings twice – 5-7.5cm (2-3in) apart in autumn, then 15-23cm (6-9in) apart in spring. Aim to keep the strongest seedlings. With mixed colour varieties, however, keep a selection of all sizes – small ones may bear unusual colours and will catch up in size later.

THINNING SEEDLINGS

When seedlings have two or three true leaves, thin them out while their roots are still small and removal won't disturb adjacent wanted seedlings. They come out more easily when soil is moist, so if dry, soak the day beforehand.

Pull out each unwanted seedling while pressing down the soil on each side with the fingers of the other hand to hold remaining seedlings firm. Transplant thinnings to a spare area or discard them.

Propagation and plant care

Raising your own new plants from existing stock is an inexpensive or even free source of young, healthy plants. The supply is potentially infinite, as each year's growth provides new material for propagation. You know just what you will get, since vegetative propagation from cuttings, division or layering produces plants identical to the parent. No special equipment is needed, only simple techniques and the right timing. And success brings a sense of achievement, as you provide enough stock to fill your own garden, give to friends and charity events, and exchange for other plants at local garden clubs.

Keeping plants healthy is an ongoing challenge. It involves adequate watering in the growing season, ideally with equipment chosen to match your garden's size and needs. Training and supporting weak or exposed plants must be done while they are still young, so they don't become unwieldy or entangled with others. Healthy plants flower well, but you can easily extend the flowering season or increase the number or size of the blooms. Pinching out the growing tips of plants such as carnations increases the number of flowering side shoots. Disbudding, or removing unwanted buds, of plants such as dahlias encourages the remaining buds to grow to flower show quality. Easiest of all, dead-heading prevents flowers setting seed and channels plants' energy into producing more blooms, as well as keeping them tidy.

Some plants, especially young ones, need protection from the ravages of wind, rain and snow; and from predators such as birds, rabbits, mice and deer, as well as pets. This chapter gives you the information you need to choose and create effective but unobtrusive barriers and deterrents.

Propagating for health Michaelmas daisies should be divided every two or three years.

PROPAGATION BY DIVISION

**Division is the easiest form of propagation
for most perennial plants – you can increase your
own stock or swap plants with friends.**

In its simplest terms, division is the process of lifting a clump of plants, complete with roots and growth buds, from the ground, pulling or cutting it into separate pieces and then replanting each in freshly prepared soil.

Each divided piece will soon grow into a new plant – each with characters identical to its parent. The process is known as vegetative propagation. Division, therefore, is a very useful means of bulking up stock of a particularly desirable variety. Growing from seed – sexual propagation – by comparison, introduces some genetic variation in the reproductive process – flower colour, size or growth habit, for instance, may vary slightly among the offspring.

Herbaceous perennials – those that die down to ground level in winter – are the easiest to divide since they have a dormant period during which most tolerate quite a lot of root disturbance.

Evergreen perennials – including many house plants – can also be increased by division, but you must take greater care in separating and replanting the roots, and spend more time on aftercare.

Most perennials should be divided every few years as a matter of routine, regardless of whether you wish to increase your stock. Old, matted clumps frequently die out in the middle and develop unmanageable shapes. Staking and tying become difficult and flower quality may be depleted. Division, therefore, serves two purposes: quick, easy propagation and an improvement in plant health.

The precise methods of division vary according to the size and type of rootstock. After lifting, small clumps or fairly young plants can easily be pulled apart by hand. Older and overgrown plants, however, whose roots have formed an entangled mass, must be levered apart or severed with a sharp implement.

Woody plants, including some true shrubs, can be divided if they produce multiple stems or suckers from ground level, rather than a single stem or trunk.

Bulbs and corms can often be increased by offsets – a special type of division in which tiny bulblets or cormlets are detached from the parent and grown on to reach maturity. New plants, however, are invariably slower to reach flowering size than with the usual division method.

Lifting

The dormant period between mid autumn and early spring is the best time to lift perennials, except during frosty weather. Slow-growing perennials and those that flower early in the year are best lifted in autumn. Choose a day for lifting plants from open ground when the soil is neither sticky – the soil shouldn't stick to your boots – nor frozen.

Push a garden fork into the ground alongside the clump of plants to be lifted. Gently lever the clump upwards until resistance is felt. Repeat this procedure on the other sides of the clump until all the roots are free. Lift the clump out of the ground – either by hand or with the fork.

Tease away as much soil from the roots as possible with your fingers, being careful not to damage any strong fleshy roots or tubers. If growth buds are still concealed by soil, wash the clump by submerging it completely in a bowl or bucket of tepid water.

◀ Overgrown perennials Tough clumps are often difficult to split up once lifted since their roots are tangled and woody. They can, however, be forced apart by inserting two garden forks back to back in the clump. Push the handles together then apart to separate the roots and crown.

DIVIDING YOUNG PERENNIALS

1 Lift the clump, using a garden fork. Pull the plants apart by hand or with a small fork. Each section should have healthy roots and strong growth buds.

2 Trim off with a knife any roots which are rotten, dead or damaged. Try to keep the healthy root ball as intact as possible.

3 Replant the divided pieces at once. Put those with six strong shoots in their permanent position and smaller ones in spare ground to grow on.

Dividing young perennials

Young, tufted perennials with fibrous roots, such as *Helianthus*, Michaelmas daisies (*Aster*) and *Rudbeckia*, are easily divided. Once lifted, they can be pulled apart by hand or with a small fork – each section should contain healthy roots and strong growth buds.

Cut off any dead roots and leaves with a sharp knife. Replant the divisions at once in their permanent positions. Tiny divisions can be planted in a nursery bed in an out of the way corner of the garden or in individual pots until the following autumn, when they can be planted out in their permanent positions.

Dividing mature perennials

Large, overgrown fibrous-rooted perennials, such as heleniums and phlox, are often difficult to divide – the crowns and shoots form a solid mass. Begin by lifting the clump –

or part of it – as before. Having lifted the clump, push the prongs of two strong garden forks, back to back, into the centre of the clump.

Most garden forks have curved prongs, so when put back to back you have a useful lever device. If you possess only one fork, borrow another from a friend or improvise by inserting a couple of stakes through the clump and into the soil below against which you can lever with one fork.

Lever the clump apart first by forcing the handles of the forks together – thus forcing the tips of the prongs apart and so separating the lower roots. Then force the handles of the forks away from each other. Repeat until the clump splits in half. Divide each half once again.

With a sharp knife, cut away and discard the woody part of each portion which came from the centre of the original clump. Separate the remainder into healthy pieces,

each containing about six buds or shoots. Also remove dead or rotten roots, then plant out. Water them if the soil is dry.

Woody-crowned perennials, such as *Baptisia* and *Rheum*, can't be split with garden forks. Instead, cut through the crowns with a sharp knife, so that each severed portion has both root and growth buds. Replant the divisions immediately.

Fleshy-rooted plants, such as *Agapanthus* and *Hosta*, are best divided by hand in the same way as young perennials – it is easier to separate the brittle roots without damaging them than if you use forks.

Dividing tuberous plants

The method of dividing tuberous-rooted plants varies according to the type of tuber.

Dig up the clump as before and gently tease away the soil – do not damage the tubers. If the soil

DIVIDING MATURE PERENNIALS

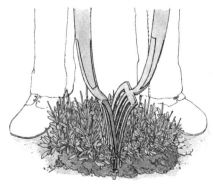

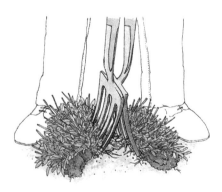

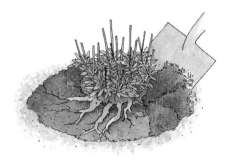

1 Mature clumps with matted roots can be split up using two garden forks back to back. Insert the forks with their prongs together into the centre.

2 Push the fork handles together so that the prongs are forced apart, thus separating the roots, then pull the handles apart to separate the crown.

3 Having divided the clump into at least four parts, discard the old material which came from the centre, then plant out each division at once.

1 Divide bearded irises every three years as a matter of routine, soon after flowering. Firstly, lift the clump with a garden fork.

2 Using a knife, cut off the younger rhizomes from the edge of the clump — each with one or two leaf fans. Some can be separated by hand.

sticks to the tubers, immerse them in a bowl of water – the growth buds must be clearly visible.

Root tubers, such as those of day lilies (*Hemerocallis*) and herbaceous peonies (*Paeonia*), have growth buds in the crown where the tubers join together. Using a sharp knife, slice downwards through the crown to divide the plant into several pieces, complete with tubers and growth buds. Plant the divisions at once.

In general, sections of single tubers with only one growth bud take longer to produce good-sized plants than those with three or four tubers and buds.

Herbaceous peonies often resent having their roots disturbed, so recovery may take a season or more. To give peonies less of a shock, divide them in autumn or early spring when the weather is not too harsh and while the tubers are dormant.

Small claw-like tubers, such as those of *Anemone* and *Liatris*, can be pulled apart by hand. Large tubers, however, may need to be cut into pieces with a knife. Make sure each piece has a strong growth bud before planting.

Dividing rhizomatous plants
Rhizomatous-rooted plants, such as *Bergenia*, *Monarda*, *Physalis* and *Polygonatum*, are quite easily lifted – their rootstocks, which are

▲ **Division of rhizomes** Perennials such as bearded irises can, once lifted, be parted by hand. In this way the attached fibrous roots remain undamaged.

really swollen underground stems, grow just below the surface of the soil.

Lift the rootstock in early spring just as new growth buds are beginning to emerge. Tease away the soil to expose the old main rhizome together with the younger underground stems coming from it.

Select side growths which have two or three strong growth buds or vigorous young shoots, as well as healthy roots. Any 5-7.5cm (2-3in) long side shoot is suitable for replanting. Remove these growths with a sharp knife, making a clean cut through rhizome and roots.

Discard the old rhizome and trim the new growths back, cutting to just below a cluster of healthy fibrous roots. Cut off any stump and rotten parts from the selected pieces. Also remove all dead leaves and leaf stalks.

Plant the sections at once. Position vertically in the soil with the root cluster downwards and fairly deep – the rhizome must be well anchored in the soil and at about the same depth as the original plant. Label the plants carefully and water in.

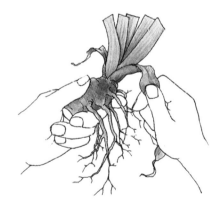

3 Using a knife or secateurs, trim the fresh foliage into a small fan and peel any withered or dead leaves from the young rhizome.

4 Replant each rhizome in its permanent site — fill in with soil but leave the top of the rhizome just exposed. Label and water the plants.

DIVIDING WOODY CROWNS AND TUBERS

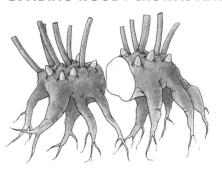

1 Tough woody crowns of plants such as lupins should be cut with a knife, each piece with roots and growth buds.

2 The swollen root tubers of dahlias don't bear buds. Split them by cutting downwards through the stem — each piece must bear a portion of the stem with a growth 'eye'.

3 Shrubs which produce their main branches from below ground can be divided by cutting into equal-sized pieces with secateurs; then replant.

Dividing shrubs

Many shrubs produce shoots from underground buds – including *Ceratostigma*, *Clerodendrum*, *Kerria*, *Romneya*, *Rubus* and *Ruscus*. The buried bases of the shoots produce their own individual roots. Such shrubs can be divided in the same way as woody herbaceous perennials.

Lift the shrub in spring – though any time between mid autumn and mid spring may be successful. Using secateurs or a small pruning saw, cut the woody base into several equal-sized pieces, each with plenty of roots and top growth attached. Replant the divisions at once.

Many trees and shrubs also produce shoots from below ground – these are called suckers. They include *Ailanthus*, *Deutzia*, *Forsythia*, *Philadephus*, *Rhus*, *Rubus*, *Spiraea* and *Weigela*.

Suckers appearing from the base of grafted shrubs are not suitable for use as propagation stock – they may be too vigorous and will not have the same characteristics as the parent. Suckers from grafted shrubs should always be removed as soon as they appear.

Remove soil from the base of the sucker any time between mid autumn and early spring. If the sucker has roots it is suitable for lifting. Using secateurs, cut the sucker close to its point of origin with the stem or root.

Plant well-rooted suckers in a permanent site in the garden. Poorly rooted suckers should be planted in a nursery bed and grown on for a year or so.

Dividing bulbs and corms

All hardy bulbs and corms left to naturalize in the ground increase steadily from offsets; eventually they form congested clumps with fewer or poor-quality flowers. Such clumps should be lifted and divided after the foliage has died down. Dig them up with a garden fork, deep enough to avoid damage to the bulbs. Ease the soil away and separate the bulbs with the fingers, taking care not to damage the bulbs. Cut away old and dead roots, discard any bulbs that show signs of disease and separate the young bulbils that have formed at the sides of true bulbs, such as narcissi and tulips. Corms, like crocus, form a new corm on top of the old and shrivelled one, as well as many tiny cormlets on top of and along the parent corm.

Narcissi, tulips and crocus need not be replanted at once but can be left to dry off until the autumn. Most other bulbs, though, should go in the ground straight after division; snowdrops are best split and replanted while the foliage is still green.

Offsets from bulbs and corms form a ready means of increase; they vary in size and very small ones can be discarded while the larger offsets are ideal for setting out in a nursery bed and growing on until they reach flowering size. They will develop roots and leaves, but no flowers, in their first season; the larger ones will produce flowers in their second or third year. Young half-hardy gladioli corms must be lifted or wintered in a frost-free place.

BULBILS AND CORMLETS

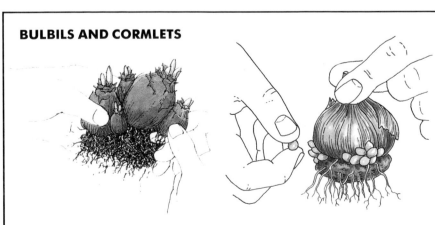

Small offset bulbils form at the side of most bulbs, especially those of narcissi and tulips. Such offsets can be removed by hand at lifting time or before planting (far left) and grown on in a spare part of the garden to reach flowering size.

Gladioli produce bulblets around the base of the new corm. When the corms have dried out, the bulblets can be gently broken off for propagation and stored separately in paper bags in a cool dry place. The old shrivelled corm should be twisted off and discarded.

PROPAGATION BY LAYERING

Layering is a simple method of increasing plant stock without the need for an elaborate propagating frame or a greenhouse

The principle of layering is based on the fact that a plant that has been cut, scraped or fractured is likely to produce roots from the wound if this portion of the plant is in contact with the soil or other rooting medium. Once roots have been formed from a stem, you have the makings of a new plant, which can be detached and grown on.

Layering is really suitable only for woody-stemmed plants – shrubs and trees, including some house plants. This method often succeeds where cuttings fail. Some herbaceous plants, notably carnations and pinks, will also respond to layering.

Many of the pendulous or lax-stemmed shrubs and trees, such as *Forsythia suspensa* and *Salix* × *chrysocoma*, layer themselves naturally when their stems touch the ground. The constant rubbing of the branch against the ground causes an injury to the bark, and roots develop from the callus formed over the wound to anchor the branch.

Simple layering

The best branches for layering are non-flowering ones that have grown in the current year – that is, the freshest, smoothest shoots. Deciduous plants are best layered in autumn or winter; evergreens in autumn or spring.

First, fork over the surface of the soil around the plant. Choose any flexible branch and bend it down until it reaches the ground 23-30cm (9-12in) from the tip, held at an upright angle. Strip the leaves off the branch where it touches the soil.

Wound the underside of the branch to restrict the flow of sap by cutting a shallow tongue with a knife, cutting towards the growing tip. Alternatively, twist the branch to injure the tissue. Dig a hole 7.5-10cm (3-4in) deep beneath the wound and part-fill it with a proprietary seed or potting compost. A light dusting of a proprie-

▼ **Layering shrubs** Flexible branches can be bent down to the ground and encouraged to produce roots by wounding the stem tissues. Buried in soil for several months, the rooted stem can be cut and grown on.

LAYERING SHRUBS

1 Select a flexible branch that has grown in the current year, checking that it will bend to the ground 23-30cm (9-12in) from the tip without undue strain. Strip off the leaves where the shoot touches the ground.

2 Using a sharp knife, wound the tissue at the point where it will contact the soil by cutting a shallow tongue into the underside of the branch, slicing up towards the growing tip. Do not cut into the heart wood.

3 As an alternative to slicing a tongue out of the branch, especially where the wood is quite thin, twist the branch sharply to break or injure the surface tissue. The heart wood should remain uninjured.

4 Dig a small hole and part-fill it with a proprietary seed or potting mixture. Bend the branch gently at the wound and peg it into the ground at the sides of the hole using a piece of bent wire or a forked twig.

5 Stake the tip upright and cover the wound with more compost. Firm in well. Anchor springy branches with a stone or brick. Keep the area watered thoroughly until the layer has rooted.

6 After about one year, check whether roots have grown successfully from the wounded tissue. If so, sever the branch with secateurs and replant directly into the chosen site.

tary hormone rooting powder over the wound may encourage quicker rooting, but is not essential.

Push the wounded part of the branch into the hole, forming a right-angle at the wound. Peg the branch to the ground with a bent piece of galvanized wire, 15-20cm (6-8in) long, and stake the upright tip. Fill the hole with more compost. Repeat with other branches. Water the area thoroughly, and ensure that it never dries out.

Check the new roots by carefully scraping away the soil. Most ornamental shrubs take six to twelve months to root sufficiently, though magnolias and rhododendrons require up to two years before they can be severed from the parent plants. If roots are well established, sever the new plant from the parent, lift with a good ball of soil and plant elsewhere in the garden.

If the roots are not well grown, but the layer is healthy, replace the soil and leave it for a few more months before re-examining the root formation.

Tip layering

Certain plants can be propagated simply by burying the tips of their shoots in the soil – brambles such as blackberries and loganberries are particularly successful.

Towards the end of mid summer, bend down a new season's shoot and, where it touches the ground, dig a 15cm (6in) hole with a hand trowel. Plant the entire tip of the shoot in the hole and firm it in. Peg down the shoot if it is particularly springy.

By mid autumn the tips will have rooted. Sever each new plant from its parent by cutting just above a bud. Do not move the plant yet. In late autumn transfer each new cane to its permanent bed. It will bear fruit in either its second or third year.

Serpentine layering

A handy method of propagating woody plants with long pliable stems – especially climbers, such as honeysuckle, clematis and jasmine – is called serpentine layering. It should be done at the same time as ordinary layering. Use long, trailing shoots that have grown during the current year.

Bend a shoot to the ground carefully and, where it reaches the soil, dig a 5cm (2in) deep hole beneath it. Wound the shoot

TIP LAYERING BLACKBERRIES

1 In mid summer, bend down a current season's shoot and mark where its tip touches the ground at a convenient position for propagation. Using a hand trowel, dig a 15cm (6in) deep hole at this point. Plant the tip in the hole.

2 In mid autumn, when the blackberry shoot tip should have rooted, cut the shoot from its parent just above a strong healthy shoot bud. Use a sharp pair of secateurs. Trim or re-train the remaining parent branch.

3 In late autumn, lift the new plant carefully, digging out a good-sized ball of soil and roots. Replant in the garden immediately. It should bear a good crop of blackberry fruits in its second or third year.

underneath as for ordinary layering. Peg the wounded part of the shoot into the hole with a piece of bent wire or a small forked twig. Fill in the hole with a proprietary seed or potting compost.

Cover with garden soil and firm in with your fingers. Leave the next two pairs of leaves above ground and repeat the operation. Continue this way along the entire length of the shoot.

One year later, the serpentine layer should have rooted. Scrape the soil away from each buried section of the layer and, if it is well rooted, sever it from the preceding section with secateurs. (If it is not well rooted, bury the whole layer again and check it a few months later.) Each rooted section is now ready to be severed and planted out in the normal way.

Transplanting is made easier if, instead of pegging the shoots into holes in the ground, they are pegged into pots of compost sunk into the ground. When the layer has rooted it can then be severed and moved without disturbing the new roots.

Growing from runners

A runner is a type of aerial or underground stem which, when it comes into contact with moist soil, roots along the stem and forms new plants – a form of natural layering.

The runners formed by healthy strawberry plants, and other ornamental members of the genus *Fragaria*, provide an easy means of propagation. In early summer, anchor the plantlets with pegs if the plants are grown in matted rows. Let them root into the soil, removing the remainder of the runners beyond the first plant.

Alternatively, select the strongest plantlets and peg them down into pots, sunk to their rim in the soil, and containing John Innes potting compost No.1. Water the pots frequently to aid root formation and remove all other runners as they form.

The plantlets should be separated from the parent in mid to late summer and planted out from their pots. If, for some reason,

planting is delayed until the autumn, the young strawberry plants should not be allowed to fruit the first season. Pinch out the flowers as they appear.

Some house plants, notably mother-of-thousands (*Saxifraga stolonifera*) and spider plant (*Chlorophytum comosum*), also produce small plants either on the flowering spikes or on thin runners from the parent plant.

With mother-of-thousands, detach the thread-like runners, each of which bears a plantlet, from the parent plant. Nip off the runner from the plantlet. Fill a small pot with moist John Innes No.1 potting compost.

SERPENTINE LAYERING

1 Select a long pliable stem and bend it down to the ground. Wound the shoot underneath. Using a piece of wire, peg the stem into a 5cm (2in) hole and fill the hole with compost.

2 Repeat the operation leaving two pairs of leaves between each layer. Continue along the entire length of the shoot. When rooted, sever each section of stem and plant out.

AIR LAYERING HARDY SHRUBS

1 Select a branch of the current year's growth and strip off a pair of leaves — any branch will do, however high or stiff, since it does not have to be bent down to the ground as with the other methods of layering.

2 Using a sharp knife, cut off a shallow slice of wood. Ensure that the cut does not weaken the branch to such an extent that it will break. Dab a small amount of proprietary rooting powder on to the wounded area.

3 Wrap polythene sheeting around the stem just below the cut and tie it with string or raffia to form a funnel. Fill the funnel around the wound with a rooting mixture of peat, coarse sand and sphagnum moss.

4 Moisten the rooting mixture, then fasten the top of the polythene with another piece of string to enclose it firmly around the wound area. Leave the plant for at least ten weeks before examining for roots.

5 When you are sure that the wounded tissue has grown a good ball of roots, remove the polythene wrapping. Using a pair of secateurs, sever the new plant from the parent stem by cutting just below the roots.

6 Pot the new plant into a 11-15cm (4½-6in) pot, using potting compost. Stand it in a closed and shady cold frame for a couple of weeks until new growth is obvious. Harden off before planting out the following spring.

Make a shallow depression in the surface and set the plantlet in it. Firm the compost round the base of the plant. Do not water, but place a polythene bag over the pot and secure it with a rubber band. Keep the pot out of direct sunlight and at a temperature of 18-21° C (64-70°F). Condensation should ensure that the compost does not dry out; otherwise water gently.

After about ten days, the plantlet should have rooted. Remove the bag and set the pot in a lighter and cooler place.

Spider plants often bear a number of plantlets on tough stalks. These can be layered into individual small pots of John Innes No.2 potting compost and secured with wire clips. After about three weeks, the plantlets should have rooted enough to be severed.

Air layering
When branches are too stiff or too high to be layered at soil level, they may be 'layered' in the air. This can be done between late spring and mid summer. Air layering is particularly recommended for *Ficus* species, such as the common rubber plant, and for magnolias. This method of propagation is sometimes known as Chinese layering.

After some years, house plants such as dizygothecas and rubber plants may grow too tall, and will often lose their lower leaves. Rather than throw the plant out, propagate it by air layering in spring to produce a new, shorter stemmed plant.

Select a stretch of the branch of the current year's growth and strip off the leaves in the middle. Then cut off a shallow slice of wood and put rooting powder on the cut.

Wrap a sheet of polythene around the area of the cut and tie the bottom of it with raffia or string. Fill the open-topped tube with a mixture of equal parts moist peat, coarse sand and sphagnum moss. Fasten the top with more string or raffia.

The conditions needed for rooting of the air layer are constant moisture, exclusion of sunlight and restriction of the stem. Therefore, it is necessary to use black polythene and well-moistened rooting mixture. Once the polythene is sealed, no further watering will be needed.

In three to six months, when rooted – check by unfastening the top of the polythene – remove the polythene and cut off below the roots. Pot up the new plant into a 11-15cm (4½-6in) pot containing a proprietary potting compost.

Place the potted plant in a closed frame for two weeks and keep it moist, then harden it off. This entails opening the frame during the day, gradually admitting more air until the frame is left open entirely. Plant out the following spring.

PROPAGATION BY CUTTINGS

**A simple way of propagating most shrubs is by
taking mature stem cuttings, while many perennials
can be grown from tip or root cuttings.**

The increase of plants by taking cuttings is probably the most widely practised type of vegetative propagation. A section of stem with or without leaves, a section of root or a single leaf or bud of a living plant is removed and treated in such a way that it develops into a new plant.

There are various types of cuttings, each with their own requirements, but certain general rules apply. For a cutting to strike – take root – it must have adequate light, warmth and moisture. Except in special cases, very small cuttings should be avoided as they tend to exhaust their food reserves before roots can be formed. Similarly, over-large cuttings draw up too much water and soon flag.

The rooting medium for cuttings must be free-draining yet capable of retaining sufficient moisture, and it must permit free passage of air. It also has to be free of pests and diseases.

Tip cuttings

Some perennials, notably non-hardy plants such as *Centaurea gymnocarpa*, penstemon and dimorphotheca as well as foliage perennials such as chamomile (*Anthemis*) and rue (*Ruta*), are best increased from tip cuttings. Take these from the ends of non-flowering lateral shoots during late summer and early autumn. The rooted cuttings generally need protection during winter in a cold frame. Plants grown under glass can be increased from tip cuttings at any time of year.

Take the cuttings, 7.5-10cm (3-4in) long, from the tips of healthy, leafy stems, ensuring that each cutting has at least three leaf joints.

Fill a pot to just below the rim with John Innes seed compost, or a proprietary cuttings compost. A 10cm (4in) pot will take about six cuttings.

Trim each cutting just below the lowest leaf node, slicing through at right angles to the stem with a sharp knife or a razor blade. Pull off the lowest pair of leaves.

Make shallow planting holes in the compost with a pencil. Insert the cuttings so that the base of each stem touches the bottom of

---

▼ **Tip cuttings** Tender fuchsias, kept over winter in a heated greenhouse, are best increased from softwood or tip cuttings taken in spring and rooted in a propagating case.

the hole, without burying the leaves. Firm in with your fingers.

Water the pot thoroughly from overhead, and label the cuttings. Cover the pot with a plastic bag and secure with a rubber band. To prevent the plastic coming into contact with the cuttings, construct a framework of sticks or looped galvanized wires before putting the plastic in place. Set the pots of cuttings in a shaded cold frame to root. Alternatively, put the cuttings in a propagating frame with a regulated bottom heat of about 16°C (61°F).

After four to six weeks – about three in a propagating frame – the cuttings should have rooted. To check, tug them gently. If they don't yield, they have rooted and the plastic covering can be removed or the pots can be taken out of the propagator. Leave the pot of cuttings in the frame for four or five days, then remove from the pot by turning it upside-down and carefully dislodging the compost, together with the rooted cuttings, in one piece.

Separate the rooted cuttings carefully, then pot them up singly into 7.5cm (3in) pots of John Innes No. 1 potting compost. Firm in each cutting and water thoroughly. Allow the pots to drain before putting them in a shaded cold frame. Pinch out the growing tip of each plant after about a week to encourage the development of a strong root system instead of excessive top growth.

Overwinter the cuttings in a closed cold frame. Plant out in their growing positions in spring, when all danger of frost is over.

Basal cuttings
Most clump-forming perennials, such as bugloss (*Anchusa*), thrift (*Armeria*), delphiniums, heleniums, lupins and scabious (*Scabiosa*), can be propagated not only by division, but also from the young shoots appearing from the base of the plant in spring.

Cut off some of these basal shoots when they are 7.5-10cm (3-4in) long, at crown level or just below. Insert the cuttings directly

into the soil in a cold frame, or in 7.5cm (3in) pots containing a proprietary cuttings compost.

Keep cuttings well watered by spraying them from overhead, and keep the frame closed. As new growth starts to show, increase ventilation by gradually opening the frame.

After about six weeks, pot the cuttings singly in 9cm (3½in) pots of John Innes No.1 potting compost. Plant them out in their permanent positions during autumn, after hardening off.

Semi-hardwood cuttings
Many woody shrubs and trees can be propagated successfully from cuttings taken in summer. These include actinidia vines, spotted laurel (*Aucuba*), caryopteris, Mexican orange (*Choisya*) and lavender (*Lavandula*).

Semi-hardwood cuttings are made from the current year's growth which has become moderately firm and woody towards the base but is still growing, so the tips of the shoots will be soft. The

TIP CUTTINGS

1 Snip off non-flowering side-shoots from perennial plants at any time during the summer. Each cutting should be 7.5-10cm (3-4in) in length and be free from all pests and diseases.

2 Trim each cutting straight across the stem, just below a leaf node – the point at which one or more leaf stalks join the main stem – then pull off or cut away the lowest pair of leaves.

3 Using a pencil, make planting holes in a 10cm (4in) pot containing a suitable cuttings compost. Insert the cuttings, firm in with your fingers and water gently from overhead.

4 Criss-cross two galvanized wire hoops to make a framework, and cover with a polythene bag. Make a few small breathing holes in the polythene and secure it with a rubber band.

5 After four to six weeks, remove the polythene and check for rooting – cuttings should not yield to a gentle tug. Plant each rooted cutting in a 7.5cm (3in) pot of potting compost.

6 Pinch out the tip of each cutting about one week after potting individually to encourage side-branching and the formation of a strong root system. Overwinter in a cold frame.

SEMI-HARDWOOD HEEL CUTTINGS

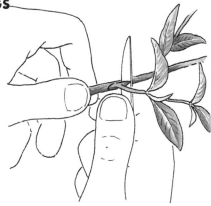

1 Most shrubs root more easily if taken with a heel – a sliver of wood from the main stem. Begin by making a slanting cut into the main stem below the join with the side-shoot.

2 Next, make a similar cut in the opposite direction to remove the side-shoot complete with the heel. A very sharp, clean knife is essential for this operation.

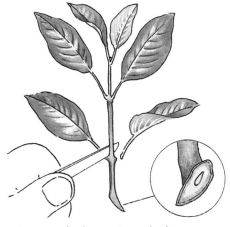

3 Remove the leaves from the lowest part of the stem, and also trim off the terminal soft tip just above a leaf joint. The final cutting should be about 5-10cm (2-4in) in length.

4 Insert the cuttings in pots of cuttings compost and provide them with a warm, humid atmosphere by covering with a polythene bag or putting them in a special propagator.

best time to take semi-hardwood cuttings is from mid to late summer. They require some attention from the time they are set out until they are rooted – their ideal position is in a cold frame, and close attention should be paid to watering and shading from the sun. A year or two must elapse before the plants are ready for their permanent quarters.

Take the cuttings by choosing 15-20cm (6-8in) long side-shoots of the current season's wood – easily identified, as the shoots will have leaves growing on them. With a knife or secateurs, cut off a shoot close to the main stem. Remove the leaves from the lower part of the shoot and sever it just below the lowest leaf node. Trim off the soft tip above a leaf so the cutting is about 10cm (4in) long.

Heel cuttings Semi-hardwood cuttings often root more reliably if they are removed with a sliver of the parent stem. Some species – including pyracantha and Californian lilac (*Ceanothus*) – will root very poorly, or not at all, if this heel-like sliver is missing. The inclusion of a heel encourages roots to form, as it prevents the sap from draining away into the soil – the sap flows down from the leaves to help form the roots.

First, cut off a main shoot carrying several side-shoots, preferably without flowers. With a sharp knife, make a slanting cut into the main shoot beneath the junction with the side-shoot. Then cut in the opposite direction to remove the shoot. Heel cuttings should be 5-7.5cm (2-3in) long. If they are longer, trim from the tip. To balance any loss of difficult-to-root plants, it is wise to take a few extra cuttings.

Once the cuttings have been

taken – with or without a heel – fill a pot to just below the rim with a proprietary cutting compost. A 7.5cm (3in) pot will take up to five cuttings, and a 12cm (5in) pot will take up to ten.

Make a hole in the compost, about one-third the length of the cutting. Insert the cutting and firm it with a dibber and your finger. Plant the other cuttings, then water them generously with a sprayer or a watering can with a fine rose.

The cuttings need a humid atmosphere to prevent them drying out. One simple method is to construct a cover from galvanized wire and a polythene bag as for tip cuttings. A box is best for a large number of cuttings, however, also covered with a polythene and wire frame. Alternatively, use a proprietary plastic propagating case, though the price may be quite high.

A cold frame is suitable for most semi-hardwood cuttings, but better rooting conditions are created if a source of heat is sup-

LEAF-BUD CUTTINGS

1 The method of making a leaf-bud cutting is much the same as for a heel cutting. Each cutting of a camellia should contain one tiny bud, one leaf and a sliver of wood.

2 Insert cuttings so that only the leaf shows on the surface. Leaf-bud cuttings of other shrubs usually include a short length of stem, rather than just a sliver of wood.

HARDWOOD CUTTINGS OF EVERGREENS

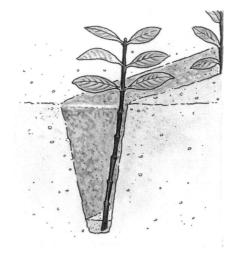

1 Make hardwood cuttings of evergreen shrubs, such as privet (*Ligustrum*), by severing just below a leaf node. Strip off most of the lowest leaves, leaving no more than six.

2 Insert the cuttings in the open ground in a V-shaped trench with a layer of sand at the bottom to assist drainage. Such cuttings will take about a year to root successfully.

plied from beneath, keeping the base of the cuttings slightly warmer than their tops. This can be done by placing the propagating container over the heating pipes in a heated greenhouse, or by using electric soil-warming cables in a cold frame. Propagating frames can be bought with built-in heating elements.

The compost above the heating source should be maintained at a steady temperature of 16-18°C (61-64°F) for most hardy plants. Cuttings generally root without bottom heat, however, but may take a little longer to do so.

After rooting, harden off the cuttings – acclimatize them to the drier or colder conditions they will meet outside by keeping them in a greenhouse or frame and raising the polythene, or piercing a few holes in it, to let in air. Keep them away from strong light.

One week later, raise the polythene still higher or make more holes in it. A further week later, remove the polythene altogether. By the following week the cuttings are ready for potting up singly.

Gently remove cuttings from the pot or box and tease them apart. Place potting compost in the bottom of a 9cm (3½in) pot. Stand the young plant on this and then fill the pot with compost to just below the lowest pair of leaves. Firm the compost so that the surface is level and about 1.5cm (½in) below the rim, then water generously.

Keep the pot in a greenhouse or

frame and never allow the compost to dry out. In three weeks, the roots should have reached the outside of the compost. Pot-on into a larger pot and place in an open cold frame. Keep those plants which are not fully hardy in a frost-free frame or greenhouse for the winter. Plant out in the spring when all danger of frost is past.

Leaf-bud cuttings
If several new shrubs are required from a limited amount of propa-

gating material, leaf-bud cuttings can be taken. Provided the material is taken at the right time, individual buds can root and break into growth more quickly than those on a traditional cutting. Camellias, in fact, are propagated more successfully by this method than by any other.

In late summer or early autumn, take cuttings from semihard lateral shoots – those which began growing in the spring. Each shoot should have several healthy leaves, with a growth bud in each leaf axil.

With secateurs, cut off the shoot near its base. Then with a sharp knife, cut through the shoot at an angle, about 2cm (¾in) below the lowest leaf.

Sever the cutting just above the bud in the leaf axil, cutting straight across. Three or four leaf-bud cuttings can be made in this way. Scrape some bark off the cutting with a knife, then dip the end and the wounded part of the cutting in rooting powder. Shake off any surplus.

Fill a pot to just below the rim with a proprietary cutting compost. Insert the cuttings so that the bud just shows above the surface. Take about 12 cuttings for each 15-18cm (6-7in) pot.

With camellias, a leaf-bud cutting should contain only a small bud with a leaf and a sliver

CHEMICAL AIDS FOR CUTTINGS

Cuttings generally root readily when taken at the correct time of year. If difficulty is encountered, various hormone rooting compounds are available which may hasten the formation of roots. These may be bought in the form of a dry powder which is dusted on to the base of the cutting, or as a gel or liquid into which the cutting is dipped. The powder types generally contain an additional fungicide which helps to limit rotting of the stem base, and may be available in different strengths – weaker for softwood and stronger for hardwood cuttings. There are also general-purpose compounds.

These hormones are present in the plants themselves, but often in such minute quantities that natural rooting is very slow. Rooting powders speed up the formation of callus tissues, the corky scar tissues that form at the base of a cutting and from where roots develop.

You can also buy small, transparent plastic tubs filled with a special rooting gel. Simply insert the cuttings directly into the gel – no soil or water is needed – and watch them take root. Follow the manufacturer's recommendations for the number of cuttings per tub and for aftercare.

Hardwood cuttings of evergreen trees and shrubs, especially conifers, may die because of rapid, excess water loss through the leaves. This can be averted by spraying the cuttings with an aerosol liquid plastic – known correctly as S-600, but often sold under a variety of trade names as a Christmas tree needle-drop protectant spray – which forms a transparent film on the leaves. It can be used also on softwood or semi-hardwood cuttings of both deciduous and evergreen plants, particularly those with large leaves, which are especially susceptible to wilting.

of wood attached – the sliver being scooped out of the parent stem with a sharp knife. Insert these cuttings in the rooting medium firming them lightly until only the leaf shows on the surface.

Water both types of leaf-bud cutting lightly after insertion. Use a small hand sprayer, or shake water on with your fingers. Cover the pot with a wire and polythene hood as before to provide a humid atmosphere, then place it in the greenhouse or cold frame.

Six months later, knock out the rooted cuttings from the pot and gently separate them. Place potting compost in the bottom of the necessary number of 9cm (3½in) pots – one for each cutting.

Stand the rooted cutting centrally in the pot, and then top up with compost so that the cutting is covered to just below the original leaf. Firm the compost so that the surface is about 1.5cm (½in) below the rim, to allow for watering. Water in generously and keep the pot in a greenhouse or frame. Never allow the compost to dry out.

In three to six weeks, the roots should reach the outside of the compost. Hardy species can now be planted out in the open. Less hardy ones should first go into a larger pot in the greenhouse, or a frame, for the following summer and winter before being planted out in the spring.

Hardwood cuttings

The simplest way of propagating a large range of popular hardy shrubs and trees is by taking hardwood cuttings in late autumn and early winter. Except for watering in dry spells and weeding, no further attention is needed for one year. The cuttings should then have strong roots, and the young shrubs or trees can be planted in their permanent sites.

Hardwood cuttings are vigorous stems which have just completed their first season's growth and have become hard and woody. They bear buds all along their length and these will grow into new shoots the following spring.

Preferably take the cuttings in mid autumn, when they have just stopped growing and are beginning the winter period of dormancy, though some shrubs will grow from hardwood cuttings taken at any time in late autumn or winter.

HARDWOOD CUTTINGS OF DECIDUOUS SHRUBS

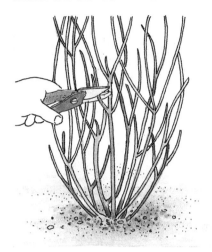

1 In mid autumn, choose a vigorous stem of the current year's growth — it should be hard and woody, and bear small, dormant buds all along its length. Using secateurs, cut the stem cleanly near its base.

2 Using a sharp knife, trim the stem to 25-30cm (10-12in) long, cutting cleanly just below a bud or joint at the base and just above a bud at the top. Cut away from your fingers or lay the cutting on a bench when trimming.

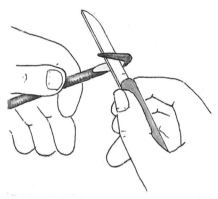

3 To aid rooting, slice off a thin sliver of bark and wood from near the base of each cutting, either on one side or opposite sides. A rooting compound may also assist rooting.

4 Plant the cuttings to at least half their length in a V-shaped trench in open ground in a site sheltered from north and east winds. A layer of sand in the bottom aids drainage.

Cut the stem with secateurs near its base and then trim it to about 25-30cm (10-12in) in length. If the shoot is a long one, two or more cuttings may be made from it. Avoid using the soft thin tip, as it may not root at all.

Sever each cutting cleanly just below a bud or joint at the base, and just above a bud at the top end. Cut evergreens below and above a leaf and remove all the leaves on the lower half.

With large-leaved plants, such as cherry laurel (*Prunus laurocerasus*), reduce each leaf by half its surface area, using a razor blade or sharp scissors. This reduces water loss until the cutting is rooted satisfactorily.

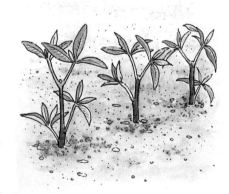

5 A year or two later, healthy shoots should have developed and the rooted cuttings are then ready for transplanting into their permanent positions in the garden.

Cuttings from difficult-to-root shrub species often respond to wounding – the removal of a thin sliver of bark on one or opposite sides near the base of the cutting. You can also encourage rooting by dipping the base of the cutting into a rooting powder, making sure to cover the wounded area. Shake off any excess powder.

Before taking the cuttings, choose a site sheltered from north and east winds and dig it thoroughly. If the soil is heavy, work in coarse sand or weathered ashes to help drainage and aeration. Make a narrow slit-like trench by pushing in a spade to its full blade depth and then pulling it forwards for several inches.

Place a layer of coarse sand 2.5-5cm (1-2in) deep in the bottom, and stand the cuttings on the sand so that the lower half or two-thirds is below ground. Plant the cuttings 7.5-10cm (3-4in) apart with 60cm (2ft) between the rows. Push soil into the trench and firm it with your foot.

After severe frosts, cuttings can become loosened. Push each cutting down with your thumb or finger so that the base is again in close contact with the soil or sand.

In early spring, firm the soil again. Hoe regularly during the summer, and water during long, dry spells. One year later, all the easier-rooting cuttings will be ready for lifting and setting in their permanent quarters in the garden. Leave species that are slower to root, or slower to grow, in the ground for a further year.

Root cuttings

Some plants, both herbaceous and woody, readily produce shoots direct from their roots as a natural process, particularly at a point where damage has occurred. Consequently, pieces of severed root can be used as cuttings. Root cuttings require less attention than semi-hardwood or softwood cuttings.

Shrubs that grow well from root cuttings include sumach (*Rhus*), smoke bush (*Cotinus*), spiraea and ornamental brambles (*Rubus*). Lift the entire plant any time from autumn to spring, using a garden fork, or unearth part of the root system of a large plant. Then, with secateurs, cut off the thicker roots close to the main stem or root.

Using a knife, cut pieces about 4cm (1½in) long from these roots.

Cut each piece straight across the top (nearest to the main stem or root), and at an angle at the base – this will help you to remember which way up to plant them.

Perennials can also be increased from root cuttings which have been taken during the dormant season. Thick and fleshy rooted plants, such as bleeding heart (*Dicentra*), oriental poppy (*Papaver orientale*), anchusa and Californian tree poppy (*Romneya*) are particularly suited to this method of propagation.

Lift the plants in the autumn and cut healthy roots into 5-7.5cm (2-3in) pieces, making a straight cut across the root nearest to the crown, and a slanting cut at the other end.

Fill pots to a level just below the rim with a proprietary potting compost, and make planting holes in the compost to the same depth as the cuttings, using a small dibber or an old pencil.

Insert the cuttings, straight cut uppermost so that the top is level with the surface of the compost. A 12cm (5in) pot will usually accommodate about six cuttings. Cover the cuttings with about 6mm (¼in) of coarse sand, and spray them with water.

Fibrous-rooted herbaceous plants are often increased from root cuttings; it is a method used particularly for the perennial phlox to prevent incidence of the dreaded stem eelworms.

Lift the plants during dormancy and cut the selected roots into short pieces about 5cm (2in) long – it is not necessary to distinguish between the top and the bottom of the cuttings. Lay them flat on the surface of a box which has been filled with John Innes seed compost, and cover lightly with sand.

All types of root cuttings should be kept in a cold greenhouse or closed frame during the winter. By spring, the cuttings should have rooted well and begun to develop leaves.

Knock them out of their pots and separate them carefully before potting them up individually in 7.5cm (3in) pots filled with a proprietary potting compost, or alternatively they could be planted out in lines in an outdoor nursery bed.

By the autumn, the young plants should be sturdy enough to be moved to their permanent quarters in the garden.

ROOT CUTTINGS

1 Lift the entire plant, or expose a section of the plant's root system. With secateurs, cut off a thick root close to the main stem, or close to a larger main root.

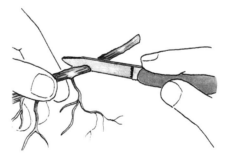

2 With a sharp knife, cut pieces of root about 4cm (1½in) long – slightly longer if the roots are thin – cutting straight across at the top, but at an angle across the bottom.

3 Plant the root pieces in pots of cuttings compost so that the tops are flush with the surface. Ensure that the angled cut ends point downwards. Cover with a thin layer of sand.

4 Six months later, move the developing plants into individual 9cm (3½in) pots of John Innes No.1 potting compost. Firm the compost well and water in generously.

WATERING AND IRRIGATION

**Rainfall is often insufficient to supply
the garden with all the water it needs. Plant
survival depends on water.**

Few plants survive for very long without water – even desert cacti and succulents, which store water in swollen stems and leaves, need a long drink from time to time. Temperature, soil condition and wind also influence each plant's water requirements.

Not only must the frequency of watering be regulated to suit your plants, but the quantity supplied at any one time, together with the droplet size, should be correctly adjusted. Excess water causes waterlogging, which is as bad for plants as drought. Under waterlogged conditions oxygen cannot reach the roots, which suffocate, killing the plant.

Insufficient water results in retarded growth. Plants can absorb nutrients from the soil only in solution with water, so they not only dehydrate in dry soils, but starve as well. In dry conditions leaf pores close to restrict water loss from the plant. In so doing, carbon dioxide intake is limited and in turn the plant is less able to manufacture sugars – food – so growth subsequently suffers.

It is essential to wet the soil deeply enough to reach the plant roots. Frequent but insufficient watering merely damps the soil surface – it does not penetrate to the soil layer where most roots are formed. It's better to water thoroughly once or twice a week than to give a little water several times a week. Even under drought conditions, a lot of water applied once a week is still the best remedy.

Before using mains water in the garden, check with your local water authority – by law, you may have to pay an extra licence fee. Even then, there may be permanent restrictions on the use of certain watering equipment, or temporary restrictions during periods of water shortage.

Susceptible plants
Newly planted outdoor plants and all shallow-rooted plants, such as bedding annuals and vegetables, are at the greatest risk from water shortage. Plants grown close to a high wall – within 60cm (2ft) – are also vulnerable, but all plants, however deep their roots, can be affected by drought.

▼ **Oscillating sprinklers** Ideal for a lawn, this type of sprinkler gives an even and gentle distribution from sprays that move slowly and automatically from side to side.

WATERING CANS AND HOSEPIPES

The choice of watering cans is huge, mostly made from plastic or galvanized iron. For garden use, 8-10 litre (1¾-2¼ gallon) cans are ideal, but smaller ones are easier to handle, especially if you have back trouble or need to stretch up or across to reach the plants.

Choose a small can with a long spout for watering hanging baskets – some have a directional rose which can be turned downwards for aiming into a high container, or upwards to deliver a gently arching sprinkle on to delicate seedlings at ground level.

Cassette hose reels are convenient to store – the hose squashes flat when not in use and rolls into an enclosed drum. They come complete with a universal tap connector and a spray nozzle. It is sometimes difficult, however, to drain out all the water before rolling back into the cassette.

Conventional hoses may be stored on a reel, which can be free-standing, on wheels or fixed to a wall. Spray lances and gun-type spray nozzles can be fitted to most hoses. These can be detached for safe storage. A number of hose couplers and accessories is available.

COLLECTING RAINWATER

Rainwater is softer than most tap-water, so it doesn't cap the soil – a common problem when watering pots from a tap. Collect it by directing the flow from a garage or shed gutter via a drainpipe into a barrel. Stand the barrel on bricks to allow room for a watering can to be placed under the drain-off tap. Always cover the top of the barrel.

Slow-growing plants, such as many trees and shrubs, need regular watering during the growing season for a couple of years after planting. Some flowering plants, however, produce a better show when kept on the dry side – moist conditions encourage leaf growth, but few flowers. These include nasturtiums (*Tropaeolum majus*) and mesembryanthemums or Livingstone daisies (*Mesembryanthemum criniflorum*).

Salad vegetables need a lot of water to grow quickly and be sweet and tender when picked. If lettuces or beetroot, for example, are too dry they quickly 'go to seed' – forming flowers and fibrous, tough growth. Excessive watering, however, can reduce the flavour of vegetables, so a balance must be achieved.

Container plants must be watered frequently. Hanging baskets are especially liable to dry out in sunny weather, and ceramic/terracotta pots lose water faster than plastic ones.

Soil types
Sandy soils and those which are low in organic content dry out fast, while clay soils hold most water but quickly become waterlogged.

Well-balanced loam holds a good quantity of water and is also open-textured and more resistant to waterlogging.

The long-term use of inorganic fertilizers can also hinder water uptake from the soil. Where possible, use organic fertilizers.

When spraying water, large droplets or high pressure break down the soil surface into a slurry. As this dries, a surface 'cap' forms which blocks the entry of subsequent water and chokes out air. On a slope, large droplet size or rapid application of water also causes erosion – valuable topsoil washes to the bottom. Good watering equipment should deliver a fine spray, or be adjustable.

When to water
Foliage becomes dull when water is lacking. This is the correct time to apply water. If you wait until leaves and stems wilt the plant will suffer. Another test is to check the soil moisture content 5-10cm (2-4in) below the surface. Dig a small hole with a trowel – the soil at the bottom should be moist to the touch and darker than the surface soil.

The amount of water needed to restore the correct soil moisture level varies considerably. Small shrubs may need about 5 litres (1 gallon) per plant and a tree may need 20 litres (4 gallons) or more. Smaller plants are best given an overall watering, about 10-20 litres (2-4 gallons) per sq m/yd.

When planting out delicate seedlings – including vegetables – set them in a shallow depression rather than level with the surface, firm in very gently, then water in with a watering can until a puddle forms in the 'well'.

Choosing watering equipment

You won't need a lot of expensive equipment for the average-sized garden. The simplest irrigation system is a watering can, but you will be surprised at how quickly a couple of gallons of water can disappear into parched soil, necessitating several trips to and from the garden tap. A can is best for localized watering of newly planted or specimen items; too little water is often worse than no water at all as it discourages deep and healthy root growth.

A better solution is to use a hosepipe, ideally fitted with an on/off control at the business end so you can turn the supply on and off as you work your way round the garden. But hand watering can be time-consuming – it may take several hours to water a large garden properly.

Better still, you can connect your hosepipe to a sprinkler – either a simple static rotary type or one of the more sophisticated oscillating or pulsating types, some of which will also travel across lawns. The advantage of even the simplest type of sprinkler over hand watering is the volume of water it can deliver unattended, but there is the drawback of having to extend and rearrange the hose run as you water different parts of the garden.

The perfect answer is a permanent in-ground watering system, which can be turned on and off as required to deliver precisely the right amount of water exactly where it is required. Such systems are a common sight on golf courses and in some public parks, but there is no reason why you should not install an irrigation system in your garden.

Watering cans are available in many shapes, sizes and colours, and can be plastic or galvanized metal. Spouts, roses and handles

SPRINKLER TYPES

1 The static sprinkler is the simplest of all. Water distribution is the same as with a standard hand-held nozzle – a circular pattern covering up to 11m (35ft) across – but the device has a spike for securing into the ground.

2 Rotary sprinklers have two or three rotating arms which produce a circular spray of fine water droplets up to 13.5m (45ft) across. Some models have a static vertical spray in the centre to complete the spray area covered.

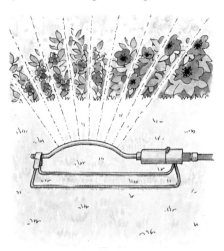

3 Oscillating sprinklers produce a rectangular spray coverage up to 17 x 12m (55 x 40ft). They have a tube or barrel bored with holes which oscillates slowly from side to side.

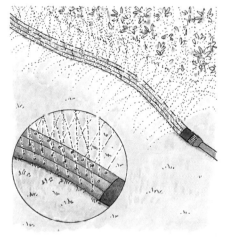

4 Pulse-jet sprinklers give an even wider coverage by spraying in one direction only at any one time. The jet rotates through 360° in a series of automatic pulses.

5 This type of sprayer holds the nozzle high off the ground and gives a gentle 'rain' of water – ideal for seedbeds and young vegetables. Several can be linked together in a chain.

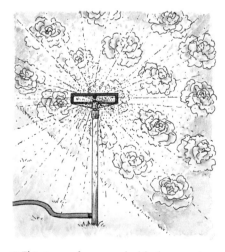

6 Sprinkler hoses give a gentle 'rain' effect and can be woven easily through flower or vegetable beds. They consist of a flat hose perforated on the upper surface with thousands of tiny holes.

DRIP IRRIGATION

This system provides plants with constant moisture – ideal in a greenhouse or vegetable plot. The drip rate can be adjusted as required by screwing in the nozzels.

vary according to brand. Some cans have detachable roses with alternative spray patterns – giving a fine, medium or coarse spray. Push-on replacement rubber roses, usually with a brass face, can be bought separately. If you intend to use the can to apply weedkillers, choose one with gradation markings to help you dilute quantities accurately. Two-handled cans are easier to balance, and for inaccessible places are easier to manoeuvre. When watering-in large plants, remove the rose and use the open-ended spout, holding it close to the planting hole.

Hosepipes provide a convenient means of applying a large amount of water to the garden with minimal effort. You can make do with a simple open-ended hose, using your thumb to regulate the flow of water, but you can greatly improve its versatility by buying a range of special hose fittings. Start with a tap connector so the hose won't keep falling off at the garden tap. Threaded types are best if the tap nozzle has an external thread; otherwise go for one with a worm-drive clip.

The nozzle secured to the other end of the hose can be adjusted to give various spray patterns or a single jet. Adjust the tap to give

▶ **Flexible irrigation** A simple arrangement of hosepipe and miniature spray heads can water plants unattended, giving them just the right amount of moisture, and saving you countless and tedious trips with a watering can.

the appropriate pressure. Lance and pistol-type nozzles are also available which incorporate an on/off valve – useful if you want to water selectively.

To avoid dragging the hose inadvertently across plants, insert short stakes at the corners of flower and vegetable beds. Slip a length of plastic pipe over each stake to form a guide roller.

Hosepipe is sold in various lengths – 15m (16½yd) and 30m (33yd) are most common – and in 13mm (½in) or 19mm (¾in) diameter (internal). Most are flexible, sturdy and weather resistant.

You can connect lengths of hose together with both straight and T-couplers (the latter allow you to run branch pipes, so you can water the lawn and the vegetable garden at the same time). The most versatile types are known as automatic connectors and come in male and female parts, rather like electrical flex connectors. With these it's a simple matter to unplug and reconnect individual sections of hose, change nozzles at will or fit sprinklers of various patterns.

Some hose connectors incorporate what is known as a water stop; this cuts off the flow of water through that section of hose if you disconnect the coupler, which is useful if you want to change components without having to walk back to the tap. However, water-stop connectors can cause water hammer in the pipework supplying the hose.

Lastly, you have a choice of spray nozzles and guns, many of which incorporate a trigger or other on/off control. Types giving a fine spray are best, since soil can absorb small droplets more quickly than a coarse spray and you are also less likely to damage delicate young plants or injure developing flower buds.

Sprinklers are available in many types. Attached to a hose pipe instead of a nozzle, they water the garden while you get on with something else. By applying a fine spray over a long period you can thoroughly moisten the soil without creating puddles and surface capping. Leave the sprinkler on until every area has had at least

INSTALLING A FIXED IRRIGATION SYSTEM

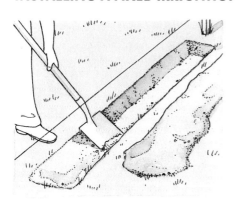

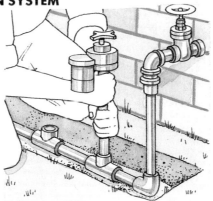

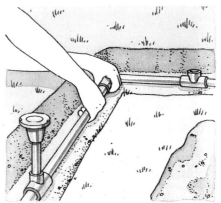

1 Mark out and stake the area of the garden you want irrigated, then dig a trench 20cm (8in) deep. Line the bottom of the trench with sand or sieved soil, keeping it as level as possible. Remove stones and any pieces of root.

2 Lay the main pipe at the bottom of the trench, then fit the anti-siphon or non-return valve at the point where you are taking the supply off the main. It is important to ensure that the join is watertight.

3 Attach the spray heads to the main pipe wherever they will be needed. Attach elbows and Ts for the branch pipes. Allow the welded joints to dry out for at least six hours, but for safety preferably longer.

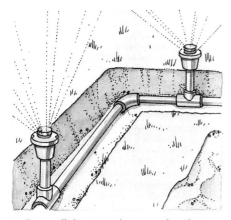

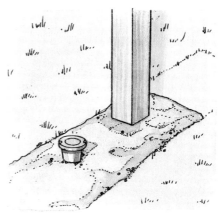

4 Once all the joints have set hard, turn on the water supply to check the anti-siphon device, to flush out any debris that may have got into the pipes, and to check for any leaks that may exist in the system.

5 Once you are satisfied that everything is working well, and there are no leaks, back-fill all the trenches with soil above ground level, taking care not to clog spray heads with loose earth or the system will not work.

6 With a timber beam or some similar object, tamp and firm down the soil around the spray heads, leaving them about 2.5cm (1in) above the surface. Take great care not to hit the heads as you do so.

2.5cm (1in) of water – stand jam jars in the spray area to check the amount. Lawns and vegetable plots in particular are best watered in this way.

You can set up two or more sprinklers at once. Use Y-connectors to join hoses; water-stop end caps turn off one branch hose until required. Water timer units are also available, though the price is high – you dial in the watering time required, set the pattern and the sprinkling is then automatic, turning off when the watering is completed.

Simple static sprinklers are the cheapest, and can often be mounted on an extender pole to allow them to be used among tall plants, but their circular spray pattern makes it difficult to get even coverage on lawns. Rotating types generally cover a larger area and can often be adjusted to vary the area covered from a narrow wedge shape to a full circle. Oscillating types deliver water in a rectangular pattern, which may be preferable if you have a square or rectangular lawn.

Drip irrigation is the most elaborate and expensive system for watering a small area. Using a complex array of plastic distribution pipes connected by cross or T-connectors, water is fed continuously to individual plants in the garden or greenhouse via special drip-feed nozzles.

Each pipe must be cut to length so that a constant water pressure can be maintained throughout the system. Nozzles are held slightly above the soil using forked or clip-type pegs. The nozzles can be adjusted to balance the drip flow, but need regular cleaning to remove lime-scale and soil blockages caused by splashing or culti-vation. You can even fit a watering 'computer' to regulate the system automatically.

Irrigation systems
The disadvantage of all these systems is that they depend to a greater or lesser extent on someone to set them out, move them around and turn them on and off. The ideal garden watering system is a permanent (or at least semi-permanent) installation which just needs turning on as required, or which can be left on permanently in really dry weather or when you go on holiday to provide a continuous supply of water.

You can install two basic types of irrigation system. The first uses a system of underground pipework which feeds fixed spray heads and other watering devices positioned at chosen intervals round the system. The second uses flexible hoses laid on the soil surface, from which other pipes are branched off using T-couplers to feed individual areas. You simply attach miniature spray heads or drip feeders wherever you want them along the branch pipes, turn on the water supply and leave the system to do its work around the garden unattended.

Fixed systems

A fixed underground system is the better choice if your garden is 'static' – if, in other words, the basic layout and the positions of flower-beds and individual plants are unlikely to change in the near future. Several manufacturers supply spray heads, drip feeders and other components; you supply and fit the system pipework, which is usually run in rigid PVC with fixed elbows and Ts, just like solvent-welded wastepipe runs inside the house.

First of all, plan where the main pipe runs will be needed. The best way of doing this is to draw out a scale plan of the garden on squared paper. Indicate where the main spray heads will be required – down each side of the lawn, for example, so their spray patterns overlap – and plan branch runs as necessary to supply drip feeders to individual areas or plants. You can then work out how many spray heads, drip feeders and other components you require, and also how much pipe and fittings to buy.

Your local water authority may require you to fit an anti-siphon or non-return valve at the point where you take your supply off the main, and they will certainly require the system to have its own stoptap. They may also increase your water rates.

The actual installation involves digging trenches about 20cm (8in) deep. Start work at the point where the system is connected to the water supply and work outwards, laying the pipe in place on a bed of sand or sieved soil and welding pipe joints, elbows and Ts for branch pipes to the main pipe run as required. Add Ts pointing upwards where necessary to supply either individual spray heads or drip feeders.

When all the welds have set hard – allow up to six hours for this – turn on the water supply and flush it through to clear out any debris in the pipes and to pro-

INSTALLING A FLEXIBLE IRRIGATION SYSTEM

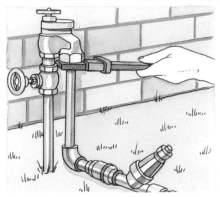

1 A flexible watering system operates on low pressure, so it is necessary to fit a pressure regulator and water filter on to the pipework just after it leaves the main supply point to adjust for the correct pressure.

2 Lay out the lateral hose pipes and attach them to the main supply hose, following your original plan. When they are securely attached, run water through the system to flush out any debris.

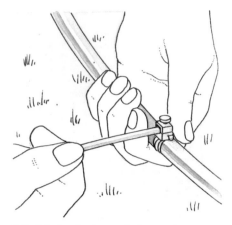

3 Drill holes in the main hose where they are needed. Insert the outlets or the transfer points. Attach points wherever they are required, taking into account the different watering requirements of your plants.

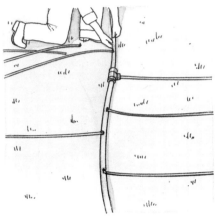

4 Complete the entire hosepipe run, flush out the system a second time, ensuring that all outlets are working. The system can be covered, but ensure the ends of the small diameter tubing remain above ground.

vide a visual check for any leaks. When you are happy that everything works, back-fill all the trenches. Make sure all the takeoff points are above ground level.

Flexible systems

Flexible irrigation systems are a better choice if your garden is in a continual state of flux, since you can easily adapt the layout accordingly. Instead of being buried deep underground, the supply pipe – in reality just special hosepipe – is laid on or just below the soil surface, with Ts supplying branches as your layout demands. Then all you have to do is to attach the spray heads and drip feeders directly to the supply hose, either using special snap-on connectors or by screwing them into holes pierced in the wall of the hose.

Various types of spray head are available, offering spray patterns of different sizes and shapes. The drip feeders can be connected to lengths of small-diameter plastic tubing to take water to individual plants some distance away from the main supply hose, and these are almost invisible if covered with a little soil.

The main difference between fixed and flexible systems is the water pressure; flexible systems operate on fairly low-pressure water – you fit a pressure regulator in the supply pipework just after it leaves the main supply point, and adjust it to give the flow rates you require at the various outlets. The other difference is that the outlets can easily become blocked by particles of grit, soil and so on, so a water filter is usually fitted just after the pressure regulator. You should clean this out at regular intervals to reduce the risk of a blockage.

SUPPORTING AND TRAINING

**Many plants need support, especially
in exposed sites. Choose a kind of staking
that is as unobtrusive as possible.**

In exposed situations, prevailing winds can do a lot of damage to any floppy or top-heavy plants – whether annual, perennial, bulbs, shrubs or trees. A few are unable to support themselves even in the most secluded spot. Others give a longer-lasting and more pleasing show when propped up, but can be left to scramble if you prefer.

In all cases, if you do have to support a plant, make sure the materials aren't unsightly – regiments of bamboo canes or wooden stakes standing above the flowers ruin any planting scheme.

Simple ties
There is a range of ties available – make sure you choose the right one for the type of plant you want to support.

Soft green twine is an ideal tie for soft-stemmed plants. It can be cut to any length and is quite strong when new – though it generally rots after one season. The colour also blends well with foliage. Rolls of twine usually contain about 30m (100ft).

Raffia is a good alternative to twine for tying indoor plants and small outdoor types, but it lacks the strength for supporting larger outdoor plants. Synthetic plastic raffia is also available; it is somewhat stronger.

Wire-cored plastic ties are available in cut pieces of suitable length for tying individual stems to a stake, or in a continuous reel form. These are strong and durable, but can cut into soft stems.

Wire split rings are useful for holding thin woody stems to a cane. Stretch the ring apart, loop it round the stem and support, then squeeze it back into a closed ring. They can cut into the stem or pull open in windy conditions, however, so are really only suitable for indoor plants.

▼ Staking border plants
Supports should be in place early in the year before tall growth has the opportunity of flopping. Galvanized wire ring supports, together with link stakes at the edge, keep many perennials upright but natural looking.

Bamboo canes

Bamboo canes are the most familiar supports for soft-stemmed border perennials, biennials, annuals and the taller bulbs, corms and tubers. They are natural in appearance, quite strong and long-lasting, readily available in various lengths from garden centres, and quite cheap. Use them to support single stems or groups of plants from 60cm (2ft) to about 1.2-1.5m (4-5ft) in height.

Canes should be tall enough to reach just below the flower spikes, so check the ultimate height of each plant before staking. Remember that you will need an extra 15-30cm (6-12in) for pushing or knocking into the ground.

For a single-stemmed plant, insert one bamboo cane firmly in the ground as close to its base as possible without damaging the root or crown. Tie the stem to the cane with raffia, twine or wire rings. These ties should be tight enough not to slip down the stem or cane, but loose enough not to cut into the stem. As the stem grows, add further ties at 15-23cm (6-9in) intervals up the cane.

For a group of stems – often produced by border perennials – insert three canes at equal distances around and close to the stems, tilting the canes slightly outwards. Knot twine to one cane about 15-23cm (6-9in) above ground, then loop the twine round the other two canes. Pull the twine taut and tie it again to the first cane. As the stems grow, tie additional lengths of twine round the canes at about 23cm (9in) intervals above the first.

Enclosure supports

Tall, floppy-stemmed plants can be supported by enclosing the stems in a cylinder of wire mesh. Galvanized mesh 20cm (8in) square is ideal and can be bought in a green plastic-coated form for an unobtrusive appearance.

Cut enough mesh to make a cylinder just wide enough to enclose the whole group of plant stems. Insert three tall canes vertically in the soil, inside the cylinder. Tie each cane to the mesh at several points. Depending on the width of mesh used, and on the ultimate height of the plant, you may need to add a second cylinder above the first. Ensure that the two cylinders are overlapped and tied to each other.

SUPPORTS FOR BORDER PLANTS

1 Galvanized steel link stakes are ideal for supporting border perennials — herbaceous or evergreen — and annuals which are planted in an irregular pattern. They can be slotted together to make small enclosures or chains to suit any planting scheme.

2 For ring supports insert a cane (about half the ultimate height of the plant) close to the centre of the plant. Push the wheel-like support over the cane — its height on the cane can be increased as the plant grows.

3 Floppy plants at the edge of a border, such as pinks and carnations, can be supported with special stakes consisting of two vertical rods with an outward-protruding hoop. The rods remain invisible behind the plant.

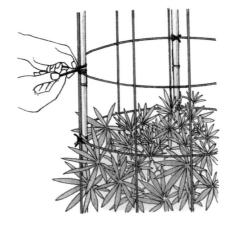

4 A wire mesh cylinder makes a good support, but install it early in the season so that some stems and leaves grow through. Insert canes just inside and tie them in to make the structure rigid.

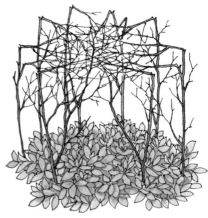

5 Pea sticks are particularly suitable for wiry-stemmed plants which are difficult to tie individually. Interlace the upper twigs to make a close framework over the plants.

Galvanized metal-link support stakes are suitable for most border plants. These consist of a vertical cane-like rod topped with a hoop socket. Proprietary models invariably come with one cross bar – which slots simply into the socket – for every upright. By slotting several together, you can construct chains – staggered or in straight lines – rings or combinations of the two to suit almost any planting scheme. Various heights of rod are available and, with some brands, it is possible to secure two or more rods on top of each other to increase their height.

Galvanized steel wire supports are also available for single stems and for small groups of low floppy stems, such as those of perennial pinks. They are springy and can be pressed open to allow stems to be slotted inside a horizontal loop at the top. Some types are adjustable in height in order to cradle heavy flowers such as those of tuberous begonias.

Metal or plastic ring supports – rather like a car steering wheel – are excellent for herbaceous border plants which send up new growths each year. Some have a central claw-like clip through which a standard bamboo cane is pushed, so holding it in a horizontal position at almost any height. Others need three canes tied around the wheel edge for support. Rings must be inserted in place in the border early in the season so that stems can grow up through the ring and conceal it.

THE CORRECT WAY TO TIE

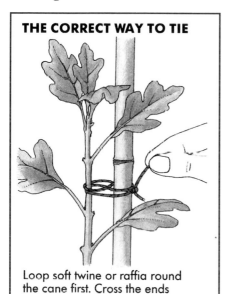

Loop soft twine or raffia round the cane first. Cross the ends behind the cane, wrap them round the stem above a leaf joint, then knot the ends against the cane.

SUPPORTS FOR TREES AND STANDARD SHRUBS

1 Plastic strap ties, sold in various sizes, are suitable for standard roses or young trees. A spacing buffer prevents rubbing and the buckle can be slackened off as the trunk swells.

2 Also adjustable in length, ratchet-grip plastic cleats provide adequate support for thinner stems against a stake. They are difficult to release once in place, however.

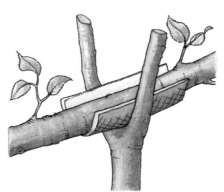

3 When using wire or stout string to tie a trunk to a stake, pad well with hessian otherwise it will cut into the bark. Wrap the hessian round the stake first, then round the stem and stake.

4 Prevent wide-spreading or old tree branches – or those heavily laden with fruit – from breaking by supporting with a forked prop. Pad the prop with thick rubber or folded hessian.

Pea sticks

Traditionally used for supporting vegetable peas, pea sticks are often available from garden centres and nurseries. They are usually the trimmings from small trees and hedges that have been cut back. Almost any tree or shrub can provide suitable twigs, but hazel, chestnut and oak are the most durable – avoid those which are brittle and break clean with a sharp snap.

Use pea sticks to support bushy plants up to 60cm (2ft) tall which tend to be floppy, or which may be exposed to wind damage – mainly annuals and herbaceous perennials. They must be inserted in spring while plants are small. Choose a day when the soil is fairly workable – pea sticks have to be pushed into the soil and cannot be hammered in. They will break if you have to apply too much pressure.

Insert two or three pea sticks as near to the centre of the plant as possible, pushing them deep enough to remain firm. If the plant is known to sprawl, or flop badly after rain, insert a few extra pea sticks around the perimeter.

At the expected height of the base of the flowers, break the tops of the pea sticks and bend them inwards. Intermesh them to form a firm top to the frame.

Wooden stakes

Upright shrubs, standard roses and young trees need sturdy stakes, especially in exposed gardens. Bamboo canes are not strong enough. Instead use wooden stakes of at least 4cm (1½in) diameter – preferably about 6-7.5cm (2½-3in) diameter for trees. Treat the lower part of the stakes with a non-toxic wood preservative.

When planting a tree or standard rose, insert the stake at the back of the planting hole, using a club hammer if necessary, before positioning the plant's root ball – never knock a stake into the

SUPPORTING CLIMBERS AND WALL SHRUBS

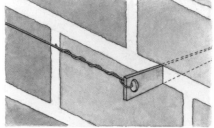

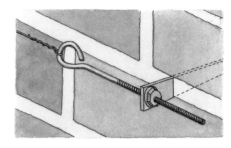

1 Woody-stemmed wall shrubs often need securing at random points. Wherever needed, fix galvanized steel screw-eyes in mortar joints in the brickwork – drill locating holes and insert plastic plugs beforehand.

2 For easy fixing of horizontal wires to a wall, hammer-in vine-eyes are ideal. These are toughened metal plates with a fixing hole at one end. When building a new garden wall bond in the vine eyes as you go.

3 To eliminate the sag from long spans of wire, fit a tensioning bolt at one end. Tighten the nut with a spanner until the wire is no longer floppy, but don't over-tighten or the wire may snap with a dangerous backlash.

ground once the plant is firmed in as you may damage its roots. Select a stake which is long enough to stand level with the first horizontal branches once inserted in the ground.

The main stem or trunk must be tied firmly to the stake. There are several proprietary tree and rose ties available, the best being made of durable plastic or webbing straps with rubber buffers. Loop the strap, at about 10cm (4in) below the branches, round the stem or trunk and through the buffer, which provides a cushion between the two. Pull the strap tight and fasten it against the stake, not against the tree trunk.

Tall trunks, or those which are not very straight, may need two or more straps at intervals to prevent the trunk from rubbing against the stake.

Self-locking straps are also available. Design varies according to manufacturer, but most consist of a plastic chain or ratchet arrangement which can be pulled taut like a buckle, but which cannot easily slip undone.

An alternative method is to wrap hessian – sacking – round the stake several times, and then wrap it round the trunk and stake so there is a protective cushion between the two. Tie the girdle in place with one or two pieces of strong string or wire.

Straps and cleats should be checked frequently – at least twice a year, and always after gales. Re-tie any that have worked loose and slacken off those which become too tight as the trunk swells with age.

Never tie a woody stem or trunk to a stake using wire alone – it will almost certainly cut into the bark, constricting the flow of nutrients up the wood from the roots and so stunting growth.

Training wall plants

Some form of support is necessary for all climbers and wall plants except ivy and Virginia creeper which are self-clinging – though even these need help at first.

The cheapest support can be made by stretching galvanized wire horizontally between vine eyes fixed into the wall or fence. Place the first wire about 1m (3ft) from the ground, and repeat every 23-30cm (9-12in) upwards.

When fixing the wire, first twist it around one vine eye then cut it to the length required. Secure the free end in the chuck of a hand drill and give it a few turns, at the same time pulling the wire taut – this will straighten out any kinks in the wire. Feed the free end through the other vine eyes and secure it to the last one by twisting it back on itself several times.

For really strong wires suitable for supporting heavy wall plants, use tensioning bolts in conjunction with the vine eyes. Tie the plant to the wires using the same techniques as for tying to a stake or bamboo cane.

Special wall cleats are available. These consist of a toughened metal spike – which is hammered into a mortar joint – with a lead or plastic collar strap for bending or tying round the plant stem. They should be positioned at random wherever needed on the wall.

Other suitable types of support include wooden trellis, panels of plastic-coated steel mesh, and all-plastic mesh. Fix all supports 2.5-5cm (1-2in) away from the wall on battens. Twining plants will then weave in and out. Others,

WEEPING ROSE TRAINER

For a really unusual and pretty effect, a standard rose can be trained into a weeping umbrella-like shape by fixing a specially shaped framework over the head of the plant. Tie in each branch to the underside of the frame – you may need to hard prune the rose to encourage new, malleable stems. Flowers and foliage will grow through and around the trainer.

such as clematis, will cling by twisting their leaf stalks around the supports.

Many wall plants, however, must be tied to their supports. Any of the ties mentioned previously will be suitable, depending on the diameter of the branches and the ultimate weight of the plant when fully grown.

Never plant close to a wall – the soil is usually too dry. Instead, plant 30-45cm (1-1½ft) away from the wall and lead the young stems to the wall with one or more canes. Position the canes in front of the stems to protect them against accidental damage until established. Alternatively, protect young, soft stems with a cylinder of wire mesh or chicken wire.

STOPPING AND DEAD-HEADING

**To promote bushy growth with a magnificent show
of flowers, many plants must be stopped, disbudded or
dead-headed, and cosseted in other ways.**

Left to their own devices, the majority of soft-stemmed plants – annuals, biennials, bulbs, corms, tubers and perennials – will develop a reasonable shape with a good display of flowers. Woody plants, on the other hand, invariably need at least some routine pruning in order to produce and maintain an attractive shape and to retain vigour for subsequent growth.

However, all plants traditionally grown for exhibition – such as chrysanthemums, dahlias and carnations – and many others besides, produce much better or larger individual flowers or heads of flowers if the growth of shoots and buds is controlled carefully from an early stage. Many foliage plants make a better and more pleasing shape when shoot growth is modified.

Stopping

Stopping is the process of removing or pinching out the growing tip of a plant to encourage the formation of breaks – side-shoots – and control the flowering habit. Chrysanthemums and carnations are commonly treated in this way, both under glass and for garden cultivation. Some side-shoots may require further stopping at a later date – known as second stopping.

When planting small, young plants into their final growing site – annuals and biennials, in particular – any which are not developing the required bushy shape naturally should be encouraged to do so by pinching out the growing tip from the main stem. However, some species, such as foxgloves and hollyhocks, only ever produce one main stem and no stopping is required.

Stopping is especially desirable where young plants have become lanky through poor cultural condi-

---

▼ Dead-heading annuals
Remove faded flowers regularly to keep plants tidy and prevent them from wasting energy in producing seeds. Dead-head with scissors or by hand.

STOPPING GARDEN PINKS

1 Young plants must be stopped in their first growing season once nine or ten pairs of fully grown leaves have developed.

2 Take the sixth or seventh joint from the base and bend the stem sharply. If the stem does not snap cleanly, cut it as close to the joint as possible.

3 Breaks or side-shoots now appear from each of the leaf joints. This delays flowering, but in so doing creates much stronger growth.

4 The result is a bushy, shrub-like plant with a succession of flowers. Do not stop garden pinks again in subsequent years.

tions in the early stages of growth – a seemingly weak, straggly plant can often be prompted to develop a better shape by pinching out the growing tip together with one third or more of the main stem. Don't be frightened of being harsh with plants in their early stages since they invariably give better results in the long run. The restriction of top growth may also encourage more energy to be put into root growth, so a transplanted specimen will get a hold quicker.

Pinched plants generally produce new, soft side-shoots immediately and these may be more tender and susceptible to damage from cold or wet than the rest of the plant. For this reason, do not stop plants any later than early autumn – the new growths will not have time to harden before the first frost. Plants should have produced several pairs of fully de-

veloped leaves before they are stopped. If they have not reached this stage by early autumn, leave pinching out until spring.

Plants bought from a nursery in the spring may already have been stopped – look to see if the growing tip has been pinched out. If they need to be stopped, wait for damp weather in the early morning when stems are full of moisture and so break more easily.

Usually the growing tip will snap out cleanly – hold the stem between finger and thumb at the base of a leaf joint, then, holding just above the joint with the other hand, bend the stem sharply down. If it does not snap, bend the stem to the other side at right angles. If this fails, do not pull at it – instead, cut it cleanly with a sharp knife as close above the joint as possible. It is best to remove the growing tip together with at least

one pair of expanded leaves, otherwise breaks may appear only near the top.

Chrysanthemums must be stopped to get good flowers – if allowed to grow naturally, they develop into bush-like plants, with a mass of small flowers. Stopping also brings the flowering season of large-flowered types forward since many varieties, if left to grow naturally, would bloom late and be spoilt by autumn frosts. Spray types usually break naturally and don't require stopping.

With large-flowered dahlias, plants send up strong centre growths, but make little side growth until the centre shoots develop flower buds. Two or three weeks after planting, pinch out the growing point – usually late spring or early summer. A fortnight later, six or more growing points will be seen developing in the leaf axils. Again remove the uppermost pair of shoots to promote vigorous growth in the lower side-shoots.

These side-shoots will each produce a bud at the tip, with 'wing' buds just below it. For large blooms, pinch off the wing buds when they are big enough to be removed without injuring the terminal bud. To promote longer-stemmed side-shoots and encourage growth in the upper part of the dahlia, cut off leaves that grow from the main stem a few inches from the ground.

Tomatoes grown outdoors must be stopped after about four good trusses of fruit have set in order to prevent further flowering. If growth continues, the fruit will not swell and ripen before autumn. Using a sharp knife, cut off the growing point two leaves above the top truss.

Disbudding
Disbudding involves removing unwanted buds so as to direct the whole of a plant's energies into a few buds. It is done to produce extra large sized blooms – particularly of carnations, chrysanthemums, dahlias and roses grown for exhibition. All buds but one on each stem are removed as soon as they can be handled – generally about the size of a pea – by rubbing them out between thumb and forefinger, or by cutting them off with a sharp knife.

When growing blooms for a specific date – an exhibition or a birthday, for instance – disbudding can be timed accordingly. To delay flowering of the main crown bud, allow side buds to grow on side-shoots up to 5cm (2in) long before removing them. The time from securing the bud until the bloom is ready varies according to the species and variety. With chrysanthemums, for example, this period is six to nine weeks, depending on the feeding programme.

Plants which naturally produce sprays of flowers can be disbudded to ensure more uniform heads. With floribunda roses, for example, remove the larger centre buds and the smallest buds from each cluster.

Protecting blooms

When growing the highest quality flowers for exhibition or cutting, it may be necessary to protect them from heavy rain, hail and high winds. Staking early and correctly will help to reduce wind damage, as will a site sheltered from the prevailing wind.

To reduce wind damage further, plant or build windbreaks around the growing area – hedging plants, timber or plastic. Rigid plastic screens with a perforated or slatted construction give the best results, allowing air to pass through, but at a significantly reduced speed. Solid structures such as fences and walls can create damaging turbulence around plants downwind of them.

For very valuable blooms, construct an open-sided timber framework with a sloping roof around and over the plants. Cover the top with tough, clear polythene or PVC sheeting once the flower buds begin to show colour – no earlier or plants may develop weak, straggly stems due to the slightly reduced light.

Flowers rich in nectar can be mutilated by birds – especially spring-flowering crocuses. A chemical spray-on deterrent is available which can remain effective for up to eight weeks, but results may be rather variable. Alternatively, construct a framework of dark-coloured, unobtrusive sticks or canes around the plants and stretch black cotton back and forth between them in a lattice-work. Few birds risk getting trapped under the cotton.

Dead-heading

Dead flower heads should be removed from plants to prevent them from setting seeds, which diverts their energy from producing further flowers. Dead-heading also gives a tidier look to the garden and prevents the build-up of fungal spores in rotting material. Seed heads which are allowed to ripen also attract seed-eating birds which can cause physical damage to other parts of the plant – African and French marigolds are often destroyed in this way.

Dead-heading of early flowering perennials, such as delphiniums, lupins and violas, will often encourage a second show of flowers later in the season.

Do not dead-head plants which are grown for decorative fruits or seed heads. Also, if you want to save some seeds for the next season, allow one or two blooms to wither on each plant. Harvest the seeds only when the pods are dry and ripe.

Soft-stemmed annuals and perennials can be dead-headed by hand. With finger and thumb, snap off flowers with a twisting motion as soon as they fade. You will need scissors or secateurs to dead-head those with tougher or wiry stems – do not tear the stem or loosen the roots by attempting to break stubborn stems by hand. Badly bruised or torn stems will die back and look unsightly or kill the whole plant. Make all cuts diagonally, sloping away from a

STOPPING AND DISBUDDING CHRYSANTHEMUMS

1 To obtain the best blooms, pinch out the main stem above the top pair of fully developed leaves in late spring or very early summer.

2 New shoots appear from leaf axils on the stem. Pinch out unwanted shoots over several days, leaving six or eight to develop.

3 In early and mid summer, remove side-shoots (which grow on the remaining side-shoots) once they are about 2.5cm (1in) long.

4 By mid to late summer a group of flower buds forms at the top of each side-shoot. Pinch out the side buds and their shoots to produce a bigger bloom on the central crown bud.

5 The result is an evenly branched, open plant with earlier and bigger flowers. A chrysanthemum left to grow naturally produces a dense, bushy plant with many small flowers.

DEAD-HEADING

1 Lilies produce flowers on upright spikes which open from the base upwards. Pinch off flowers when they fade to improve appearance and stop seed formation, which weakens growth.

2 With annuals such as marigolds, cut or snap off each flower, as it fades, between finger and thumb with a twisting motion – this encourages more blooms and increases plant vigour.

3 Regularly dead-head multi-flowered roses, such as the shrub roses, climbers and ramblers, by hand. Use a twisting action to maintain tidiness, unless hips are required in autumn.

4 Hybrid tea roses and floribundas should be dead-headed using secateurs. Cut just above a leaf which has an outward-facing bud in its axil, making a cut away from the bud.

5 With rhododendrons, break off the entire flowerhead once it has faded, gripping it between finger and thumb. This will help to produce the maximum number of flowers next year.

6 Perennial plants with bare flower stems, such as red-hot pokers, should be dead-headed to ground level. If the stems bear foliage, however, trim to just below the top leaves.

---

growth bud, so that water runs off.

Dead flower heads should not be put on the compost heap – any seeds which have ripened may remain dormant for up to several years and germinate in unwanted places when the compost is distributed around the garden. Preferably burn this material instead.

The dead flower heads of certain plants can look attractive in autumn or winter and these can be left intact. The heads of many hydrangeas, for example, take on bronze and purple hues as the petals dry out. In addition, they afford some protection from winter frosts for sensitive dormant growth buds – leave them on the plant until the following spring. The dead flower heads of summer heathers are also attractive.

Other factors

Rich, fertile soils generally produce the largest, lushest plants, but in some cases they encourage luxuriant foliage at the expense of flowers. Many annuals, including nasturtiums (*Tropaeolum majus*), can be disappointing on well-prepared soils. A sunny, quite dry spot with relatively poor soil can give much showier displays of flowers. Succulent plants, such as stonecrops (*Sedum*) and mesembryanthemums, are also reluctant to flower well when the soil is too moist – in nature they may only flower and subsequently set seeds when the life of the plant is threatened by drought or intense heat. For the same reason do not use fertilizers high in nitrogen on shy-flowering plants.

In recent years, F1 hybrids –

especially of annuals – have become popular. Many of these produce larger, showier flowers which may also be more resistant to rain, wind and disease. Where any of these problems have occurred in previous years, switch to an F1 hybrid selection. It is pointless to save seed from such annuals; they do not breed true.

Aspect is often very important in determining the display of flowers. A sun-loving plant grown in shade may produce a reasonable amount of healthy foliage, but few or no flowers.

F2 hybrids – second generation hybrids – also have improved flowering qualities over the open-pollinated varieties. They are not quite as spectacular as F1 hybrids, but the seeds are somewhat cheaper to buy.

PROTECTING GARDEN PLANTS

**Having spent time and money getting the
garden in order, damage by bad weather or animals is
disheartening. Prevent this with suitable protection.**

It is not just fungal diseases and insect pests which can damage garden plants – larger animal pests and adverse weather conditions are often equally destructive. While most of us have few qualms about destroying 'lower forms of life', when it comes to animals such as rabbits, deer, squirrels, cats and dogs – even if they *are* ravenous pests – we prefer to try to deter them from the garden rather than to kill them. Similarly, we cannot control the weather, but can ward off its more harmful effects.

Plants may be damaged at any time during their life, from the seedling or cutting stage right through to maturity – seeds can even be unearthed or eaten by rodents before they germinate.

Each garden or regional area will, however, show certain trends in the type and cause of damage. For instance, rural gardens with adjacent fields may be troubled by rabbits, but an urban garden will not. Similarly, pigeons may be a menace close to woodlands or in inner cities, but be unfamiliar in open country. If you live in a mild region, severe frosts will not be a problem, but gardens in a frost pocket or sites exposed to biting winds will suffer losses every year unless precautions are taken.

The following pages show you how to prevent undue damage by each of the major animals and weather 'pests', but you need only carry out measures against the few that are known to be likely in your garden. If you are new to a particular area, ask neighbours whether there are rabbits, deer, and so on in the vicinity, or check for tell-tale droppings. Weather maps and charts may be available from regional or national meteorological offices which show the extremes of weather you are likely to experience, based on data from previous years.

Protection against frost

Several decorative shrubs and perennials, while not hardy enough to withstand severe weather outdoors during the winter months unprotected, can be grown successfully if they are sheltered from extreme cold. Freezing or very cold winds cause the most damage.

The ideal situation for tender plants is on the south side of a wall or fence 1.8m (6ft) or more high. A dense evergreen hedge can also provide enough shelter. Plants that tolerate shade will usually be protected from the worst winds if planted among trees.

Shelter is not enough, however, during severe weather – further protection will be necessary. During a very cold spell, protect bushy shrubs by wrapping straw around the branches, binding it in place with sheets of hessian sacking, tied with twine.

Wall shrubs and climbers can be protected by mats made of straw sandwiched between two sheets of fine chicken wire. Simply squeeze a 10-12cm (4-5in) layer of material between two pieces of chicken wire, then join the edges by twisting the wires together. Hang the 'mats' in front of the plants in bad weather.

Free-standing shrubs – newly planted evergreens are especially at risk – can be protected during

◀ **Winter protection** A cludding of clear polythene, packed with straw and held in place with nylon twine, provides adequate frost and wind protection for most half-hardy evergreen perennials and shrubs.

123

PROTECTING PLANTS FROM SEVERE WINTER WEATHER

1 Protect tender wall shrubs by screening them with straw sandwiched between two sheets of chicken wire and secured to canes.

2 Protect the crowns of tender herbaceous perennials by covering them with a 15-23cm (6-9in) layer of straw, weathered ashes or forest bark throughout the winter months. To keep the material in place, lay a few dead rhubarb, rheum or fatsia leaves on top and weight them down.

3 Upright free-standing shrubs can be protected by wrapping them in a wigwam made from bamboo canes and hessian, stuffed with straw.

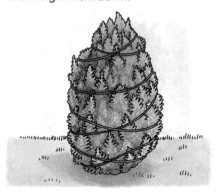

4 Bind dwarf conifers with twine or soft rope during snowy weather to prevent their branches from sagging or breaking under heavy loads of snow.

the winter by using a strip of the same construction. Stand it on end around the plant like a collar. During the coldest weather a lid of similar material can be put on top.

Bamboo canes and a polythene bag with the bottom slit open will also give a fair amount of protection. Insert four canes around the plant in a square. Lower the bag over the canes to cover the plant.

Plants which produce new shoots from the base each year – tender herbaceous perennials, and certain shrubs such as fuchsias – should have the crowns protected. Put a 15-23cm (6-9in) layer of mulch such as straw, weathered ashes, coarse sand or forest bark around and over the crown of the plants in late autumn. Anchor this material with a few rocks or pieces of rubble if necessary. Clear away this layer in early spring.

An alternative is to use bamboo canes and straw. Form a wigwam of canes by inserting about six at equal distances around the plant and tying them together at the top. Also loop string halfway down each cane, all around the wigwam. Stuff straw or even crumpled newspaper into this framework and, if necessary, tie it with more string. Another method is to tie hessian around the wigwam.

In cold or exposed areas, do not cut down the dead top-growth of herbaceous perennials in the autumn. Instead leave this tidying-up job until the spring – the old stems will afford some winter protection for the delicate dormant shoots in the crown. It is also a good idea to leave the dead-heading of susceptible shrubs such as hydrangeas until the spring, since the broad clusters of dead flowers form a useful insulation layer and a sort of 'umbrella' against snow.

The best frost protection of all is to move tender plants under glass – into a greenhouse or cold frame. Plants which cannot be moved can be protected *in situ* by placing a glass or plastic cloche over them. Leave some ventilation and do not remove the cover too quickly when

the weather turns milder – instead, increase the ventilation steadily over a few days to harden off the plants.

Often, the damaging effects of frosts are not so much caused by the low temperature as by the speed at which the frost melts when early morning sun strikes it. Camellias are notoriously susceptible to petal scorch within the unfurling flower buds in late winter when planted in a spot where morning sun falls on them. The best solution is to plant such species either in full shade or continuous dappled shade, or against a west-facing wall, where the rate of melting will be slower.

Surprisingly, a layer of ice over new shoots actually protects them against extreme cold, so if you find a prized tender shrub covered in thick white frost, a gentle spray with cold water before the sun strikes will reduce the chance of permanent damage. Never spray with warm or hot water, however.

If shrubs, trees or evergreen perennials do become damaged by cold or other weather conditions in winter, leave them alone until the spring when new growth starts to appear. Pruning in winter will often promote the premature emergence of tender growth which can then be damaged further by a late frost. If the plant looks dead right down to the ground, don't despair – wait until the summer before you grub it out, since new growth may appear from ground level given time. The so-called hardy fuchsias, for instance, invariably die down to the ground every winter, but vigorous shoots burst out from the crown in spring. Trim off the dead wood as soon as new shoots appear.

Protection against snow
As with ice, snow can actually insulate tender plants against extreme cold – that is why many alpine plants are able to survive on even the coldest mountains. However, a heavy load of snow can cause physical damage to plants. The branches of evergreen trees and shrubs can be broken under the weight. Those branches which are weighed down but do not break may not resume their original position when the snow melts – this can ruin the shape of a compact, formal plant such as a dwarf or prostrate conifer.

If heavy snow is expected, bind

PROTECTING PLANTS FROM STRONG WINDS

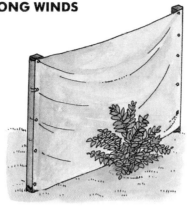

1 Wattle hurdles make good windbreaks since they allow some air to pass through the weave – solid fences create wind turbulence which can defeat the purpose of the barrier.

2 Hessian sacking secured between wooden posts or stakes makes an adequate temporary screen to protect newly planted shrubs from undue wind-rock which would loosen the roots.

3 Proprietary windbreak cladding made from durable high density polyethylene can be erected simply on conventional fence posts to provide a most effective permanent windbreak.

the branches of evergreens with garden string or rope until all danger is past. If branches get weighed down before you have a chance to bind them, shake or brush loose snow away immediately and tie in the branches if further snow is expected or if the branches don't fall back into place.

Gently brush snow off cloches, cold frames or greenhouse roofs, since a prolonged covering will reduce the light levels inside quite dramatically.

Protection against wind

High winds can damage plants at all times of the year, causing the roots to become dislodged from the soil by rocking and growth to become lop-sided by bud death on the exposed side.

Check all newly planted specimens after a storm and re-firm the root ball if necessary. Ensure that young trees and standard-trained shrubs are securely staked; replace ties as necessary.

In an exposed garden, provide protection for floppy or unstable plants by erecting a windbreak of some kind. This can be a permanent feature such as a hedge or fence, or a temporary barrier to be removed once the plants have developed a strong root system.

Do not use solid materials, such as continuous timber or bricks, for a windbreak – currents of air will simply blow over the top, swirling as they go, and often create even worse turbulence behind the barrier. Instead choose a material which will allow some air to pass through it, but at a reduced speed. Wattle hurdles, sacking, slatted 'interference' fencing, or even wire mesh offers the best protection.

Proprietary windbreak material gives the best protection of all. This is usually made from lightweight, tough, highly durable polyethylene. The mesh construction is designed to reduce wind speed by about 50% to a distance of four times the height of the barrier, and by 33% to a distance of eight times its height. As well as reducing physical damage by high winds, such windbreak materials also reduce the wind-chill factor.

Polyethylene windbreak mesh is easy to erect – simply batten it directly to timber support posts spaced at about 3m (10ft) intervals, following the manufacturer's instructions. More elaborate fixing methods may be advised for permanent windbreaks, but are usually simple to install.

Protection against rain

Excess rainfall can cause waterlogging of the soil, but the only way of preventing this problem is

SPECIAL RAIN PROTECTION

1 Protect the petals of chrysanthemums grown for exhibition by 'bagging' in greaseproof bags. Use two bags, one inside the other, the outer one with holes at the base to allow any water that soaks through to drain away.

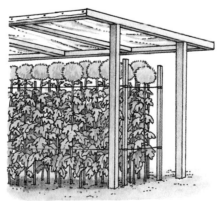

2 Construct an open-sided framework of timber and heavy-grade polythene – with a slightly sloping roof – to prevent heavy rain from spoiling the blooms of exhibition plants. Don't cover until the buds show colour.

3 Prevent water from accumulating in the leaf rosettes of alpine plants during winter by securing a small pane of glass on wire or plastic clip-pegs a few centimetres above ground. Tilt the glass slightly so water runs off.

by good soil preparation and cultivation – curative measures are generally impossible.

Tiny plants such as the true alpines and many rock garden plants which hate being soaked by heavy rain – their rosette leaves collect water resulting in rotting at the neck – can be given individual protection by covering them with a small sheet of glass supported on wire clip pegs. Tilt the glass slightly to one side so the water runs off away from the delicate plants. Put a good surface layer of coarse grit around alpine plants to drain away any surplus water from their collars.

Perfect blooms grown for exhibition can be given more elaborate protection with paper bags or umbrella-like roofs.

Protect strawberries from rainsplash by tucking clean straw beneath the ripening fruit and round the plants – unprotected fruit can be ruined by mud thrown up by heavy rain. Alternatively, use proprietary or home-made strawberry mats – collars of polythene or synthetic whalehide which fit under and around each individual plant.

Protection against animals

Dogs and cats can foul the garden, scrape up and trample plants and dig holes in seedbeds, and their urine can scorch grass and other plants. The best means of coping with these problems is to train your own pets to use a small plot of unused garden, away from the lawn and flowerbeds. Proprietary repellent pepper dusts and sprays may also keep pets – and other animals – away from a particular area or group of plants, though the effects are rarely long-lasting.

Many birds eat seeds and seedlings. The best method of protecting a seedbed is to insert low stakes around the perimeter, tie black thread to one of them and loop it criss-cross over the bed. Alternatively, nylon mesh or netting can be spread over the bed, supported on stakes. Erect a fruit cage over soft fruit bushes to keep birds off, making sure there are no holes in the construction – a single trapped bird can do a great deal of damage.

Bird scaring devices such as scarecrows, bangers, glitter strips and recorded distress signals may be used to limit bird damage, and several chemical bird repellents

GUARDING AGAINST ANIMAL DAMAGE

1 The bark of young trees and woody shrubs is often gnawed in rural areas by rabbits, hares or deer. Use a proprietary wrap-round tree guard or enclose the trunk in wire mesh.

2 Proprietary pepper dusts and foul-scented repellent pellets and sprays may be used to deter pets and other animals, including some birds, from approaching particular garden plants.

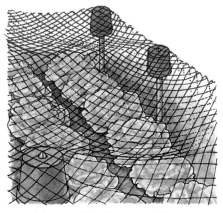

3 Rabbits and birds are troublesome pests of vegetables. Cover the plot with strong netting supported on canes with upturned plastic pots. Weigh down the edges with timber planks.

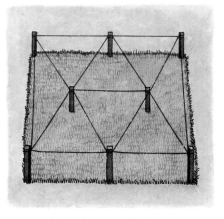

4 Deter birds from seedbeds or re-seeded lawn patches by stretching black thread criss-cross between short stakes – most seed-eating birds won't take the risk of getting trapped.

are also available, but none of these methods is fully effective.

The bark of young trees and woody shrubs may be gnawed by rabbits, hares or deer. Such damage can kill trees or seriously stunt their growth, and secondary fungal infections can also take a hold in the wounds. Plastic tree guards can be bought, the design varying enormously according to the manufacturer – all are cylindrical, usually perforated with holes to allow the bark to breathe and prevent condensation, and range from about 30cm (1ft) long to 90cm (3ft) or more.

You can make your own tree guards from chicken wire or wire mesh bent into a cylinder to suit the size of the tree.

Rabbits can be kept away from juicy young vegetables by covering the plot with netting, though a determined rabbit will get

through all but strong wire mesh. A high fence – 1.5m (5ft) or more – all around the garden should keep rabbits and deer out, but you will have to keep a constant check for holes. Bury wire mesh under the fence to a depth of at least 30cm (1ft) to prevent rabbits from burrowing underneath.

Mice often devour peas, beans and other seeds in the garden before they have time to germinate, or climb cropping plants to raid the pods; and they sometimes dig up and eat bulbs. Conventional mousetraps are effective – though keep pets away from them – and proprietary poisons may be used to control severe infestations. Squirrels are virtually impossible to control and the only effective safeguard against their damage to ripe fruits, and shrub and tree bark and buds, is by netting valuable plants.

Pruning

Correct pruning benefits the health and well being of trees and shrubs, as well as improving their appearance. The vast majority of woody plants respond to pruning by producing fresh growth from immediately below the cut so that, in effect, a well pruned plant is continually being rejuvenated. Most trees and shrubs also flower and fruit best on shoots of the current or previous season, so flowers and fruits are more reliable, prolific and often larger on regularly pruned plants. Shrubs with coloured bark produce the brightest freshest tints; trees such as eucalyptus continue to produce attractive juvenile foliage; and trees such as paulownia produce their enormous, exotic-looking leaves only if cut back hard regularly.

Correct timing is vital, and a mistake can lead to the loss of a whole year's flowers. Timing depends mainly on individual flowering habits; with few exceptions, those plants that flower on the new season's growth are pruned in late autumn, winter or early spring, and those which flower on the previous season's growth are pruned immediately after flowering. Weather is also a factor. Pruning in early autumn can result in soft new growth, unable to withstand winter cold, while pruning in frosty conditions can lead to die-back. A few plants, such as cherry, are vulnerable to disease at certain times of the year, so their pruning schedules should be adjusted accordingly.

Techniques involve deciding roughly how much to remove, exactly which stems or branches to cut and where to make each cut. By choosing pruning points with care, you can ensure that new growth occurs in the desired direction. Maintenance pruning helps to tidy up crowded, thin, dead or diseased wood.

Perfect roses Stunning summer displays depend on a rigorous spring pruning programme.

PRUNING ROSES

**Probably no aspect of gardening causes
as much needless anxiety as pruning – particularly
the annual cutting back of roses.**

The method of pruning differs slightly for each of the main categories of roses – hybrid teas, floribundas, polyanthas, miniatures, climbers, ramblers and shrub roses – and they undoubtedly perform best when treated appropriately. But most roses flower well after only light pruning, as long as you follow the three basic steps outlined here.

Roses are pruned to maintain a healthy, well-shaped plant and to encourage flowering shoots to develop. Pruning methods vary because cultivated roses don't all replace old and exhausted stems in quite the same way, nor do they all flower on wood of the same age.

Basic pruning principles apply to all roses whatever their classification as bush, shrub, climbing or rambling types and serve as the starting point for all surgery.

Pruning equipment
Sharp secateurs cut most stems. Many experienced gardeners prefer two-bladed models, but single-bladed secateurs with an anvil action are adequate if the blade is sharp. Cut thick stems with a saw or long-handled loppers; use a sharp knife to trim the edges around rough cuts, and always wear gloves for protection.

When to prune
Major pruning is done during the dormant period. Despite the increasing availability of container-grown roses, which can be planted at any time of the year, the main planting season is still

▼ **Pruning tools** Essential equipment (clockwise from top) include pruning saws, double-bladed secateurs, long-handled loppers, single-bladed secateurs, pruning knife and gloves.

from autumn to spring. This is also the time when bare-rooted roses are put in. All newly planted stock should be pruned in late winter or early spring.

Normally it doesn't matter what time established roses are pruned during the dormant season. Very harsh winter weather may damage those that have been pruned in autumn, so they may need additional trimming in the spring. It's advantageous to trim and tie in long stems before they are lashed about by autumn gales. In mild areas where new growth starts early, prune sooner rather than later.

Dead-heading

Dead-heading during the flowering season is a form of pruning which, with repeat-flowering roses, encourages a second flowering. With those that flower only once, it will save the strength of the plant being put into the development of seed. Don't dead-head roses which produce showy hips – the display will be lost.

With hybrid teas, cut off spent flowers above a strong outward-facing bud. Later in the season,

cut back to the first bud below the flower; at the end of the season simply remove the flower stalk. With floribundas, remove the whole spent flower cluster, cutting back to the first bud. Burn all prunings to prevent the spread of disease.

Correct pruning cuts

Two kinds of cuts are used in pruning. When removing a complete stem, for instance the weaker of two stems that cross, cut close to the base then trim off any stumps.

To shorten a stem, cut to just above an outward-facing growth bud or eye. Choosing such an eye ensures that the centre of the bush won't be cluttered by criss-crossing stems. Vigorous types such as hybrid teas can be hard pruned – cut almost to the ground – each year. With ramblers and climbers, cut to an eye or bud that will grow in a direction suitable for training along a support.

Right   Wrong

The three basic steps

There are three pruning steps that apply to all roses, whether established or newly planted. Treat them as routine whenever you are planting or pruning. Many roses will need very little further attention.

1 Remove all dead, damaged or diseased stems. Cut back to just above a bud on healthy wood or take out the stem completely, cutting back to a junction with a healthy stem or even the rootstock itself.

2 Remove weak or thin stems. These are unlikely to produce flowers, yet they will take strength that the plant could put into other, better growth. Cut back to a join with a healthy strong-growing stem or to the rootstock.

3 Take out the least vigorous of stems that cross or rub. Either cut the stem right out or prune back to a growth bud below the point where the two stems cross. With ramblers and climbers, cut out some overcrowding stems and remember that training and tying will be needed to avoid rubbing.

ROSE CLASSIFICATION

	TYPE	GROWTH HABIT	FLORAL CHARACTERISTICS	POPULAR EXAMPLES
BUSH ROSES	**HYBRID TEAS**	Bushy, compact, 60-120cm (2-4ft)	Large, elegant, double, high-centred, to 10cm (4in) across, one or few per stem	'Alec's Red', 'Ernest H. Morse', 'Fragrant Cloud', 'Mischief', 'Peace', 'Super Star'
	FLORIBUNDAS	Bushy, small, 60-90cm (2-3ft)	Cluster-flowering, 6cm (2½in) across, double or semi-double	'Allgold', 'City of Leeds', 'Lilli Marlene', 'Masquerade'
	POLYANTHAS	Bushy, small, to 60cm (2ft)	Cluster-flowering, to 2-4cm (¾-1½in) across	'Cécile Brunner', 'The Fairy'
	MINIATURES	Bushy, dwarf, 20-30cm (8-12in)	Mostly double, up to 2.5cm (1in) across	'Anna Ford', 'Baby Masquerade', 'Heidi', 'Rosina'
SHRUB ROSES	**MODERN SHRUB ROSES** Including Musks and Rugosas	Medium to large shrub, 1-1.5m (3-5ft), dense, vigorous, many good for hedging	Single or clusters, each flower 5-8cm (2-3in) across, very free-flowering; showy hips	'Constance Spry', 'Buff Beauty', 'Fred Loads', 'Roseraie de l'Hay', 'Frühlingsgold'
	OLD GARDEN ROSES Including Albas, Bourbons, Chinas, Gallicas and Hybrid Perpetuals	Medium to large shrubs, 1-1.8m (3-6ft), variable habit, often lax and open, suitable for general shrub plantings	Variable according to parentage, double or single, some repeat- or perpetual-flowering, mostly 5-7.5cm (2-3in) across	'Rosa Mundi', 'Mutabilis', 'Königin von Dänemarck', 'Paul Neyron', 'Ferdinand Pichard', 'Henri Martin', 'President de Sèze'
	SPECIES/WILD ROSES	Medium to large, open shrubs, to 1.8-2.5m (6-8ft), often wiry or arching, good for mixed plantings.	Usually single with five petals, some semi-double or double, once-flowering; showy hips	*Rosa rugosa*, *R. rubrifolia*, *R. californica* 'Plena', 'Canary Bird', *R. moyesii*, *R. × harisonii*
OTHERS	**CLIMBERS** Including lower-growing Pillars	Scrambling, tall shrubs, 3-9m (10-30ft), permanent framework, little or no new basal growth	Large, borne singly or in small clusters, double, mostly 8-10cm (3-4in) across	'Paul's Scarlet Climber', 'Paul's Lemon Pillar', 'New Dawn', 'Zéphirine Drouhin', 'Kiftsgate'
	RAMBLERS	Scrambling, tall shrubs, 3-7.5m (10-25ft), with thin, flexible canes growing from base each year	Clusters or trusses, mostly single, small, to 4cm (1½in) across, best on year-old shoots	'Albertine', 'Dorothy Perkins', 'Veilchenblau', 'Goldfinch', 'Temple Bells', 'Wedding Day'

INITIAL PRUNING

Whatever kind of rose you are planting, begin by following the three basic pruning steps.

Hybrid teas and hybrid perpetuals must be pruned hard to outward-facing buds about 10cm (4in) above ground. Prune floribundas less hard, to buds about 15cm (6in) from the ground; reduce dwarf varieties to 7.5cm (3in). Hybrid teas and floribundas grown as standards can be pruned even more moderately.

Prune the increasingly popular miniature roses to leave stems about 5cm (2in) high. Cut back the stems of polyanthas, such as 'The Fairy', by about one third.

Old roses need no pruning other than the basic steps. Remove about 7.5cm (3in) from the tips of species roses, modern shrub roses, climbers and ramblers.

▶ **Reward for pruning** Annual pruning will ensure abundant flowers.

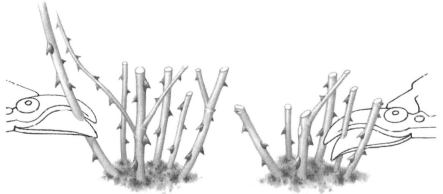

Newly planted hybrid teas

1 Carry out the three basic pruning steps — remove dead, damaged, diseased or weak stems and any that cross or crowd the centre of the bush.

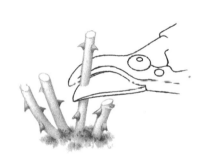

2 Cut all stems down to 10cm (4in) from the ground, above an outward-facing bud. This encourages an open, well-balanced bush.

▲ **Hybrid tea roses** Prune hybrid tea roses such as 'Fragrant Cloud' hard during the dormant season to produce a balanced bush with shapely blooms.

▲ **Floribunda roses** Reduce strong shoots on floribunda roses such as 'Anne Harkness' for a good framework bearing flowers throughout summer.

Newly planted floribundas

1 Carry out the three basic pruning steps. Floribundas are more vigorous and free-flowering than hybrid teas and need less severe pruning.

2 Then cut remaining stems down to outward-facing buds at about 15cm (6in) above ground level. Always use sharp tools and make clean cuts.

PRUNING BUSH ROSES

The hybrid teas, floribundas, polyanthas and miniatures, together with the standards derived from these groups, make up a large category of roses which are all pruned in much the same way.

Reduce the stems of hybrid teas and hybrid perpetuals by about one third. This moderate pruning is adequate to give a good garden display. Hard pruning to within three buds of the base results in fewer but better flowers.

Hybrid teas grown for exhibition are normally hard pruned. The very vigorous kinds may occasionally need hard pruning to check tall growth which might get damaged in high winds.

In autumn, trim the top growth of tall bush roses to reduce the risk of wind damage. Do not hard prune standard hybrid teas.

1 A bush rose in need of pruning will have a mixture of wood – dead or old unproductive stems, diseased and weak stems, and some that cross.

▲ **Miniature roses** Usually, miniature roses such as 'Anna Ford' need only light or moderate pruning. Reduce main stems by a quarter in early spring.

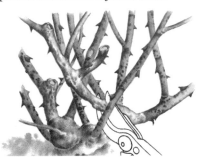

2 Cut back a dead stem to the point where it meets a healthy stem. Cut back any part of a stem which is diseased to just above a bud on healthy wood.

3 Cut out thin or weak stems to their point of union with a strong stem or with the rootstock to allow more nourishment to reach vigorous wood.

4 Cut out stems that cross or rub. Remove the weaker of the two, cutting to a growth bud below where they cross, to prevent a crowded centre.

5 Every spring, prune bush roses of average growth lightly, to ensure a good display. In general, prune weaker varieties and thin shoots more severely than vigorous ones.

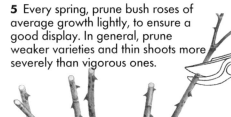

▲ **Bush roses** Prune polyanthas (such as 'The Fairy') and floribundas less severely than hybrid teas. Cut back by about a quarter during dormancy.

6 Hard prune a bush rose every year if you want to grow large, well-formed blooms, though few in number. Always begin pruning with the three basic steps.

PRUNING SHRUB ROSES

Old and modern shrub roses, and the species roses, require only light pruning.

After completing the three basic pruning steps, check plants to see if any vigorous new shoots have developed from old stems. Where this has occurred, cut back the old stem to the junction with the new shoot. Check for any exceptionally long stems which distort the shrub's balance. If there are any, cut them back by about one third. Cut back all laterals that flowered the previous summer to a strong bud about 10cm (4in) from the main stem. Lastly, cut back the tips of all main stems by 10-15cm (4-6in) to encourage side shoots which will bear flowers during the following year.

► **Modern shrub roses** These flower best on side-shoots. Tip main stems and laterals of shrub roses such as 'Constance Spry' to encourage growth of sub-laterals.

▲ **Old garden roses** Most, including Gallicas such as 'Président de Sèze', flower on shoots of the previous season. Prune lightly, tipping the main shoots after flowering.

▼ **Species roses** Prune very lightly, to maintain shape. Do not dead-head hip-bearing types like the Albas, the Moyesiis and this Rosa rugosa.

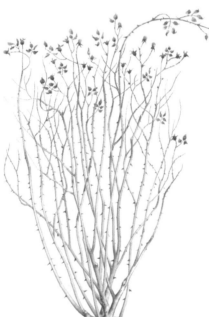

1 A shrub rose ready for pruning. Remove all dead and diseased stems.

2 Cut back all long shoots by about one third to prevent drooping.

3 Cut old exhausted stems back to the junction with new healthy laterals.

4 From the base, cut out dead stems and any that cross in the centre.

5 Finally, lightly tip all remaining stems to promote strong lateral growth.

PRUNING CLIMBERS

The pruning of the vigorous climbing roses and the shorter-growing pillar roses needs to go hand in hand with training. These roses flower on the previous season's wood. Most do not shoot readily from the base – new wood appears higher up the old stems of the leaders.

In summer, trim stems that have borne flowers back to a new bud. In winter, cut main stems (or leaders) back to vigorous new shoots. However, if no new growth has formed, cut back leaders and laterals (the stems growing from the leaders) by about half. As far as possible, train new shoots to grow horizontally – this will stimulate the growth of flower-bearing side-shoots.

1 Prune a climber in early winter, after its flowering twigs have been trimmed back in summer. Remove spindly wood, but retain a framework of new shoots for the next year's flowers.

2 Summer pruning after the climber has flowered. Trim back the flowered twigs to selected new buds. Don't let hips form — they drain the rose's energy.

◄ **Pruning climbers** Prune climbers such as 'Paul's Lemon Pillar' in winter to maintain a good framework. Cut out old stems and replace with new laterals.

3 In winter, remove old wood, cutting back the leaders to strong new shoots.

4 If no new shoots have grown from a leader, prune it and its laterals by about half to encourage new side-shoots.

PRUNING RAMBLERS

The ramblers are lax-growing scramblers producing a single but profuse crop of flowers in the summer. The long flexible canes which develop from the base of the plants bear flowers in their second year.

Begin pruning in early autumn by carrying out the three basic steps. With those ramblers that produce new canes from the base, cut old flowered canes right out from the rootstock and tie in new canes to replace them. In some ramblers, the new stems spring not from the base, but from some point along an old stem. With these, cut back the old cane to where the new stem is growing away. Tie it in place.

The tangling vigour of ramblers can make pruning difficult. Cut out old canes in sections rather than in one piece.

1 Prune ramblers after flowering or as soon as new canes sprout freely.

2 Cut flowered stems back to the base, or junction with a new cane.

▲ **Pruning ramblers** True ramblers like 'Albertine' have one glorious display, on canes produced the previous year. Flowered stems must be removed annually and replaced by new ones.

PRINCIPLES OF PRUNING

**Pruning is a means of maintaining shape
and vigour by removing weak, crossed, diseased or
dead growth from shrubs and trees.**

Large shrubs and climbers with straggly, untended or diseased branches look unattractive and often fail to produce a good show of flowers or fruits. Though regular pruning may not be essential for many popular shrubs, growth may be improved if light is let into the centre by cutting away old branches. Some shrubs will produce larger – though generally fewer – flowers if pruned each year. Dead or diseased branches should be cut away immediately to prevent the spread of infection.

Three tools are used in pruning: secateurs for removing shoots and small stems; long-handled loppers for large stems; and a pruning saw for large branches. A sharp knife may also be needed for trimming large wounds.

When shortening branches, cut just above an outward-facing bud or shoot. Cut diagonally, parallel with the angle of the bud or shoot. When removing entire branches, cut flush with the trunk or main branch. Then trim the raw area with a sharp knife and paint it with a proprietary wound-sealing compound. This will prevent disease spores entering the shrub through the wound.

Shrubs which have been hard pruned – especially when this is an annual operation – benefit from a 5cm (2in) thick mulch of garden compost or decayed manure after pruning, plus 55g (2oz/2tbsps) per sq m/yd of a general-purpose fertilizer such as Growmore.

Young shrubs, whether evergreen or deciduous, seldom require pruning except for the removal of crossing branches or damaged shoot tips. Frosted and dead shoots should be cut back to healthy wood in spring. Young conifers may occasionally fork, in which case the weaker of the two leading shoots should be cut out at the base in early or mid spring. Sometimes a young shrub produces a fast-growing main stem; cut this back to induce branching.

Dead or straggly wood

This method of pruning applies to most shrubs, and may involve only the removal of a small piece of damaged branch. It can be carried out at any time of year – after a long, straggly branch has developed, or after a storm when a branch has been damaged, for instance. Or, you might prefer to carry out a routine examination of all shrubs in the garden every spring.

Remove any dead or damaged wood, cutting back to a healthy, outward-facing shoot or bud. Then remove shoots that are particularly weak, cutting right back to a main branch. If any branches have grown straggly and unsightly, prune them by half to a strong shoot or bud facing outwards.

Do not remove any well-formed, healthy wood, or you are likely to cut off many of the buds that would produce flowers later.

Popular shrubs which need such regular pruning include camellias, rock roses, daphnes, euonymus, hebes, shrubby cinquefoils (*Potentilla*) and viburnums.

◀ **Thinning out** Fast-growing shrubs such as forsythias produce numerous shoots from the base every year. Unless removed, old stems will crowd the shrub and impede flowering.

Overgrown plants

Some shrubs, particularly evergreens, should not be pruned at all until, after many years, they become overgrown or bare at the base. Then, in spring, cut all the main branches down to within a few inches of the ground with a pruning saw or bow saw.

Mulch with garden compost or rotted manure and apply 55g (2oz or two tablespoons) per sq m/yd of a general-purpose fertilizer, such as Growmore. The shrub will not flower once again until the following year.

Popular shrubs that may require this treatment include the cherry laurels (*Prunus laurocerasus* and *P. lusitanica*), daisy bushes (*Olearia*), pernettyas and pieris, and the deciduous mock oranges (*Philadelphus*).

Flowers on new shoots

Some shrubs flower mainly on shoots that have grown in the current season. To restrict their size, or to encourage larger but fewer flowers, they can be pruned in spring, just as growth is beginning to show.

Cut all last year's shoots back to two or three buds or shoots from their base. Unless you want to remove a branch altogether, do not cut back into the older wood, as this might prevent new shoots from developing.

After pruning, mulch with a 5cm (2in) layer of garden compost or well-rotted manure and apply

REMOVING DEAD AND STRAGGLY WOOD

1 A mature shrub may look untidy when a few branches grow longer than the rest, or when random branches die out. Cosmetic pruning can be carried out at any time of year to improve the shrub's overall appearance.

2 First, cut out any dead or damaged wood and very weak stems right back to strong, healthy growth. Then shorten branches that have grown straggly and unsightly. Cut them back by half to an outward-facing bud or shoot.

55g (2oz or two tablespoons) per sq m/yd of a general-purpose fertilizer, such as Growmore.

Shrubs that can be pruned by this method include *Buddleia davidii*, caryopteris, ceratostigmas, coluteas, *Cytisus* × 'Porlock', fuchsias, indigos (*Indigofera*), deciduous Californian lilacs (*Ceanothus*), lippias, passion flowers (*Passiflora*), potato vine (*Solanum crispum*), santolina, Spanish broom (*Spartium*), most spiraeas and *Tamarix pentandra*.

Flowers on last year's shoots

Some shrubs flower on shoots grown the previous year. These can be pruned each year immediately they finish flowering – whether in spring, summer or winter. The pruning is aimed at keeping the shrub in bounds, or promoting larger but fewer flowers.

Cut each shoot that has borne flowers back to two or three shoots or buds from its junction with the parent stem. The new shoots will

CUTTING DOWN OVERGROWN SHRUBS

1 Regular pruning of most evergreens is unnecessary – they are generally slow-growing and neat in habit. Once they have outgrown their allocated space, however, they can be cut right down to encourage new compact growth.

2 Begin pruning an old, overgrown shrub by clearing away the top growth with long-handled loppers – an essential tool for pruning thick branches which are beyond the capacity of ordinary secateurs.

3 Once access to the base of the shrub is established, saw off all the branches close to the ground, leaving short stumps from which new shoots will appear. Paint large wounds with a proprietary sealing compound.

PRUNING SHRUBS THAT FLOWER ON NEW SHOOTS

1 *Buddleia davidii* is one of the most popular shrubs flowering on shoots grown in the current year. Pruned annually, it will produce large flower spikes.

2 In late winter or early spring, cut the previous year's shoots to two or three buds from their base. Unless you want to remove a branch entirely, do not cut back into the older, thicker, darker-coloured wood as this may not readily sprout new shoots. The pruned shrub will have a low framework of branches from which shoots will grow rapidly to produce flowers in summer.

produce flowers in the next season.

Buddleia alternifolia, ornamental brambles (*Rubus*), brooms (*Cytisus* except *C.* × 'Porlock'), deutzias, kerrias, *Prunus glandulosa*, *Prunus triloba*, *Spiraea* × *arguta* and weigelas can all be pruned by this method.

Removing old wood
Some shrubs, most notably the common *Hydrangea macrophylla*,

benefit from having some of the oldest growth removed almost at ground level each year.

In spring, cut out all three-year old stems, which are rough-looking and have sub-laterals as well as lateral branches. Make the cut within 2.5-5cm (1-2in) of the ground. You can also cut away some of the two-year old stems, which have lateral branches but no sub-laterals.

Other shrubs which benefit from this method of pruning when they have become overgrown include barberries (*Berberis*), beauty-bush (*Kolkwitzia amabilis*), clethras, cotoneasters, flowering currant (*Ribes sanguineum*), forsythias, genistas, shrubby cinquefoils (*Potentilla*), snowberries (*Symphoricarpos*), Himalayan honeysuckle (*Leycesteria*), abelias and weigelas.

PRUNING SHRUBS THAT FLOWER ON LAST YEAR'S SHOOTS

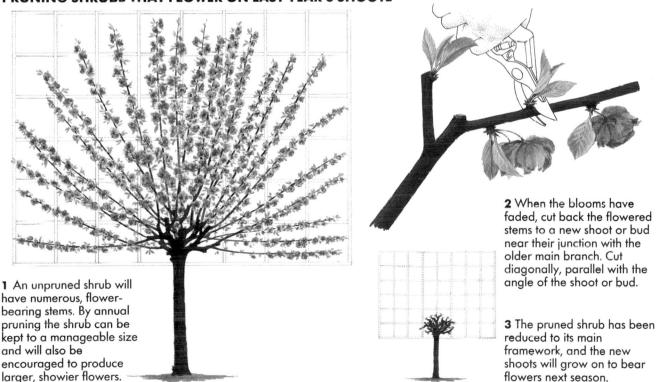

1 An unpruned shrub will have numerous, flower-bearing stems. By annual pruning the shrub can be kept to a manageable size and will also be encouraged to produce larger, showier flowers.

2 When the blooms have faded, cut back the flowered stems to a new shoot or bud near their junction with the older main branch. Cut diagonally, parallel with the angle of the shoot or bud.

3 The pruned shrub has been reduced to its main framework, and the new shoots will grow on to bear flowers next season.

CLEARING OLD WOOD FROM THE CENTRE

2 In spring, cut away almost to ground level the stems that are more than three years old — those with sub-laterals as well as laterals. Some two-year-old stems can also be removed.

1 An unpruned shrub, such as this *Hydrangea macrophylla*, has many old stems with lateral and sub-lateral branches which are overcrowding the space, and preventing light penetrating to the centre.

3 One-year-old, and some two-year-old, growths are left to flower in summer. The centre is now open to sun.

Controlling climbers

Leave most woody climbers unpruned until they get too large, then prune them after they have flowered. Prune non-flowering climbers in spring or summer.

Self-clinging climbers, such as ivies (*Hedera*) or climbing hydrangea (*Hydrangea petiolaris*), can be trimmed as necessary on the wall. Climbers that use supports, such as honeysuckles (*Lonicera japonica* and *L. periclymenum*) and clematis, should first be detached from the supports. Then remove all side growths, leaving just the main stems.

If the main stems look extremely old, cut them out and tie in their place some of the younger ones – either shoots growing from ground level or from low down on the old stems.

Other woody climbers requiring this method of pruning once established include actinidia vines, *Clematis armandii*, *Clematis macropetala*, *Clematis montana*, ornamental grape vine (*Vitis*), Russian vine (*Polygonum baldschuanicum*), trumpet creepers (*Campsis*) and Virginia creepers (*Parthenocissus*).

RESTRICTING CLIMBERS

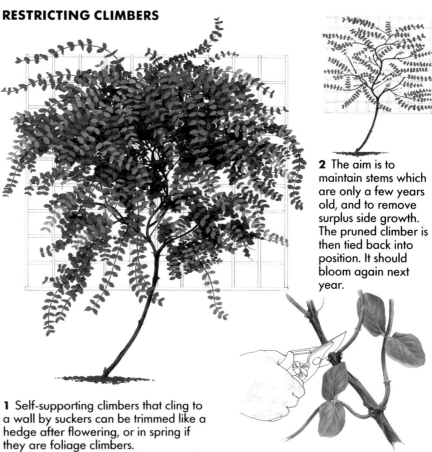

2 The aim is to maintain stems which are only a few years old, and to remove surplus side growth. The pruned climber is then tied back into position. It should bloom again next year.

1 Self-supporting climbers that cling to a wall by suckers can be trimmed like a hedge after flowering, or in spring if they are foliage climbers.

Climbing shrubs that are supported by trellis or wires should be removed carefully from the supports before pruning is begun, after flowering.

3 If the main stems are very old, cut them back to young shoots lower down near the base.

PRUNING POPULAR SHRUBS

Deciduous shrubs in particular need regular pruning to keep them healthy and well-balanced but their specific requirements vary.

Shrubs are grown for the beauty of their flowers or foliage, or for the quality of their fruit, their brightly coloured winter stems or branches, their characteristic shape or outline, or a combination of these. The aim of regular pruning is to make the most of these attributes; the timing depends on the shrub's flowering habits.

Not all shrubs need regular annual pruning – many, especially when grown as single specimens, require only occasional light trimming to maintain their shape. The necessity for regular pruning can also be reduced by care and forethought at the time of planting, by ascertaining the eventual size and shape of the shrub, and by allowing ample room for growth. Overcrowded shrubs require drastic pruning each year to prevent them becoming weakened and misshapen as they compete for the available root space, light, food and water.

The health and vigour of a shrub is maintained by correct pruning. It is important to remove all dead or damaged wood immediately it is noticed. The longer dead wood is allowed to remain on a shrub, the greater is the risk of disease spores entering it, multiplying and eventually spreading to healthy tissue. In severe cases, extensive damage and even death of the whole shrub may occur. Branches that cross or rub against one another are also a potential source of damage, and should be cut away before diseases can enter through the wounds.

Thin, weak growths are of little use, especially if they are produced in the centre of a bush, where they are starved of light and air. Well-ripened branches stand up better to severe weather and to disease. Consequently, the purpose of pruning is also to keep the centre of a shrub fairly open so as to allow light and air to circulate freely round the branches.

Make pruning cuts cleanly, leaving no ragged edges, torn bark, or bruising and crushing of the stems, since this results in the tissues dying. The pruning will heal more rapidly if the cut is made nearly horizontally across a branch. As the buds are the only points from which further growth can develop along a stem, make pruning cuts as close as possible to a bud without damaging it, starting the cut on the side opposite to the bud and finishing immediately above it so that the cut face slopes downwards away from the bud. This ensures that water runs off the cut without rotting the bud.

Cut unwanted or damaged shoots flush with the main stem from which they arise – on no account leave a short length of branch, or snag, as this will almost certainly die back or produce unsightly clusters of short stems. Trim off the edges of any large pruning cuts using a sharp knife. Painting the cut surface with a bituminous wound-sealing paint may also prevent subsequent disease infection, but this is less important than with pruned or lopped trees.

Coloured leaved and variegated shrub varieties, such as *Spiraea × bumalda* 'Goldflame', sometimes produce shoots which lack the characteristic colour – golden-leaved varieties in particular tend to produce a few all-green shoots from time to time. These must be removed as soon as they appear, since they are frequently more vigorous than the coloured shoots and will ruin the effect of the plant. Cut out the rogue branch completely.

◀ **Winter stems** Many willows and dogwoods are grown for their brightly coloured bare stems in winter. As on this scarlet willow, coloration is most prominent on young stems; hard prune in alternate years for new growth.

Buddleia alternifolia

A graceful shrub with long, weeping branches, which produces lavender-blue flower sprays on the previous year's shoots.

As soon as the blooms fade, cut the flowered stems back to strong new shoots. On young plants keep most of the older wood for the first few years to build up a good framework. As the shrub ages, cut back harder.

Caryopteris x clandonensis

A bushy, thin-stemmed shrub with small bright blue flowers on shoots of the current year. It becomes straggly unless pruned each spring.

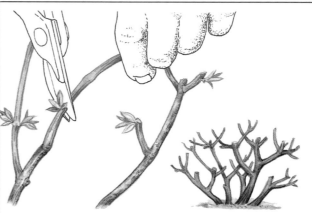

In late winter or early spring, cut all of the previous year's shoots back to new shoots about 2.5cm (1in) from the old wood. Remove all dead, weak and straggly or overcrowded shoots from the base.

Ceanothus species and hybrids

Evergreen Californian lilacs need no regular pruning, but deciduous types should be pruned each spring.

In mid spring, cut back the previous year's shoots of all deciduous *Ceanothus* species, varieties and hybrids to two or three pairs of buds from the base. On young plants, prune more lightly until a strong framework has built up.

With the evergreen Californian lilacs, merely shorten leggy, untidy stems by about half after flowering; cut back late-flowering types the following spring.

Ceratostigma willmottianum

Shrubby Chinese plumbago does not need regular pruning, but can be constrained by severe pruning in spring.

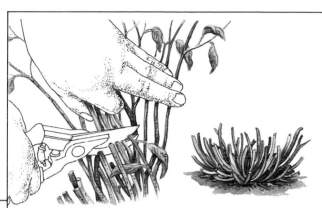

Overgrown plants can be cut back to within 2.5-7.5cm (2-3in) of the ground in early to mid spring. Cut all the stems, both old and new. The new shoots that spring up will flower in the autumn.

The related *Ceratostigma plumbaginoides* dies down each winter and so needs no pruning.

Chaenomeles species and hybrids

Free-standing Japanese quinces (japonicas) need no regular pruning, but wall-trained plants must be kept within bounds.

When it is grown against a wall or fence, tie in the leaders of Japanese quinces each year until the space is completely filled. In mid to late spring after the flowers have faded, pinch out or cut back all the young shoots not wanted for training to four or five leaves from the older wood.

Cornus alba and *C. stolonifera* varieties

These dogwoods are grown chiefly for their coloured stems in autumn and winter; young shoots produce the best effects.

In early spring, hard prune the previous year's shoots, cutting back to a few inches from the base. To renovate an old bush, remove some stems completely and cut strong shoots back to a framework 30cm (1ft) high.

Cytisus species and hybrids

Most garden types of broom flower on shoots of the previous year. Prune annually to prevent them becoming leggy.

Pruning must be started early in the plant's life, before the main branches become old. In summer, after flowering has finished, remove the growths that bore flowers, cutting back to young shoots. Never prune old wood, as new growth rarely sprouts.

Deutzia species and hybrids

Left unpruned, deutzias will become dense and untidy, with progressively fewer flowers, so prune annually in mid summer.

After the flowers fade, thin weak stems out completely at ground level in order to admit light and air into the centre. Cut the stems which have flowered back to a point low down where new shoots are developing.

Forsythia species and hybrids

Any sparse-flowering wood on forsythias should be replaced regularly. They produce new branches from ground level.

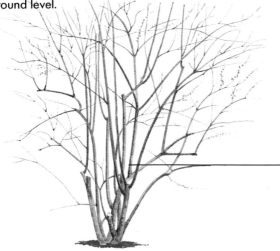

Once the shrub is 3 years old take out old branches every year or two after flowering. On a neglected bush (shown), cut out half of the old stems to encourage new shoots, then cut the rest next year.

Fuchsia magellanica

Though the rootstocks of this attractive shrub are hardy, top growth often dies back to near ground level each winter.

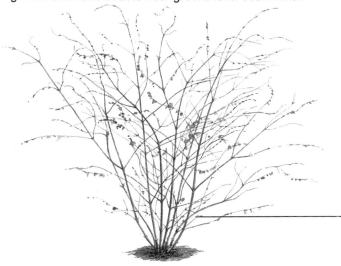

Where growth is killed, buds appear from near soil level in spring. At this time, prune dead shoots to just above a new bud. When branches survive, prune laterals to one or two buds from their base.

Hypericum calycinum

Rose of Sharon is usually grown as a low ground cover. Pruning is made quicker and easier by using garden shears.

In very late winter or early spring, cut the old shoots back to within 5-7.5cm (2-3in) of the base. At the same time, clear away dead leaves and garden debris from between the twiggy stems. Young shoots will quickly develop and flower in summer.

Hypericum **shrubby species and hybrids**

Prune tall-growing hypericums, such as *Hypericum* 'Hidcote', in early spring to remove dead and spindly wood.

Cut back dense or straggly wood to where young shoots are appearing. They will form a new framework, but won't give their best show of flowers until the next year. In future years, shorten all strong branches.

Indigofera species

With shrubby indigo, winter frosts may do the pruning for you; if not, they can be cut hard back each spring.

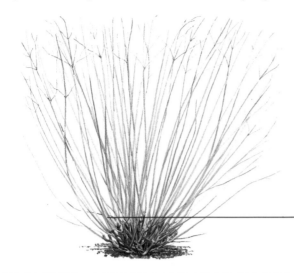

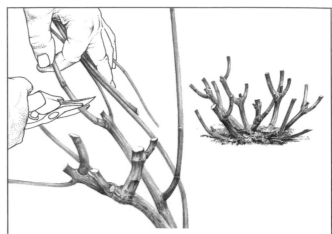

If shoots are killed down to ground level in winter, simply remove the dead wood in late winter or early spring. Cut back living stems almost to their junction with older wood. New shoots flower the same year.

Jasminum nudiflorum

If left to itself, winter jasmine soon becomes a dense and unsightly tangle of growths with relatively few flowers.

In early spring, cut back the shoots that have flowered to two or three buds from their junction with the main branches. Cut away all dead and weak growths to allow air to circulate. With white jasmine (*Jasminum officinale*) just remove any crowded or dead stems.

Kerria japonica

Jew's mallow produces new shoots from ground level each year, which flower the next season and then often die back.

Remove the old flowered stems when the flowers fade in late spring or early summer. Cut right back to near the ground or, on stronger stems, to where healthy new shoots are developing.

Lavandula angustifolia

Without pruning, lavender becomes leggy and bare-stemmed, so is best trimmed annually with secateurs or garden shears.

In early to mid spring, cut down the dead flower spikes plus about 2.5cm (1in) of top growth. Do not cut into old wood as die-back can result. To tidy plants for winter, old flowers can be cut off in autumn.

Leycesteria formosa

This shrub produces strong shoots from the base which flower the same year, and gives a display of pea-green winter stems.

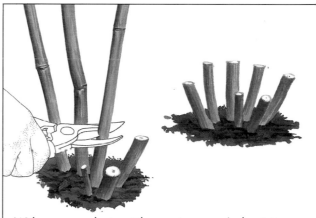

With a young plant, cut the previous year's shoots to within two or three buds of the base in early spring. With an old, neglected plant, use long-handled loppers to cut the oldest wood down to ground level.

Lippia citriodora

Lippias may develop a permanent woody framework in mild areas, but branches often die back in winter.

Shorten main branches which survive the winter to within 30cm (1ft) of the central stem in late spring. Cut back side-shoots to within 5-7.5cm (2-3in) of the main branches. Prune frost-killed stems back to healthy buds.

Philadelphus species and hybrids

Old mock orange plants invariably become dense and untidy, so prune them after flowering in mid summer.

Remove all dead and weak growth completely. Then cut back old stems to where young shoots are growing. Very old branches can be cut right down to ground level, so that none are more than five years old.

Rhus species and varieties

The ferny leaves of sumachs turn fiery orange in autumn, but the best display is achieved only by regular pruning.

In late winter, cut the previous year's growths back to within 10cm (4in) of the old wood. By this method, a low, well-structured framework will gradually be built up, bearing extra-large and attractive leaves.

Ribes sanguineum

If a flowering currant becomes too large it can be cut hard back immediately after flowering, generally in mid spring.

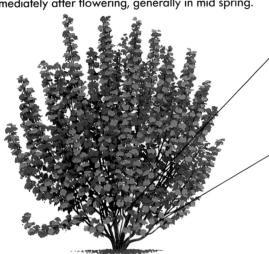

Cut the old stems hard back to live buds near the ground (*top left*). Last year's shoots need only be shortened to strong shoots lower down (*above left*). In future years, remove one-third of the older stems.

Rubus species and hybrids

Rubus cockburnianus is grown for its white winter stems. Those remaining after pruning will flower the next summer.

In mid summer, cut out the stems that have flowered. Other species can be pruned in the same way, either after flowering or after fruiting. *R. × tridel* and *R. deliciosus,* however, need a framework of older wood.

Salix alba varieties

Varieties of the white willow are often grown for their winter display of brightly coloured young stems.

To produce a fresh crop of stems cut them all back almost to their base every second year in late winter, as the buds are breaking. Or, cut half the stems every year. Red or yellow shoots will sprout from the stumps.

Sambucus species and varieties

Elders grown for their foliage (not flowers or fruits) can be cut hard back to produce large, colourful young leaves.

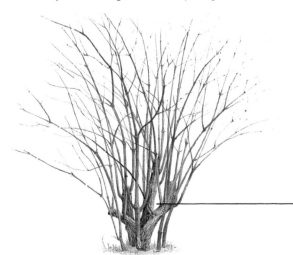

In early to mid winter, cut all stems to a few centimetres from the ground if possible; otherwise to 5-7.5cm (2-3in) from their base. Cut out weak shoots completely. Use a pruning saw for thicker shoots.

Santolina species and varieties

All santolinas tend to become straggly with age and to lose their compact shape unless they are pruned annually.

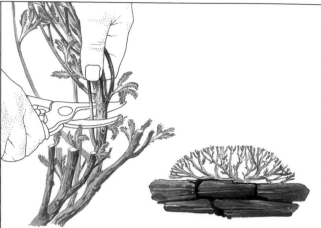

Prune hard in mid spring, cutting each long growth back to where clusters of young shoots appear near the base. Flowers will form on the young shoots. Clip hedging plants in spring and summer.

Sorbaria species

Most species of sorbaria produce many suckers, which have to be removed to keep the plant within bounds.

Between early and late winter, prune all stems back hard — to within 10-23cm (4-9in) of the base. Vigorous new shoots will develop quickly and produce larger leaves and flower heads.

Spartium junceum

Old Spanish brooms can become very dense and cluttered, but annual pruning helps form a more compact plant.

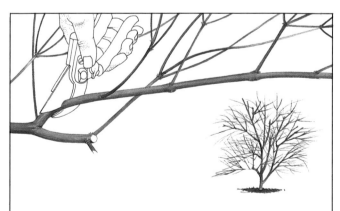

Renovate old plants in early spring by cutting hard back into old wood — as far back as you wish. In later years, prune the previous season's growths to within 2.5cm (1in) of the older wood. Very young plants should have the previous year's growth cut by half.

Spiraea × arguta

Some spiraeas, including *S. × arguta* and *S. thunbergii,* produce flowers on stems that grew the previous year.

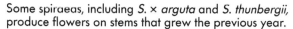

Renovate an old plant after the flowers fade, usually in late spring. Cut back old stems to where younger shoots are growing (*top left*). On all plants, cut away the part of the stem which has flowered (*above left*).

Spiraea japonica

Other spiraeas, including *S. japonica* and *S. × bumalda,* flower on the current year's shoots.

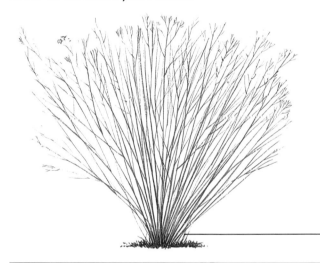

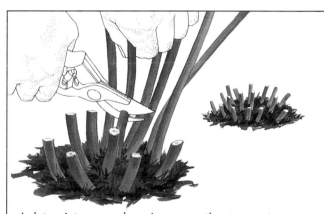

In late winter or early spring, prune the strongest stems to within 5-7.5cm (2-3in) of the ground. Cut out all weak stems completely. New shoots will spring up to flower in mid to late summer. Dead-head. Remove shoots with all-green leaves from coloured varieties.

Stephanandra tanakae

This shrub is grown for its autumn leaves and coloured winter stems. Pruning lets in light and produces bright new stems.

After the plant has flowered in early or mid summer, cut the flowered stems down to strong young shoots sprouting lower down the stem, or right down to the ground. Remove weak stems completely.

Tamarix species

In good conditions, tamarisks may develop into straggly, top-heavy shrubs, so need regular pruning.

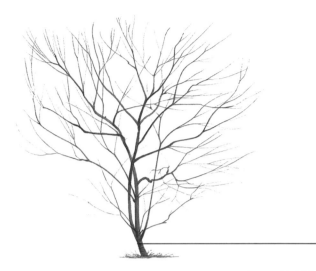

Prune summer-flowering species (*T. pentandra* and *T. ramosissima*) in late winter. Cut last year's growths to 5cm (2in) from the old wood. On an old, overgrown plant, cut strong stems to 5cm (2in) from their base and remove dead, weak and straggly shoots. Prune spring-flowering species (*T. tetrandra* and *T. parviflora*) after flowers fade. Shorten lax stems; remove weak ones.

Weigela florida and hybrids

Weigelas can quickly become dense and crowded, with fewer flowers, so prune them annually after flowering in summer.

Prune back flowered stems where young shoots are developing lower down. Cut out dead and weak growths. With an old, neglected plant, the oldest branches can be cut down nearly to the ground.

Wisteria species and varieties

In summer, the long leaders of wisterias must be trained in the direction you want this vigorous wall shrub to spread.

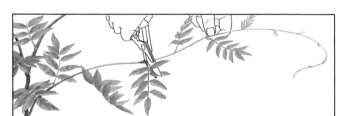

To encourage flowering spurs, cut back unwanted growths to 15-30cm (6-12in) from their base. In winter, shorten them further — to two or three buds from their base. Or, to provide more flower buds, work over the plant every few weeks throughout summer, pinching back all growths not needed for extending the coverage. Pinch the shoots back to 10cm (4in), and later pinch back any extension growth to two leaves — each shoot may be pinched back three times during the season. No winter pruning is then needed.

TREE SURGERY

**In general, ornamental trees require no regular
pruning, but they may become too large or get damaged
during a storm and need remedial attention.**

Left alone, most trees normally develop into a well-proportioned shape which is characteristic of the particular species. However, in certain circumstances it may be desirable to modify their shape or size by pruning. A tree growing in a confined space, for example, may become unbalanced. One which is close to a house may have to be restricted to prevent structural damage and to let in more light.

There are several other reasons for pruning a tree – for instance, it is necessary to tidy up broken branches after a storm to restore the tree's attractive appearance and to prevent fungal diseases taking a hold in the wounds.

On shallow, rocky soils tall trees may become unstable and need to be kept in check. Trees which have been planted too close together often look better if they are thinned out as they mature, either by felling some of them or by removing a few selected branches from each.

Some gardeners also like to encourage artificial growth habits in their trees – a form of topiary on a large scale – perhaps to make an otherwise rather ordinary tree into a real eye-catcher, or to establish a very formal atmosphere in the garden.

A mature tree won't be harmed by the sudden loss of an individual limb and the tree's energy will be diverted to branches elsewhere. If a branch has to come off for whatever reason – it may simply be growing at an awkward angle – don't be afraid of removing it. However, the important thing is to cut it right back to the point where it joins the trunk and not to leave a stump which will later die off and encourage disease.

Legal requirements

Before attempting *any* pruning or felling of trees – regardless of whether they are on private property – check with your local authority that a Tree Preservation Order is not imposed on them. Also ensure that you are not in a registered conservation area. In both cases, there are strict restrictions on tree surgery and written notice and authorization must be exchanged between yourself and the appropriate authority before work commences. Always seek advice – there are heavy penalties for illegal tree surgery.

The correct tools

The branches and trunks of living trees consist of wood and bark, the density and hardness of which varies from species to species. Even when trees are dormant in winter, this wood is relatively moist and has different physical properties from the dried timber used in carpentry.

For this reason, carpentry saws are not suitable for living tree surgery of any kind – their teeth are too fine and close-set and soon get clogged with damp sawdust, making for unnecessarily strenuous work.

Small branches can be trimmed with secateurs, but anything thicker than a finger should

◄ **Winter pruning** A long-armed tree pruner is invaluable for trimming high branches without the need for a ladder. The secateur-like cutting head can be used to remove surplus twigs from mature fruit trees. This will divert the tree's energies into producing fruiting spurs.

TREE PRUNING HAND TOOLS

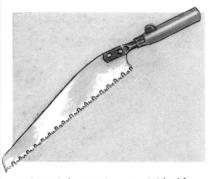

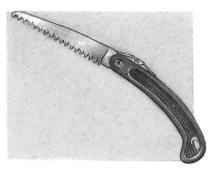

▲ **A straight pruning saw** is ideal for cutting branches 2.5-13cm (1-5in) thick. The teeth cut on the backward stroke — the strongest stroke when you are working at shoulder height. This saw has an interchangeable long or short handle.

▲ **A folding pruning saw** is more portable than any other type and is safer when not in use — the teeth are shielded inside the handle when the saw is folded in half. The blade is short and suitable for 2.5-7.5cm (1-3in) diameter branches.

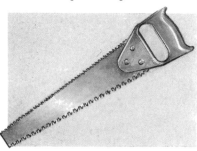

▲ **A double-edged pruning saw** can be used for both coarse and fine work, depending on which edge you use. Take care not to slice wanted branches with the unused edge. The blade is long and will cut quite large branches.

▲ **A Grecian pruning saw** has a slender, curved blade. This shape affords easier access to branches which are in confined spaces and the teeth cut deeply into the wood on the backward stroke with relatively little effort.

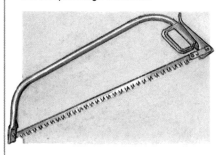

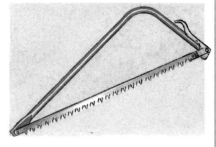

▲ **A bow saw** is the best tool for cutting trunks, boughs and felled logs. The teeth are coarse and cut on both the forward and backward strokes. The bow-shaped handle gives the blade sufficient clearance to cut about 20cm (8in) deep.

▲ **A triangular bow saw** serves the same purpose as an ordinary bow saw, but the pointed nose allows better access to closely packed branches. It is less suitable for cutting trunks, boughs or logs over 13cm (5in) in diameter.

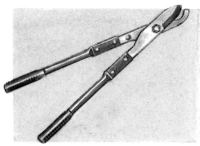

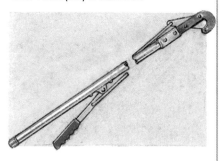

▲ **Long-handled loppers** are ideal for cutting branches which are too large or tough for secateurs, but not large enough to warrant using a saw. The handles are about 30-45cm (1-1½ft) long, providing good leverage on the blades.

▲ **Long-arm tree pruners** are used to cut high branches up to 2.5cm (1in) in diameter without the need to use a ladder. Some have a single arm about 1.8m (6ft) long; others have extension arms totalling 3.6m (12ft).

be cut with long-handled loppers, a pruning saw or a bow saw.

If you are experienced in their use, chain saws can provide a much quicker and less laborious solution to tree pruning and felling, but they are far too dangerous for use by a casual, inexperienced gardener. In fact, no garden tree is too large to be dealt with using hand tools alone.

To gain access to the upper branches of a large tree you will need a sturdy ladder. For safety, tie the top of the ladder to the tree with rope before starting work. Get someone to stand on the bottom rung of the ladder until you have secured the top.

Aluminium alloy ladders are lighter to carry around the garden, and those with serrated rungs provide extra protection against slipping if you are wearing muddy shoes or boots.

Look out for overhead electricity supply or telephone cables when manoeuvring a ladder around a tree, especially if the ladder is made of metal.

Dealing with branches

As with all garden plants, dead, diseased or damaged branches must be removed from trees as soon as they are spotted. Failure to do this can result in further unsightly dieback or even the death of the entire tree. Any branch which crosses and rubs against another when the wind blows should also be removed, since damaged bark can lead to cankers and other forms of decay.

To gain more access under a tree and to allow more sunlight to reach plants growing below it, remove some of the lower branches back to the main trunk or to a large bough. If you wish to reduce the overall weight of the tree's crown to minimize the chance of storm damage, remove some of the upper branches. This will also reduce the amount of shade cast by the tree.

Remove heavy branches in two pieces, taking the weight off the tip before attempting to make the final cut close to the trunk. The most important reason for doing this is to prevent the possibility of the bark tearing away from the main trunk as the branch falls — such a wound will take a long time to heal and may become infected. To reduce further the chance of the bark tearing, make the first cut to

REMOVING A TREE BRANCH

1 Detach the bulk of the branch about 45cm (1½ft) from the main trunk or bough. Make the first cut on the underside of the branch (*inset*), then cut down into the first cut to sever the branch. This will ensure that the bark which is to remain is not torn as the branch falls.

2 Remove the stump in the same way, first undercutting it, then sawing down into the first cut. Saw flush with the main trunk, but not so close that you make an excessively broad wound in the remaining bark. The inset illustration shows how the bark could tear if you did not undercut the branch first.

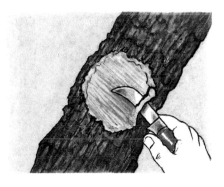

3 Using a sharp pruning knife or penknife, pare away the surface and edges of the cut to make it perfectly smooth – rough wounds left by a coarse-toothed saw accumulate fungal spores and are more likely to rot. Either hold the knife with both hands or keep your free hand away from the blade.

4 Paint the cut surface with a proprietary bituminous wound sealer within minutes of completing step 3. This will shield the growing wood from disease infection and provide cosmetic cover for the scarred tree. With a very large wound, it may be better to leave the centre unpainted to let it breathe.

DEALING WITH SUCKERS

1 Basal suckers may sprout from the rootstock of grafted trees. If not removed, they could outgrow the tree and look unsightly. Wearing gloves, simply tear them away from the rootstock. Don't use secateurs or pruners as you will leave buds beneath the soil which will regrow.

2 Healed-over pruning wounds may sprout tufts of thin shoots, known as water or epicormic shoots. Apart from looking unsightly, these tap the supply of water and nutrients to the tree's crown and weaken its growth. Using secateurs, cut them away every autumn to late winter.

all branches on the underside, then saw down into the first cut to complete the job.

There is some controversy regarding the use of wound sealing paints on severed branches. The exposed sapwood will be prone to disease infection until a callus has grown over it and a coating of paint will reduce this risk. But paint can also slow down the rate at which the callus grows.

On balance, it is probably best to coat all cuts larger than 2.5cm (1in) in diameter with a proprietary bituminous wound sealer as soon as possible, preferably within minutes of cutting. Painting a wound of an hour or more in age could seal in air-borne fungal spores which have already settled. On large wounds, it is better to paint just the outer 2.5cm (1in) of the surface to seal the living tissues, leaving the inner dead tissue completely bare.

Household paint can be used to seal pruning cuts, but may not be fully effective, especially in hot weather when the wood expands – unlike bituminous types, these paints aren't very elastic once dry and soon crack or flake.

Boughs and trunks

If it is necessary to cut the tree's main support framework of boughs or trunk, special care must be taken. Such surgery may be for cosmetic purposes or to eradicate diseased and insecure wood.

Heartwood at the centre of a trunk or bough can rot before any outward symptoms are evident, and this seriously weakens the tree – it can fall during a gale and damage surrounding property. If large, flattish, fan-shaped fungal growths, known as bracket fungi, appear on the bark this is a sure sign that internal rotting is at an advanced stage and the bough or trunk must be felled.

Root pruning

Trees often have substantial roots which extend beyond the spread of the top growth. These can cause damage to the foundations of buildings and walls, and to paths and drains. The larger the root system grows the more vigorous is the top growth, and this may be undesirable in a small garden.

To limit the tree's development of spreading branches and its ever-increasing height, winter root pruning is a useful practice.

THE ART OF POLLARDING

1 Pollarding is a special pruning technique adopted either as a means of reducing the size of the crown of a mature tree, or to develop an unusual, often formal growth shape. The tree should have more or less reached its ultimate required height before pollarding begins in winter.

2 Using a bow saw, lop the entire crown of the tree, leaving just short stumps with lots of dormant growth buds. Or cut out selected branches and reduce the others to desired lengths or shapes — like bonsai, pollarding techniques are largely a matter of taste. Coat all the cuts with a wound-sealer.

3 In spring, tufts of new shoots will grow from the cuts. These may have colourful bark and will bear lush foliage. In one to three years, or as soon as the new shoots have outgrown the desired space, prune back to the original wounds. After repeated pollarding, the stumps become gnarled.

Dig out a trench around the tree, about 1.5m (5ft) from the trunk, putting the soil to one side. Try not to damage too many small roots with your spade, but aim to expose all the thickest outward-growing roots. Using a pruning saw, sever only the largest roots. It is not necessary to dig up the cut ends, unless they are causing a nuisance.

Finally, refill the trench with the original soil and firm it well. With a large tree it is best to sever the roots on one side of the trunk one year and those on the other side the next year, otherwise growth will be seriously weakened and dieback may occur.

Pollarding

Repeated severe lopping of a tree's crown, cutting back to the established main trunk or to main branches, is known as pollarding. The effect is to produce a single tight ball of leafy growth at the top of the tall trunk or lots of tufts of fresh growth along a framework of gnarled branches.

Pollarded trees have a unique, almost grotesque appearance and can be used to great effect in a formal garden. This type of pruning is also useful where trees are planted close to a building and a broad-spreading crown would occupy too much space. Street trees are frequently pollarded to allow the free passage of traffic beneath their crowns.

Lime trees (*Tilia*) are favourite subjects for pollarding, since they rapidly regenerate a head of lush green leafy growth after being cut back. Coloured-stemmed varieties of the white willow — *Salix alba* 'Britzensis' (scarlet) and *S. a.* 'Vitellina' (bright yellow) — produce their brightest bark when pollarded annually.

FELLING A SMALL TREE

1 Take heed of the legal note on page 151. Start by tying a sturdy rope to the crown of the tree. Get someone to maintain a firm pull on the rope in the required direction of fall, standing beyond the danger zone — the tree will fall towards your helper. Make the first cut a metre (3ft) or so up on the side facing your helper, sawing horizontally one-third through the trunk.

2 Saw out a wedge of wood by cutting downwards at about 30-45° to the horizontal into the back of first cut. At this point, the tree should still stand securely on its own, but your helper must maintain a firm grip on the rope. Ensure that the area all round the tree is clear of people or valued possessions — keep young children and pets safely indoors from this point onwards.

3 Make the final cut on the side behind the direction of fall. Saw downwards at an angle of about 30° to the horizontal towards the inner edge of the wedge cavity. As the tree loses its balance it will fall into the wedge. As soon as you detect movement, step clear and allow your helper to guide the falling tree. Having cleared the debris, sever the roots and lever out the stump.

Garden tools and safety

The old saying, 'a craftsman is only as good as his tools', applies as much to gardening as to any other activity. Having the right tools for the job, keeping them in good condition and using them correctly can mean the difference between a quick, easily accomplished task and an arduous one, inefficiently done. Top quality, stainless steel tools, well cared for, can last for years, if not a lifetime, and buying the best tools you can afford is more satisfying and economical, in the long run than buying a series of cheap but short-lived ones.

Before buying tools, check that the handles are comfortable, and that large tools suit your size and strength; so-called 'lady's spades', for example, hold smaller, lighter loads. Clean tools after every use, oil metal parts occasionally, especially before winter storage, and keep tools somewhere clean, dry and secure.

Common sense dictates that sharp tools and all power tools should be used with care. Thoughtless acts, such as filling a petrol mower with the engine running or cobbling together electrical extension leads, can cause accidents.

Keep tools and equipment out of reach of children, and garden chemicals, especially herbicides and pesticides, away from both children and pets. Remember that young children can climb on one object to reach another. Make sure chemicals are clearly labelled and in their original containers, never in lemonade or other bottles. Safety with chemicals extends beyond the garden, too. Never flush unwanted chemicals down the drain, but take them to the council depot instead.

Tools of the trade The right tools for the right job take the backache out of gardening.

GARDEN TOOLS & EQUIPMENT

A multitude of hand and power tools are on offer as labour-saving devices. Some are essential, others may be a waste of money and time.

Certain tools are essential for all gardening jobs; others are only needed for more specialised tasks. Many gadgets are only useful on rare occasions, and it is inadvisable to invest in heavy-duty equipment for the average garden (it can be hired more cheaply on a daily basis).

Buying a small number of traditional good-quality tools which will last a lifetime is better value for money than spending your entire budget on so-called 'bargain' products which are often inferior in use and may break down or wear out quickly.

Hand tools

Almost every gardener will need a spade, fork, rake, hoe and trowel, and a pair of secateurs in his basic toolkit. If a lawn forms a large part of the garden, a lawn rake, half-moon edging iron, edging and lawn shears will be useful in addition to the essential mower. Hand shears will be needed for trimming a hedge (mechanical trimmers are a more expensive alternative or addition).

Well-known brand names are the safest buys, but use your own judgement to decide whether a particular product is suitable for your needs. Handle the tool before you buy it, checking for weight, strength and comfort of handling – one brand or model may be ideal for a tall or very strong person while another may be better for a short or less fit person. Secateurs, in particular, must feel comfortable in your palm – there are many different grip sizes and shapes to choose from and inappropriate ones will give you blisters after prolonged use.

Spades and garden forks usually have carbon steel heads and are given a coat of paint to protect them from rusting initially. Once the paint wears off, regular wiping with an oily rag will keep the head in good order. Stainless steel and chromium plated types are available at extra cost, which, provided the surface is not scratched unduly, will maintain their shine for many years – polished surfaces are easier to push into the soil than pitted, rusty ones.

Tool handles may be metal or wooden. Both are durable and should be strong enough for normal garden use. Spade and fork handles are invariably plastic nowadays and can be replaced if necessary. Plastic is strong, smooth to the touch and has a long life, so is not used simply for cheapness. Make sure that the handle is fixed securely to the shaft and that the shaft is fixed securely to the head. The rivets or fixing screws must be flush with the surface and should feel smooth to the touch.

Looking after tools

Clean thoroughly all tools after use – never put them away caked with mud or grass clippings. Wipe metal surfaces with an oily rag, and treat bare wood with linseed

◄ **Heavy-duty secateurs** Also known as loppers, long-handled secateurs are useful for pruning thick-stemmed, woody shrubs and small trees. The handles provide leverage and allow access to the centre of a dense plant. Use a bow saw for larger branches.

oil from time to time. Don't store tools on a concrete floor – they will become damp and rust. Hang them by their handles on hooks secured to the shed wall. Treat wooden handles with respect – splintered handles are dangerous.

Sharpen the blades of secateurs and shears regularly – blunt blades make the cutting action tiring and produce ragged cuts which in turn can lead to plants becoming diseased.

Special hand tools

If age or physical fitness are not on your side – or if you have a disability – certain gardening jobs may be difficult or impossible. There are, however, several hand tools on the market which can either make a particular job more manageable or render an otherwise impossible one within your capability. The following information refers only to normal production tools, not to specially adapted tools made to order for an individual handicap.

Star-wheeled cultivators can be used to cultivate light soils. They consist of star-shaped wheels mounted on a frame which incorporates a hoe blade. The unit is mounted on a long handle and is pushed over the soil surface, producing a fine tilth while at the same time cutting down small weeds. Depth of cultivation is regulated by the angle at which the handle is held. This implement requires the use of one hand only.

Two-handled spades make soil lifting easier. A second D-shaped handle is mounted mid-way down the shaft allowing you to pull the spade head upwards from a standing or sitting position rather than having to bend down to reach the base of the shaft.

Long-handled grabbers consist of a pair of boards fixed to the ends of two long handles, mounted together on a scissor-like hinge. They can be used to gather up garden debris without bending.

► **Digging made easy** A lever-action spade eliminates the need for bending and powerful muscles when you are digging. A pedal attached to the base of the spade shaft makes it easier to push the blade into the soil. The shaft is mounted to the blade via a pivot – by pulling backwards on the handle, soil is thrown forwards automatically. A fork head can be fitted in place of a spade.

Long-handled weeders are useful for extracting weeds from inaccessible places and eliminate the need for bending. Unlike ordinary hoes, these devices combine a hand-operated grabber which will pick up the weeds once loosened from the soil.

Long-handled loppers are a powerful type of secateur able to cut branches up to about 30mm (1¼in) in diameter. The handles are generally 45 or 55cm (18 or 22in) long, allowing you to reach into the centre of the plant.

Long-arm tree pruners give easy access to tree branches. The arm may be in one piece or consist of three lock-together sections for convenient storage. A cutting head at one end is operated via a steel rod from a hand lever at the other end. Long-arm fruit pickers are a modification of this tool –

they incorporate a small bag under the cutting head into which the cut fruit falls.

Bow saws provide the best means of cutting large branches or trunks. A replaceable blade is tensioned across a broad, bow-shaped handle, giving clearance to cut trunks up to 30cm (1ft) across.

Grass hooks, scythes and sickles consisting of variously shaped blades attached to short or long handles, are useful for cutting down long, rough grass and weeds.

Turfing irons consist of a large rounded blade attached to a long handle, angled appropriately to undercut and lift lawn turf.

Before buying a special tool of any kind, consider whether it will have enough use to warrant its cost. You may be able to improvise with other tools or it may be cheaper to hire a specialist tool.

Tools for the disabled

Special tools and equipment are available for disabled gardeners, including the Easy-kneeler stool with sturdy handles to facilitate movement to and from a kneeling position, and barrows designed for hitching on to wheelchairs. Lightweight aluminium hand tools are moulded in one piece, with grips for finger and thumb.

Power tools

Garden power tools used to mean just lawnmowers and chainsaws. In recent years, though, there has been an expansion of powered labour-saving appliances that promise to simplify almost the whole range of gardening chores.

Like lawnmowers, the advantage of the new power tools over traditional hand tools is the speed and ease with which they perform strenuous, time-consuming tasks.

An example of this is the power weeder designed to limit the back-breaking work of weeding. The tool – a long rod with a control-handle linked to a powered weeding device – allows you to stand comfortably upright while removing weeds.

However, the power weeder also illustrates the limitations of some power tools. The discomfort of kneeling down and probing for a weed's roots is banished – along with the thoroughness of doing it by hand. The tool rips a weed out of the ground, often snapping off the roots, which may regrow.

Power supplies

The power source for all garden tools is usually either petrol or electricity. Electric tools are generally cheaper and are useful in small to average-sized gardens; the need for power cables restricts their range. Effective cordless models for all but the most menial tasks are still beyond the grasp of manufacturers.

Petrol-driven tools mostly have higher specifications, a higher price-tag, and are aimed at larger gardens and professional users.

The initial higher cost of a petrol-driven tool should be judged against its longer working life. Manufacturers admit that generally petrol appliances last 10-15 years while equivalent electric models last 5-10 years.

Electric models may also require you to buy both an extension lead to bring parts of your garden

within reach and a residual current circuit breaker to protect against electric shock. Circuit breakers are highly recommended for anyone using electric power tools – death or injury caused by electrocution from a power garden tool are all too common. A circuit breaker will largely remove this threat. Even so, electric power tools should never be used in rainy or very damp weather.

Be warned that petrol tools are more mechanically complex so bills for parts and labour can be heavier than for those that run on electricity. What's more, electric models are easier to start and you won't need to refill the fuel tank.

Weight is another factor worth considering. Electric models tend to be constructed mostly of light-weight, high-density plastic that makes them easy to manage.

Petrol models have internal

▲ Mechanical lawn edgers
Nylon-line trimmers or 'shimmers' are useful if expensive gadgets suitable for trimming lawn edges and cutting grass round and among trees.

combustion engines, petrol tanks, and metal parts to protect against the corrosive petrol; as a result they weigh much more. If the tool you intend to buy has to be lifted around or, like hedgetrimmers or chainsaws, held in the air for several minutes at a time, make sure you will be able to control safely the extra weight a petrol engine involves.

Most manufacturers recognize the need for petrol models to be easily manageable – petrol nylon-line trimmers, for example, are specially balanced to counteract the engine weight which would otherwise make them unwieldy.

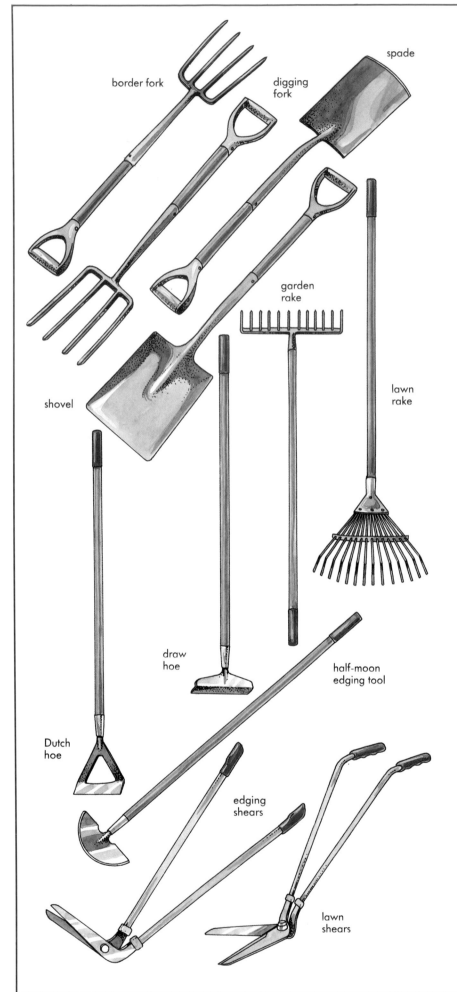

LONG-HANDLED TOOLS

Garden forks are sold under a variety of names, depending on their size — 'digging', 'border', 'lady's', for instance — but these names do not correspond to standard specifications. Forks are used primarily for breaking up and preparing the soil prior to planting or sowing, but are useful also for moving debris or compost, and for general cultivation and lawn aeration. Border forks are smaller than digging forks and are used for more shallow cultivation of planted areas. Most digging forks have square prongs, tapering to a point. Forks with flat prongs are used for potato lifting.

Spades may also be called 'digging' or 'border', depending on their size. They are used for deep soil preparation and for making large planting holes.

Shovels are similar to spades, but have the sides of the blade curved upwards to form a scoop. They are used for shifting sand, soil or other materials.

Hoes are used to cut down small weeds growing among other plants and for breaking up 'capped' or crusted soil surfaces. The Dutch hoe has a D-shaped steel blade attached to a long shaft and is used with a push-pull action. The draw hoe has a backward-angled blade attached by a swan-necked stem to a long shaft and is used for loosening heavy weed growth and taking out seed drills. Shafts are generally lightweight, some having moulded handgrips.

Rakes consist of a row of metal, wooden or plastic tines — prongs — mounted on a horizontal head attached to a long handle. They are used for general seedbed preparation and soil levelling. Lightweight alloy shafts make easier work of raking, but cost more than ordinary ash wood handles. Lawn rakes are designed for removing moss and dead grass. Their heads are fan-shaped, with springy wire prongs. Lawn rakes can also be used for collecting fallen leaves.

Half-moon edging tools with a rounded blade are used for cutting a lawn back to a new, straight edge.

Edging shears are used to trim grass blades along the lawn edges once a straight edge has been cut. The blades are angled in such a way that you can cut the grass from a standing position without the need to bend over.

Lawn shears are used for trimming the surface of a lawn where it is inaccessible to a lawnmower. As with edging shears, they are operated from a standing position.

SMALL HAND TOOLS

Hand trowels are used for setting out small plants and for digging out weeds. Avoid those which have a thin neck — it will bend during use.

Hand forks, short or long-handled, are used for weeding and cultivating the soil around plants. They may have three or five tines, and these may be curved or flat — the latter are generally the best.

Hand cultivators, with three or five hooked tines, are used for loosening compacted soil. Three-tined models are best for heavy soil.

Onion hoes are used for general surface cultivation between rows of seedlings or other small plants.

Secateurs are hand-held, spring-loaded shears used for cutting small stems up to 1.2cm (½in) in diameter. Some have one blade which cuts against an anvil head, others have blades which cut with a scissors action. They range in size from small flower-gatherers to large heavy duty types, but one general-purpose pair should be adequate.

Hand shears are used for trimming hedges and for cutting long grass. The blade edges may be straight or serrated — the former being easiest to sharpen, but the latter are better for cutting woody stems.

Bill hooks are used for cutting down coarse weeds and undergrowth among overgrown plant borders and for rough pruning of woody plants.

Pruning saws, which come in various shapes and sizes (including folding models), are used for pruning or cutting back woody branches which are too large for secateurs but not large enough to warrant the use of a bow saw. Some have fine teeth on one cutting edge and coarse teeth for rougher work on the other.

Bulb planters are useful for planting bulbs, especially in grass or among other plants. They consist of a metal cylinder with a serrated cutting edge which is pushed into the soil by means of a handle.

Garden lines, consisting of a reel of string fastened at each end to a spike, are used for marking out seed drills and straight edges.

Dibbers are used for making planting holes. They may be pencil-sized sticks used for inserting small plants or cuttings, or larger versions up to 2.5cm (1in) in diameter for planting vegetables.

Daisy grubbers are small, fork-tipped implements designed specially for extracting daisies and other rosette-forming weeds from lawns.

Paving stone cleaners are scraping tools used for slicing off weeds and moss growing between paving stones.

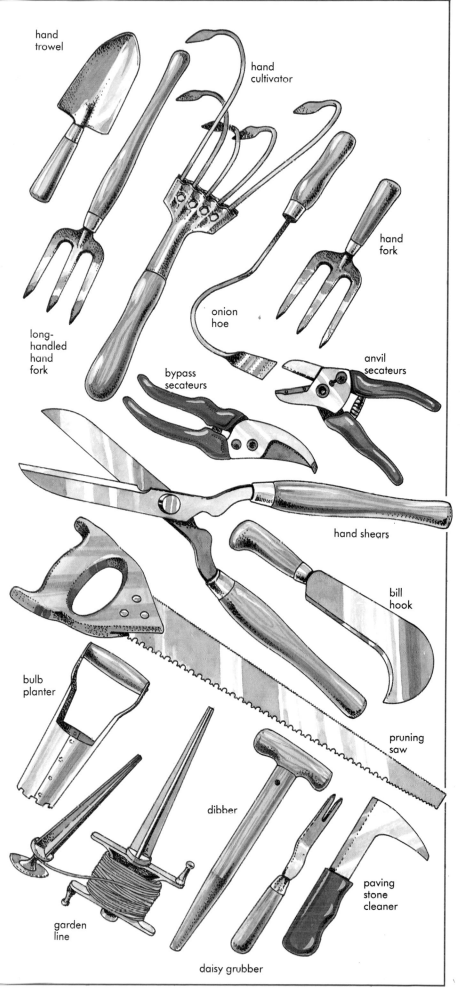

hand trowel

hand cultivator

hand fork

onion hoe

long-handled hand fork

bypass secateurs

anvil secateurs

hand shears

bill hook

bulb planter

pruning saw

dibber

garden line

daisy grubber

paving stone cleaner

POWER TOOLS

Hedge trimmers should have reciprocating blades — two blades that move at the same time. Those which have just one vibrate uncomfortably. Machines can also be divided into those that have teeth on both sides of the blades and those with teeth along just one edge — the latter is not as versatile.

Generally the closer the teeth the cleaner the finish. Close teeth are fine for maintaining Lawson cypress hedges, but wider gapped teeth are more suitable if you want to prune woody stems and branches.

Power hedge trimmers are the source of many accidents so safety is vital. Machines fitted with lock-off switches have a two-step starting procedure which prevents the machine being activated accidentally. Make sure the machine will also turn itself off when you relieve pressure on the on-button.

Nylon-line trimmers are popular with gardeners, not least because they perform several tasks. The machines are ideal for cutting grass where lawnmowers can't reach, such as the corners and edges of lawns. The machine will also edge a lawn, though not as neatly as some edging tools.

Some trimmers are equipped with devices to feed the nylon line. As the line may snap during use, a feeding mechanism avoids interruption.

Chainsaws of professional specification are best left to the professionals. Smaller, electric models are useful for removing small to medium-sized branches and help fell small-stemmed or young trees.

Choose the machine according to the guidelines for safety described above for hedge trimmers.

Power weeders are designed to eliminate the chore of bending and pulling weeds. The prongs dig and cut out small weeds with shallow roots easily but are not so effective for deep-rooting weeds.

Power shredders help recycle your garden refuse — woody tree and shrub prunings, for instance — by reducing it into shredded matter ready for the compost heap. Electric and petrol models are expensive but do help provide high grade compost.

Hand shearers are one of the easiest means of trimming lawn edges and they give a very clean cut. They can be fitted with an extension rod to prevent you having to stoop.

Being battery powered, they require regular recharging — you could run out of power in the middle of a task. They are not suitable for lawns of more than 30 sq m/yd.

Lawnmowers See page 40.

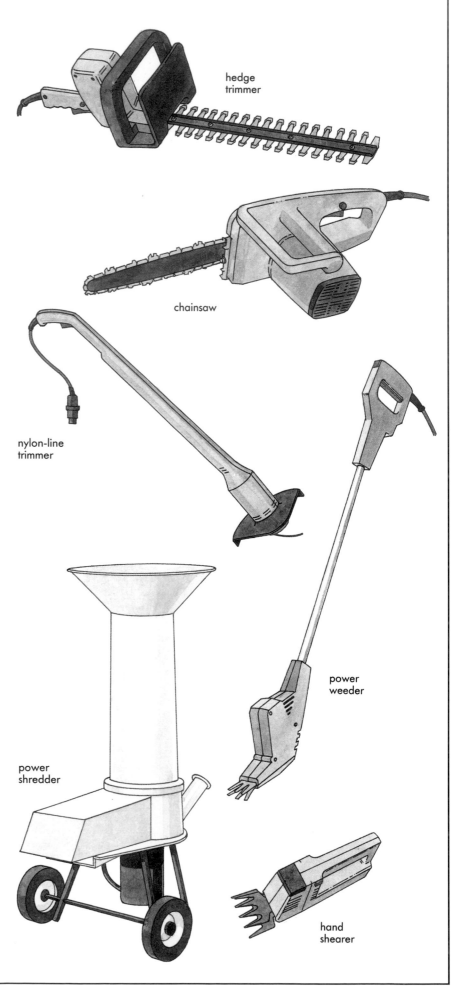

hedge trimmer

chainsaw

nylon-line trimmer

power weeder

power shredder

hand shearer

GARDEN SAFETY

Many gardening activities are potentially hazardous, so take precautions to safeguard yourself and your family.

Thousands of accidents occur in gardens every year and statistics show that all age groups, irrespective of gardening experience, are involved. Almost all of these accidents are avoidable and gardening will be as safe as any other leisure activity so long as a few basic precautions are taken.

General precautions

Unless you are very fit or manual work is an everyday activity, take plenty of time with strenuous jobs such as digging or pushing a cylinder lawnmower. Take frequent breaks to do something more leisurely. Never set yourself a massive task like digging the entire vegetable plot, making a determined effort to finish it in an afternoon come-what-may – you could end up with muscular pain for weeks afterwards.

Wear stout gloves to protect your hands from thorns, splinters and rough or sharp materials. Wear sturdy shoes or boots at all times, preferably with reinforced toe caps. Never do any gardening in bare feet or wearing open topped footwear. Don't strip off down to sunbathing attire when gardening in full sunshine, unless your skin is well tanned, since you can easily spend much longer in the sun than you think.

Additional safety garments should be worn for particularly hazardous activities. When cutting paving slabs with a bolster and hammer, for example, protect

▲ **Safety first** Use all power tools, such as hedge trimmers, with care. Hold them with both hands and keep the cable across your shoulder or clipped to a belt. Don't lean over a hedge from wobbly step ladders.

your eyes with plastic goggles. Wear rubber gloves when handling chemicals and don't spray on a windy day. If some wind drift is unavoidable wear a face mask.

Tidy up after each operation and never leave tools lying about to trip over. Keep a watchful eye on children and pets and don't allow them to play where you are working, especially if you are using mechanical or power tools.

Safety with hand tools

Take your time and do not rush jobs – accidents happen much more often when you hurry.

Hold secateurs firmly in the palm of your hand, getting a good grip before you make pruning cuts. Different sized models are available to suit your particular hand size – choose the right one to avoid getting blisters or pinching your skin between the pivot or spring mechanism. Use a pruning saw to cut large stems – never struggle with secateurs since you will blister your hand and strain the tool. Wear gloves if your skin is soft or if you are pruning thorny plants. Secure the safety catch on secateurs when they are not in use.

◄ **Pool covers** Stretch strong rigid wire mesh over ponds and pools to prevent children and pets from falling in. Aquatic plants will soon grow through and above the mesh.

PROTECTIVE CLOTHING

1 Wear strong gardening gloves when pruning thorny or woody plants, especially roses. They also provide some protection against rubbing blisters in the palm of your hand if you have soft skin.

2 Wear stout shoes or boots preferably with reinforced toe caps, when digging or using machinery. Never stab a fork into the soil – place the prongs on the soil surface then push the fork into the ground with your foot.

3 When using long-handled electric coarse-grass trimmers, wear long boots to protect your shins, ankles and feet from the rotating whip-cord blades even though all models have a guard around the back of the cutters.

4 Wear stout gloves and footwear when doing any construction work around the garden. Also wear plastic goggles to protect your eyes when cutting paving slabs with a bolster, or chipping up stone or concrete.

When using shears to cut long grass, check first that there are no electric cables or other objects concealed in the way, then cut carefully and methodically. Take similar care when using a scythe, and make cutting strokes away from yourself to avoid injuring your legs. Wear long sleeves and gloves when dealing with coarse weeds which may include nettles and brambles.

Ensure that the blades of all cutting tools are closed together when not in use. Tree pruners are dangerous if the blade is left open against the counterweight of the lever handle – you could lose a finger while handling them.

When digging with a garden fork, place the prongs on the ground first, then push into the soil using your foot. Never stab the fork into the ground – you could put it through your foot.

Do not leave a rake lying on the ground with its prongs pointing upwards – if you tread on the prongs the handle may catapult into your face. The same is true for garden forks.

Safety with power tools

Used correctly, electricity is a safe power source, but careless use can burn, paralyze or even kill. In the event of a break in an electric cable, you will be safe-guarded from shock if an earth wire is securely connected to the equipment – colour-coded green, or green and yellow striped. Many garden tools are double insulated, however, and need no earth wire. Check the manufacturer's specifications before wiring or re-wiring power tools.

Extension cables must be in good condition with no cuts in the outer casing, and be as short as possible, free from kinks and absolutely dry. When using cables stored on a reel, unroll them to their full length before plugging in power tools – heavy electrical loads cause coiled cable to get hot and create a fire risk.

Ensure that the mains plug contains a fuse of the correct rating – if in doubt consult a competent electrician. Use a residual-current circuit breaker adaptor at the power point to provide extra safety from electric shocks if your main fuse board does not incorporate an overall circuit breaker.

Never plug several tools into the same socket, or join cables together with tape – use properly connected extension leads. Don't use power tools in wet conditions or drag the cable through water. If there are several people in the garden, keep the cable away from paths where they may be trodden on or crossed by wheelbarrows or vehicles. If the cable pulls taut while you are working, switch off the tool immediately – it may be caught in a door or snagged on a sharp surface.

When using an unfamiliar tool for the first time, read the manufacturer's instructions carefully before plugging it in. Do not wear loose clothing when using tools with rotating or oscillating parts, and tie up long hair which may get caught in moving parts. Ensure that the chuck is tight and that the chuck key has been removed before starting an electric drill, and don't lay it on the ground until the chuck has stopped rotating.

Put the mains cable across your shoulder when using a power lawnmower or hedge trimmer to reduce the risk of cutting through it by mistake or tripping over it. Never run over a cable with a lawnmower, and take special care to avoid running over your own toes, especially when using a 'hover' mower or working on a slope. Always wear protective footwear – modern mowers won't slice into tough leather, but you could lose a toe in an accident if you are not adequately shod.

Safety with water

Adults are unlikely to find water a hazard in the garden, except with regard to the use of electricity. Young children, however, can drown in even quite shallow water.

Encourage children to play

ELECTRICAL SAFETY

1 Outside mains electricity cables must be enclosed in conduit along their entire length. Wherever mains sockets are exposed to the weather or moisture, they must be fitted with a weatherproof faceplate which should be secured when the socket is not in use.

2 To avoid cutting through the mains cable by accident when using an electric lawnmower, put the cable across your shoulder so that you are always walking with it trailing behind you. Work systematically over the lawn and never cross the cable.

3 When you run a cable across a patio, make sure it can't rub against a wall. Make a roller from a wooden stake and a piece of plastic drainpipe or a washing-up liquid bottle to keep the cable clear of sharp edges. Avoid getting kinks in the cable.

---

away from ornamental ponds, swimming pools or water butts. Use strong, rigid wire mesh to cover all expanses of water if you have small children – green-coated types are fairly unobtrusive. Always keep the top of a water butt or tank covered with a strong lid – which is preferably locked in place.

Safety with chemicals

Store chemicals – pesticides, fungicides, weedkillers, disinfectants, fertilizers, fuel oil and petrol – out of reach of children. A cupboard under lock and key or a high shelf in a garage or shed is

ideal. Never store chemicals in a hot place such as a greenhouse where they may catch fire or give off toxic fumes.

Flammable liquids such as petrol and oil should be stored in metal cans – plastic ones are suitable only for short-term carriage of flammable liquids – and the quantity restricted to no more than a couple of gallons. Preferably keep them in a brick or concrete garage, which will help to contain an explosive fire, rather than in a timber shed.

Mix up only as much solution as you will need for one application. Do not store diluted chemicals.

Always keep chemicals in their original container so that they are accurately labelled – most chemicals are sold with clear instructions on the label for their correct use and how to deal with an emergency. Never put a chemical in an unmarked bottle – or worse still, in an incorrectly labelled container such as an old lemonade or squash bottle.

Wash out thoroughly all equipment after using chemicals. Dispose of any left-over solution safely by tipping it down an outside sewerage drain – not a rainwater soakaway drain. Do not tip chemicals on to the soil. If no suit-

LIFTING HEAVY WEIGHTS

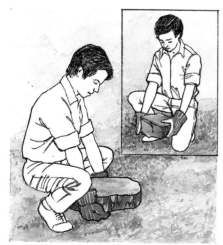

1 Lifting heavy weights can cause back or groin injury if done incorrectly. Crouch down to the object with feet apart and one foot alongside the load. Keep your back straight and let your leg muscles do the lifting work.

2 Never attempt to lift awkward shaped or very heavy items by yourself. To minimize the actual height to which the load must be lifted, use rope or sturdy straps as handles. Again, let your leg muscles do the lifting.

3 When taking a heavy sack from a lorry or from a platform it is best to carry it on your back. Get a firm grip with both hands and keep your back straight by raising the top of your head slightly and by tucking in your chin.

USING LADDERS SAFELY

1 When moving a ladder, rest it on one shoulder and lift it by the rung just below your normal reach. Find the correct balance before moving.

2 When erected, a ladder should stand at a 75° angle. If, for example, the ladder reaches 4m up a wall, it should stand 1m from the wall to give the correct 75° angle. Extension ladders with a closed length of up to 4.5m (15ft) must be overlapped by two rungs; longer ones by three or four rungs.

3 Ladders over 3m (10ft) tall should be fixed either at the top or at the bottom. Lash them to secure positions — never to a pipe or gutter. Alternatively, ask someone to stand on the bottom rung to steady the ladder.

POISONOUS PLANTS

Teach children not to pick or eat *any* berries, seeds, leaves or flowers unless they are known to be harmless. The following plants are poisonous — some causing stomach-ache, others being deadly — so do not eat any part:

Anemones (*Anemone* species)
Autumn crocuses (*Colchicum* species)
Box (*Buxus* species)
Buttercups (*Ranunculus* species)
Columbines (*Aquilegia* species)
Daphnes (*Daphne* species)
Daturas (*Datura* species)
False acacia (*Robinia pseudoacacia*)
Foxglove (*Digitalis purpurea*)
Globe flower (*Trollius europaeus*)
Hellebores (*Helleborus* species)
Hemlocks (*Conicum* species)
Holly (*Ilex* species)
Ivies (*Hedera* species)
Kingcup (*Caltha palustris*)
Laburnums (*Laburnum* species)
Larkspurs (*Delphinium* species)
Laurel (*Prunus laurocerasus*)
Lily-of-the-valley (*Convallaria majalis*)
Lupins (*Lupinus* species)
Monkshoods (*Aconitum* species)
Potatoes (green tubers, leaves and fruits only are poisonous)
Primulas (*Primula* species)
Privet (*Ligustrum ovalifolium*)
Rhubarb (*Rheum* — leaves only)
Spindle (*Euonymus europaeus*)
Spurges (*Euphorbia* species)
Sumachs (*Rhus* species)
Sweet peas (*Lathyrus* species)
Tomatoes (leaves and stems only)
Yew (*Taxus* species)

able drain is available, empty the chemical into a deep hole in the garden away from any plants, ponds or watercourses, and fill in with soil. Take old oil to your nearest fuel-oil garage for safe disposal. Wash your hands after handling any chemical.

Safety with bonfires
Keep children and pets away from a bonfire and never leave it unguarded. Position it away from fences, sheds or overhanging plants. Burn only small quantities at a time – large bonfires easily get out of control, especially in hot weather. Don't use petrol to start a fire as it is explosive. If newspaper and a match prove inadequate, a little paraffin can be added, but light it safely at arm's length or with a taper.

Paths and patios
Lawns or sand-pits are the safest places for children to play – concrete, rough paving and brickwork can cause painful cuts and grazes.

Apply moss-killer regularly to steps and paths. Keep overhanging branches pruned back to prevent constant water drips and shade, which encourage slippery moss and algal growth. Sweep leaves off paths and steps.

HEDGE TRIMMING SAFETY

When trimming a tall hedge, work off a scaffold board supported by two step ladders or trestles. Position the steps as close to the hedge as possible and on firm, level ground. Boards 38mm (1½in) thick can span 1.5m (5ft); boards 50mm (2in) thick can span 2.5m (8ft).

The Gardeners' Calendar

**Container-grown plants can be planted
at any time of year – but what about bulbs and seeds?
Which are the best months to prune, feed or mulch? This calendar
pinpoints the essential tasks of the seasons and
suggests plants to provide colour
throughout the year.**

Early spring

Lawns Rake vigorously and mow with blades set high. Spike badly drained lawns and brush sandy compost into the holes. Feed lawn to help grass recover from winter and apply mosskiller if this wasn't done in late winter. At end of month sow grass seed for new lawns. Turf can still be laid but it must be watered well to prevent shrinking.

Trees and shrubs Continue to prune winter-flowering shrubs as the blooms fade, and also species flowering in late summer. Mulch with garden compost or bark and apply a dressing of general fertilizer. Remove winter protection from tender shrubs. Keep weeds between shrubs and under hedges under control with a hoe or weedkiller. Plant or transplant conifers.

Roses Prune established plants, then spray branches and surrounding soil with a fungicide to destroy any overwintering spores. Feed with a rose fertilizer and mulch with garden compost or manure at end of month.

Perennials Fertilize beds and apply a thick mulch. Finish dividing and replanting established plants. Remove winter protection from tender perennials. Towards end of month, when the weather is mild and the soil drier, plant out perennials. Propagate summer-flowering chrysanthemums from new shoots on the stools (root clumps) stored over winter in a frost-free place.

Annuals Finish preparing the ground for seeds. Allow a couple of weeks for the soil to settle and then sow hardy annuals. Scatter slug pellets. Sow half-hardy annuals under glass for planting out in early summer. Start begonia tubers into growth in boxes of moist compost with gentle bottom heat.

Bulbs Dead-head spring-flowering bulbs. Towards the end of the month plant gladioli and acidantheras in succession. In cold areas plant De Caen anemones for summer flowering. Divide snowdrops. Remove dead leaves of bearded irisis and apply fertilizer to soil around the plants. Plant hardy indoor bulbs that have finished flowering outside, discarding those grown in bulb fibre. Place cloches over young lily shoots to protect from frost. Spread a light mulch of leaf-mould or well-rotted compost over beds of lilies.

Fruit Finish planting fruit trees and bushes only container grown ones can be planted after early spring. Prune acid cherry trees. Fertilize apples, cherries, peaches and pears; also red, white and black currants, gooseberries and raspberries. Mulch both fruit trees and bushes to keep the soil moist and free of weeds.

Vegetables Sow first vegetable seeds under cloches: onions, broad beans, parsnips, radishes, lettuces, carrots, round-seeded peas. In prepared seed bed sow cauliflowers, Brussels sprouts, broccoli and cabbages for later transplanting to a permanent site. Plant shallots and early potatoes. Scatter slug pellets among young plants.

Herbs Sow salad burnet, chervil, common fennel, dill, lovage, marjoram, parsley, rosemary, sage and thyme. Plant bay trees and tarragon.

Flower colour Dutch and species crocus, *Iris reticulata*, polyanthus, saxifrage, anemone, primrose, spring snowflake, *Tulipa kaufmanniana*, forsythia, camellia, flowering currant, Japanese quince, *Daphne mezereum*, hyacinths and *Magnolia stellata*.

Mid spring

Lawns Continue to sow grass seed for new lawns. Mow established lawns with blades set at medium height. Apply a fertilizer, followed two weeks later by a selective weedkiller.

Trees and shrubs Plant and transplant evergreen trees – especially conifers – and shrubs. As soon as flowering is over, prune forsythia, flowering currant and other spring-flowering shrubs. Lightly shear winter heathers. Cut back any frost-damaged hebes. Continue to mulch shrubs and trees with forest bark, well-rotted manure, compost or leaf-mould.

Roses Apply mulch of manure/leaf compost.

Perennials Sow perennials in a seed bed for flowering the following year. Prepare ground for outdoor-flowering chrysanthemums.

Annuals Complete sowing of hardy and half-hardy annuals. Plant out sweet peas.

Bulbs Continue planting summer-flowering bulbs such as gladioli and acidantheras. Dead-head early flowering bulbs. Stake tall lilies as flower buds form. At the end of the month plant out dahlia tubers in mild areas.

Fruit Spray pear and apple trees before they are fully in blossom with a combined insecticide/fungicide. Spray strawberries and raspberries with insecticide and gooseberries with fungicide. Water all fruit trees and bushes which were planted during the winter. Apply fertilizer to fruit bushes. Mulch established raspberries.

Vegetables Remove cloches from seeds sown the previous month (onions, broad beans, parsnips, radishes, lettuces, carrots and round-seeded peas). Sow more of these vegetable seeds to ensure a steady supply through the summer months, and also start sowing spinach, summer, autumn and Savoy cabbages and sprouting broccoli. Finish planting early potatoes. Plant onion sets and maincrop potatoes. Under glass, sow ridge cucumbers and outdoor varieties of tomato. Also sow celery and French beans.

Herbs Sow parsley, lemon balm, borage, chervil, coriander, dill, pot marjoram and sage. Plant bay trees.

Flower colour Daffodils, tulips, grape hyacinths, lily-of-the-valley, wood anemones, aubretia, alyssum, arabis, gentians, brooms, magnolias, ornamental crab apples, barberries and spiraeas.

Late spring

Lawns Mow at least once a week. Feed poorly growing grass. Apply a selective weedkiller.

Trees and shrubs Prune brooms, weigelas and other spring-flowering shrubs that have finished blooming. Mulch trees and shrubs if you have not already done so.

Roses Regularly spray against greenfly, mildew and blackspot. Apply a rose fertilizer.

Perennials Weed borders regularly. Provide support for tall plants such as delphiniums and sea holly. Pinch out growing tips of Michaelmas daisies, golden rod, heleniums and other vigorous plants. Plant outdoor-flowering chrysanthemums early in month; remove centre tip a week later to encourage bushy growth.

Annuals Plant out half-hardy annuals after risk of frost has passed. Thin seedlings of hardy annuals.

Biennials Sow Canterbury bells, foxgloves, sweet Williams and wallflowers.

Bulbs If space is needed, lift bulbs which have finished flowering.

Fruit Place straw or spread black polythene around strawberry plants, and put netting over them to keep off the birds. Prune leading shoots on apple and pear trees.

Vegetables Continue to keep a check on weeds with a hoe or weedkiller. Sow more broad beans, parsnips, carrots, peas, broccoli, lettuces, radishes, spinach, turnips, winter and Savoy cabbages and also swedes. Transplant the cauliflowers, Brussels sprouts, cabbages and broccoli that were sown in a seed bed in early spring. Harden off the tomatoes that are under glass and plant out at the end of the month. Also plant self-blanching celery. Prepare outside beds for courgettes, marrows and ridge cucumbers. Under glass, sow celery, leeks, ridge cucumbers, courgettes and marrows in pots. Early in the month, prepare ground for runner beans and put up support canes or netting. Sow runner beans towards the middle and end of the month. Earth up early potatoes.

Herbs Harden off basil and marjoram and plant out a fortnight later.

Flower colour Pulsatillas, star-of-Bethlehem, wallflowers, spurges, forget-me-nots, pyrethrum, sun roses, Spanish gorse, azaleas, rhododendrons, wisteria, laburnums, clematis.

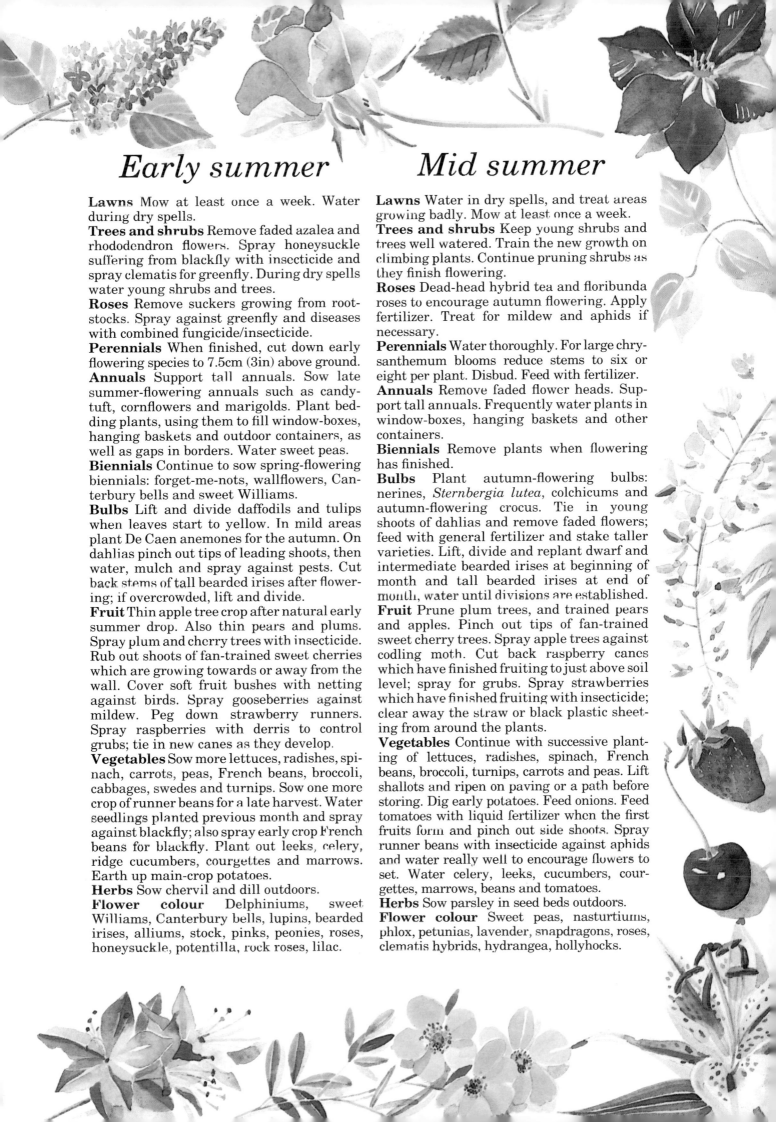

Early summer

Lawns Mow at least once a week. Water during dry spells.

Trees and shrubs Remove faded azalea and rhododendron flowers. Spray honeysuckle suffering from blackfly with insecticide and spray clematis for greenfly. During dry spells water young shrubs and trees.

Roses Remove suckers growing from rootstocks. Spray against greenfly and diseases with combined fungicide/insecticide.

Perennials When finished, cut down early flowering species to 7.5cm (3in) above ground.

Annuals Support tall annuals. Sow late summer-flowering annuals such as candytuft, cornflowers and marigolds. Plant bedding plants, using them to fill window-boxes, hanging baskets and outdoor containers, as well as gaps in borders. Water sweet peas.

Biennials Continue to sow spring-flowering biennials: forget-me-nots, wallflowers, Canterbury bells and sweet Williams.

Bulbs Lift and divide daffodils and tulips when leaves start to yellow. In mild areas plant De Caen anemones for the autumn. On dahlias pinch out tips of leading shoots, then water, mulch and spray against pests. Cut back stems of tall bearded irises after flowering; if overcrowded, lift and divide.

Fruit Thin apple tree crop after natural early summer drop. Also thin pears and plums. Spray plum and cherry trees with insecticide. Rub out shoots of fan-trained sweet cherries which are growing towards or away from the wall. Cover soft fruit bushes with netting against birds. Spray gooseberries against mildew. Peg down strawberry runners. Spray raspberries with derris to control grubs; tie in new canes as they develop.

Vegetables Sow more lettuces, radishes, spinach, carrots, peas, French beans, broccoli, cabbages, swedes and turnips. Sow one more crop of runner beans for a late harvest. Water seedlings planted previous month and spray against blackfly; also spray early crop French beans for blackfly. Plant out leeks, celery, ridge cucumbers, courgettes and marrows. Earth up main-crop potatoes.

Herbs Sow chervil and dill outdoors.

Flower colour Delphiniums, sweet Williams, Canterbury bells, lupins, bearded irises, alliums, stock, pinks, peonies, roses, honeysuckle, potentilla, rock roses, lilac.

Mid summer

Lawns Water in dry spells, and treat areas growing badly. Mow at least once a week.

Trees and shrubs Keep young shrubs and trees well watered. Train the new growth on climbing plants. Continue pruning shrubs as they finish flowering.

Roses Dead-head hybrid tea and floribunda roses to encourage autumn flowering. Apply fertilizer. Treat for mildew and aphids if necessary.

Perennials Water thoroughly. For large chrysanthemum blooms reduce stems to six or eight per plant. Disbud. Feed with fertilizer.

Annuals Remove faded flower heads. Support tall annuals. Frequently water plants in window-boxes, hanging baskets and other containers.

Biennials Remove plants when flowering has finished.

Bulbs Plant autumn-flowering bulbs: nerines, *Sternbergia lutea*, colchicums and autumn-flowering crocus. Tie in young shoots of dahlias and remove faded flowers; feed with general fertilizer and stake taller varieties. Lift, divide and replant dwarf and intermediate bearded irises at beginning of month and tall bearded irises at end of month, water until divisions are established.

Fruit Prune plum trees, and trained pears and apples. Pinch out tips of fan-trained sweet cherry trees. Spray apple trees against codling moth. Cut back raspberry canes which have finished fruiting to just above soil level; spray for grubs. Spray strawberries which have finished fruiting with insecticide; clear away the straw or black plastic sheeting from around the plants.

Vegetables Continue with successive planting of lettuces, radishes, spinach, French beans, broccoli, turnips, carrots and peas. Lift shallots and ripen on paving or a path before storing. Dig early potatoes. Feed onions. Feed tomatoes with liquid fertilizer when the first fruits form and pinch out side shoots. Spray runner beans with insecticide against aphids and water really well to encourage flowers to set. Water celery, leeks, cucumbers, courgettes, marrows, beans and tomatoes.

Herbs Sow parsley in seed beds outdoors.

Flower colour Sweet peas, nasturtiums, phlox, petunias, lavender, snapdragons, roses, clematis hybrids, hydrangea, hollyhocks.

Late summer

Lawns Mow regularly, water during dry spells. Apply weedkiller and lawn fertilizer.

Trees and shrubs Keep soil around shrubs and trees well watered. Clip lavender bushes after flowering. Cut back wisteria.

Roses Prune ramblers after flowering. Continue to spray against mildew and watch out for and pull up suckers.

Perennials Make sure perennials never dry out, particularly autumn-flowering species such as Michaelmas daisies, golden rod and heleniums. Dead-head all faded flowers not needed for their seeds. Keep chrysanthemums well supported and tied in; continue to disbud.

Annuals Dead-head regularly and water well during dry spells.

Biennials Dead-head regularly and water well. Remove plants that have finished flowering.

Bulbs Plant crocus corms as soon as available from stockists; replant any established bulbs previously moved to make room for annuals in the position you want them to flower. Continue to dead-head and tie in dahlias; rub out young buds on side shoots.

Fruit Continue summer pruning of trained apple and pear trees. Prune peach trees after fruiting and tie in replacement shoots. Plant new strawberry plants, and plant runners from established plants. Continue to cut back raspberry canes after fruiting to just above soil level; support new canes and sprinkle fertilizer on surrounding soil. Prune black currant bushes.

Vegetables As you harvest your vegetable crops, prepare the ground for more cultivation. It is still possible to sow lettuces, radishes, spinach and turnips. Sow onions and carrots – to be covered with cloches later – for harvesting in winter. Early in the month sow spring cabbages and winter greens. Feed Brussels sprouts with general fertilizer. Water runner beans, spray them against blackfly and give them a liquid feed. Spray brassicas against cabbage white caterpillars and aphids. Earth up trench-blanching celery. Start lifting maincrop potatoes. Fumigate greenhouses to eradicate pests and diseases.

Flower colour Early flowering chrysanthemums, begonias, heleniums, marigolds, lobelia, sunflowers, lilies, gladioli, hibiscus, fuchsias, heathers, buddleias, St John's wort.

Early autumn

Lawns Sow new lawns before the start of the cold weather; re-sow worn areas. Aerate and top-dress existing lawns. Mow with blades set at medium height.

Trees and shrubs Plant or transplant all types of evergreen trees or shrubs apart from conifers. After gales, check climbers and young trees are still secure.

Roses Dead-head to encourage late flowers. Tie in new shoots on climbers, and watch for diseases.

Perennials Dead-head and cut down all dead stems. Move late-flowering chrysanthemums to greenhouse and dig up stools of early types and put in cold frame. Plant young hardy border carnations.

Annuals Clear away annuals that have finished flowering.

Biennials Plant out biennials grown from seed in separate beds.

Bulbs Plant spring-flowering bulbs: narcissi, anemones, scillas, grape hyacinths, Dutch, English and Spanish irises. Pot indoor bulbs such as prepared hyacinths, daffodils and tulips for flowering in winter and spring. Water dahlias in dry spells.

Fruit Prepare ground for winter planting of fruit trees and bushes. Prune any secondary growth on apple and pear trees. Cut away dead wood on sweet cherry trees and shorten the shoots pinched back in early summer.

Vegetables Sow winter lettuces and spring cabbages. Lift onions and ripen off under glass. Pick French beans and runner beans. Earth up trench-blanching celery again. Feed leeks again with general garden fertilizer. Spray Brussels sprouts, Savoy and winter cabbages, cauliflowers and broccoli against caterpillars and cabbage whitefly. Encourage the last tomatoes to ripen by removing some of the leaves on the plants. Continue digging up maincrop potatoes. Remove greenhouse shading and reduce ventilation.

Herbs Outdoors, plant rue and thyme and sow angelica and lovage. Gather fennel seed heads for drying. Under glass sow summer savory. Root sage cuttings in a cold frame.

Flower, leaf and berry colour Dahlias, agapanthus, gladioli, Japanese anemones, golden rod, crocosmia, autumn cyclamen, colchicums, sedum, autumn snowflake, tamarisk, caryopteris, mountain ash, hawthorn.

Mid autumn

Lawns Lay turf for new lawns. Apply weed-killer on established lawns. Increase height of mower blades for cutting. Keep lawn clear of debris. Top-dress with sand.

Trees and shrubs Plant deciduous and evergreen shrubs and trees (not conifers); protect in exposed sites with plastic sheeting and canes. Prune conifers. Take hardwood cuttings of all shrubs.

Roses Plant at end of month. Take cuttings of species, ramblers, and some floribunda roses.

Perennials Tidy borders, cut back plants and remove old stems and leaves. Divide and replant overgrown perennials that have finished flowering. Scatter slug pellets before slugs start laying eggs. Lift stools of outdoor-flowering chrysanthemums and store in boxes of old soil in cold frames or greenhouses. Bring in other tender plants.

Annuals Finish clearing annuals.

Biennials Complete planting of forget-me-nots, wallflowers, pansies, Canterbury bells and sweet Williams.

Bulbs Continue planting spring-flowering bulbs such as snowdrops, *Iris reticulata*, miniature daffodils, crocus and chionodoxa. Tulips can be left until late autumn. Divide overgrown clumps of lilies; cut off stems when they begin to fade. Feed bearded irises with potash. Cut down dahlias, lift tubers and store. Cut down stems of gladioli, lift, and store in a frost-free place.

Fruit Start planting new fruit bushes and trees. Take hardwood cuttings of gooseberries.

Vegetables Sow more winter lettuces. Cover carrots sown in late summer with cloches. Feed Brussels sprouts and winter cabbages. Draw soil up stems of Brussels sprouts. Pick off yellowing leaves of cabbages. Gather last runner beans and marrows before the frosts set in and clear away plants. Lift last of maincrop potatoes. Dig up maincrop carrots, swedes and turnips. Fumigate greenhouses.

Herbs Raise new plants of lemon balm by division. Plant tarragon. For a winter supply, sow chervil under glass and pot some roots of mint, placing them in a sunny window.

Flower, leaf and berry colour Colchicums, nerines, *Amaryllis belladonna*, Michaelmas daisies, maples, strawberry trees, shrub roses, Japanese quinces, sumachs, smoke trees, ornamental cherries, Virginia creeper.

Late autumn

Lawns Make one final cut with blades set high and apply fertilizer. Top-dress with sand. Rake to keep clear of dead leaves. Avoid walking on frozen lawns – the grass can become damaged. Laying turf is still possible, weather and soil permitting.

Trees and shrubs Continue planting deciduous shrubs and trees. In cold gardens give winter protection to tender shrubs. If it is particularly cold, bring container shrubs indoors. Take hardwood cuttings.

Roses Prune climbing roses. Plant new roses as soon as they arrive. Take cuttings.

Perennials Plant and divide perennials. Remove remaining weeds from borders. Protect perennials in exposed sites and any plants that are slightly tender by covering with straw or newspaper. Place cloches over Christmas roses to encourage early flowering. Ventilate stored chrysanthemum stools in cold frames unless the weather is freezing; keep the stools just moist.

Biennials Keep plants free of wet leaves.

Bulbs Plant tulips, lily-of-the-valley and hardy lilies. Cover nerine bulbs with a thick layer of straw or leaves to protect them from winter frost. Examine bulbs potted in early autumn for indoor display. Move those with 2.5cm (1in) high shoots to a cool room, cold frame or greenhouse. Keep compost just moist. Examine stored dahlia tubers for signs of rot.

Fruit Continue planting fruit trees and bushes. Prune apples and pear trees before cold weather sets in. Prune red and white currants. Begin forcing rhubarb by lifting one or two plants and exposing their roots to frost to make the plants dormant.

Vegetables Dig soil, and leave in large clods, to be broken up by frost. Incorporate well-rotted manure where no root crops will be planted. In mild areas sow broad beans and round-seeded peas for late spring crop. Check maincrop potatoes in store and remove any diseased ones. Keep greenhouse glass clean.

Herbs Sow chervil under glass for a winter supply. Cover late-sown parsley and chervil with cloches. Bring bay trees growing in containers inside during cold spells.

Flower, leaf and berry colour Chinese lanterns, mountain ash, *Skimmia japonica*, pyracanthas, barberries, pernettyas, viburnums, snowberries, *Vitis coignetiae*.

Early winter

Lawns During mild spells, prepare sites for spring sowing. In dry weather lightly rake established lawns to remove dead leaves and scatter wormcasts. Aerate badly drained areas. Apply mosskiller if necessary.

Trees and shrubs Continue planting deciduous species during mild spells; otherwise heel in young plants until conditions improve. Take hardwood cuttings if you haven't already done so. Firm shrubs loosened by wind and stake if necessary. Remove dead, diseased and untidy branches.

Roses Complete planting during mild weather. Begin to prune floribunda and hybrid tea roses in mild regions.

Perennials Order plants and seeds for spring planting. Examine stored chrysanthemum stools for signs of rotting and withering; ventilate on mild, dry days.

Biennials Keep overwintering plants free of leaves and debris. After severe frosts, firm any plants that have been loosened.

Bulbs Move potted daffodil, hyacinth and tulip bulbs with shoots into the house or put them in a cool greenhouse. Make sure they do not dry out. Frequently check stored dahlia tubers for rotting or withering; if they are withering, soak in tepid water overnight. Plant hardy lilies when the soil is not too hard or waterlogged.

Fruit Continue pruning fruit trees. Spray them with winter wash to kill moss, lichen and overwintering pests. Protect buds on fruit bushes with bird repellant – if the bushes are in a fruit cage this is not necessary. Feed and mulch red, white and black currant bushes. Look out for big bud mite on black currant bushes; remove infested buds and burn. Force rhubarb by putting crowns lifted in late autumn in boxes of moist compost.

Vegetables Continue to dig the ground, incorporating well-rotted manure where root crops are not to be cultivated. Harvest cauliflowers, Brussels sprouts, parsnips, leeks, celery and winter cabbages. Place cloches over winter lettuces, and over some of the spring cabbages for an early crop.

Flower colour Christmas roses, *Iris unguicularis*, *Viburnum grandiflorum*, cotoneasters, winter-flowering heathers, hollies, winter-flowering jasmine, euonymus, *Mahonia bealii*, aucubas.

Mid & late winter

Lawns Turf new lawns. Treat established lawns with mosskiller.

Trees and shrubs If the soil is not frozen, plant deciduous species. Prune deciduous summer-flowering shrubs such as clematis, buddleia, potentilla and hardy fuchsia. Prune winter-flowering shrubs once blooms are over; mulch and apply a general fertilizer. Cut suckers growing from the bases of trees.

Roses Continue planting roses in suitable weather. Prune in mild or sheltered gardens.

Perennials Lift and divide lupins, Michaelmas daisies, delphiniums, and any other hardy border plants that have been left for three years. Apply general fertilizer to other hardy perennials. Firm plants lifted by frost. Fork over the soil between plants. Examine stored chrysanthemum stools for signs of rotting. Ventilate on sunny days.

Annuals In suitable weather dig and manure sites for sowing. Lightly fork over ground dug in autumn and work in a general fertilizer if it wasn't manured. Sow half-hardy annuals in a cold frame or greenhouse late in the winter.

Biennials Dress with a general fertilizer. Lightly fork soil around them. Firm any plants that have been lifted by frost.

Bulbs Deter birds from eating crocus buds by stretching dark cotton, supported on sticks, across the area occupied by the bulbs. Spray stored dahlia tubers showing signs of mould. Pot lily bulbs for early display indoors or under glass.

Fruit Plant fruit trees and bushes in mild spells. Feed all fruit trees with fertilizer. Every third year, paint tar oil wash on apple and pear trees. Prune raspberries, gooseberries and red and white currants. Prepare beds for rhubarb crowns and plant.

Vegetables Place cloches in position to warm soil for seeds sown in early spring. Outdoors, plant shallots. Feed winter brassicas with general fertilizer.

Herbs Plant or divide chives, thyme, sage and mint. Cut back frost-damaged sage.

Flower colour Christmas rose, snowdrops, crocus, winter aconites, dog's tooth violets, chionodoxa, *Iris reticulata*, lungwort, *Prunus cerasifera*, *Viburnum burkwoodii* and *V. tinus*, *Lonicera fragrantissima*, winter sweet, dogwood, Chinese witch hazel, cornelian cherry.

INDEX

ACKNOWLEDGEMENTS

Photographer's credits
Heather Angel, 10, 131(b), 133(t,c), 134(t); Linda Burgess 79(b); Simon Butcher/Eaglemoss 11; Brian Carter 132(t); Eric Crichton 25, 32(b), 34(b), 45, 56(b), 89, 97, 99, 103, 105, 109, 163(t); Robert Estall 163(b); Garden Picture Library 39, (Brigitte Thomas) 2-3, (Steve Wooster) 62; John Glover 35(t), 45, 52; Jerry Harpur 32(t), 33, 34(t), (J. Stephenson) 31; Neil Holmes 85, 87; Patrick Johns 159; Lamontagne back cover, 54(t,b), 55(b), 59, 77, 79(t), 80, 119; Andrew Lawson 17, 53, 73, 74, 75, 91, 128, 151; Tania Midgley 12(t), 156; Philippe Perdereau 81,

131(t); Photos Horticultural 12(c,b), 35(b), 55(t), 56(t,c), 57(t,c), 63, 68, 69(t), 86, 115, 123, 135, 157; Nick Rebbeck 9(tl), Harry Smith Collection 21, 88, 95, 112, 131(c), 132(b), 133(b), 134(b), 139; Chris Stephens/Eaglemoss 129; The Soil Survey 9(c,r,bl), John Suett/Eaglemoss front cover; Michael Warren/Eaglemoss 69(b), 70-71; Elizabeth Whiting and Associates 81, (Karl-Dietrich Buhler), 94, (Jerry Harpur) 4-5, 8, (Harpur/design: Cobblers Garden) 6, (Spike Powell) 30; Wolf Tools 158.

Illustrators
Sophie Allington 152-154; David Ashby 162; Alison Christie 16(t); Elisabeth Dowle 26-28,

104-108, 140(c), 141(t), 143(b); Terry Evans 78-79; Ian Garrard/Readers' Digest 136-138, 144-150; Will Giles 10, 82-83; Christine Hart-Davies 18-19, 22-24, 36-38, 40-44, 46-48, 50-51, 60, 61, 64-66, 74-76, 86-87, 89-92, 96-98, 100-102, 110-112, 115-118, 120-122; Ron Hayward 164-166; John Hutchinson 160-161, Sean Milne/Readers' Digest 52; Stan North 13-15, 16(b), 113-114; Charles Pickard/Readers' Digest 130-134; Readers' Digest 140(t,b), 141(c,b), 142, 143(t,c), 144; Charlotte Wess 167-172; Ann Winterbotham 124-126; Cathy Wood 70, 72.

Index compiled by Christine Bernstein

Typesetting SX COMPOSING, ESSEX; Printing & Binding PRINTER INDUSTRIA. GRÁFICA S.A. BARCELONA
Separations COLOURSCAN OVERSEAS CO PTE LTD, SINGAPORE

53-002-2